D1605940

THE POLITICS
OF THE SECOND FRONT

CONTRIBUTIONS IN MILITARY HISTORY
Series Editors: Thomas E. Griess and Jay Luvaas

THE POLITICS
OF THE SECOND FRONT

American Military Planning
and Diplomacy in
Coalition Warfare, 1941-1943

MARK A. STOLER

CONTRIBUTIONS IN MILITARY HISTORY, NUMBER 12

GREENWOOD PRESS
WESTPORT, CONNECTICUT • LONDON, ENGLAND

Acknowledgments

Material from Winston Churchill, *The Second World War,*
Houghton Mifflin Company, 1948-1953, is quoted with
permission of the publisher.

Material from Robert E. Sherwood, *Roosevelt and Hopkins,*
Harper & Row, Publishers, 1950, is quoted with permission
of the publisher.

Material from Henry L. Stimson, *On Active Service in Peace
and War,* Harper & Row, Publishers, 1947, is quoted with
permission of the publisher.

Library of Congress Cataloging in Publication Data

Stoler, Mark A
    The politics of the second front.

    (Contributions in military history ; no. 12)
    Bibliography: p.
    Includes index.
    1. World War, 1939-1945—Diplomatic history.
2. United States—Foreign relations—1933-1945.
3. Great Britain—Foreign relations—1933-1945.
4. Russia—Foreign relations—1917-1945. 5. Operation
Overlord. I. Title. II. Series.
D748.S76   940.53'22   76-47171
ISBN 0-8371-9438-5

Library of Congress Catalog Card Number: 76-47171
ISBN 0-8371-9438-5

First published in 1977

Greenwood Press, Inc.
51 Riverside Avenue, Westport, Connecticut 06880

Printed in the United States of America

For my parents
and for Michael

It is not possible in a major war to divide military from political affairs. At the summit they are one.

Winston S. Churchill[1]

These [old] definitions [of strategy] seemed to me all too limited. . . . In our complex modern world, in which the dividing line between military and economic, scientific, technological, political and psychological factors has almost disappeared, I thought that a far broader concept of strategy was essential to survival. . . . "Grand Strategy," I said, "is the art and science of employing all of a nation's resources to accomplish objectives defined by national policy."

General Albert C. Wedemeyer[2]

I repeat again that I doubt if there was any one thing except the shortage in LSTs that came to our minds more frequently than the political factors. But we were very careful, exceedingly careful, never to discuss them with the British, and from that they took the [view] that we didn't observe those things at all. But we observed them constantly, with great frequency, and particular solicitude, so that there is no foundation in that. We didn't discuss it with them because we were not in any way putting our necks out as to political factors which were the business of the head of the state—the President—who happened also to be the Commander-in-Chief.

General George C. Marshall[3]

Nothing could be more mistaken than to believe that General Marshall's mind was a military mind in the sense that it was dominated by military considerations, that is, considerations relating to the use of force. . . . When he thought about military problems, nonmilitary factors played a controlling part.

His opponent in the debate, Mr. Churchill, was moved by political considerations too. . . . My point is not which political consideration is more valid in the light of knowledge then available, but that the decision in favor of the cross-Channel attack was not the triumph of the "military mind" over political insight.

Dean Acheson[4]

CONTENTS

PREFACE

War, as Carl von Clausewitz perceived, is an instrument of policy, and military strategy should be geared to the accomplishment of national political goals. According to popular belief, Americans have traditionally rejected such a concept, naively insisting that their wartime strategy be geared solely to achieving quick and decisive victory while politics awaited the peace conference. Following this unrealistic duality during World War II, the United States supposedly gave no thought to the importance of placing troops in key areas for bargaining purposes once the war ended, and vehemently opposed British attempts to follow such a "politically inspired" strategy. The State Department, which should have pointed out the necessity of controlling key areas, refused to meddle in what it considered "purely military" matters. Thus, it excluded itself from the decision-making process during the war and left the president with only military advice from the joint chiefs of staff.

According to this interpretation, the American military chiefs thus wound up determining foreign as well as military policy without ever realizing it—and with disastrous results. Their victory in the long and bitter strategic debate with Britain, signified by the Normandy invasion in June 1944, insured decisive victory over Germany. But the political cost of such blindness to reality was a dangerous extension of Soviet power, thereby denying the United States the fruits of victory and adding another chapter to the supposed American tradition of winning the wars but losing the peace.[1]

While such an explanation of events appears correct on the surface, it actually raises more questions than it answers. Why, for example, were the president and the joint chiefs so intent upon defeating Germany as quickly as possible? Was "military efficiency" the sole reason for the Army's almost fanatical adherence to the cross-Channel concept and opposition to British Mediterranean plans? Did the State Department totally ignore what had become by 1942 the biggest political as well as military issue of the war? How could a president known for his incredible political acumen, and military leaders trained in Clausewitzian and Mahanite principles of warfare, totally ignore the political aspects of strategy?

Careful examination of American military and political records for the war years casts doubt upon the validity of traditional assumptions regarding American naivete during the war. From its very inception, the second-front issue was highly political and was so recognized by the leadership in Washington. The United States developed and backed this concept not simply as a way to win the war as quickly and decisively as possible, but as a way to win it on American, rather than British or Soviet, terms. Furthermore, the military did not develop its concept in a political vacuum. It asked for and received advice from political agencies, increased its contact with the president, and politicized itself to an unprecedented degree during the war. If the "military mind" did triumph with the Normandy invasion, it was a military mind very concerned with and knowledgeable of the political aspects of strategy-making.

* * *

Sources consulted for this study include unpublished records of the War, Navy, and State Departments, files of the joint and combined chiefs of staff and their subcommittees, Office of Strategic Services documents, presidential papers, and manuscript collections of American political and military leaders. Use of these records raises numerous problems for the historian and requires much time, money, and expert assistance. Financial aid was originally provided by Ford Foundation research funds distributed through the Graduate School and History Department of the University of Wisconsin. Later grants from the University of Vermont and the National Endowment for the Humanities made possible revisions and additional research into newly declassified material.

Archivists and librarians too numerous to mention individually gave the needed assistance. My deepest appreciation goes to all of them, but in particular to Mrs. Hazel Ward of the National Archives, without whose knowledge, patience, and aid this study would not have been possible. Expert assistance was also provided by retired American officials and officers and by historians at the Army's Military History Office and the Universities of Wisconsin and Vermont. I would like to express my sincere thanks to all of them for their time and knowledge, and particularly to Professor John A. DeNovo, under whose patient direction I began this study at the University of Wisconsin. Special thanks also go to Mrs. Carolyn Perry for her invaluable typing and editorial assistance.

In a separate category is my wife, Jennie. Her time, aid, patience and encouragement, offered in the midst of pursuing her own research and fulfilling her teaching obligations, were crucial in the revising of this manuscript for publication. Beyond that, her presence gave meaning to the entire effort.

The aid provided by these agencies and individuals improved the quality of this study. Final responsibility for the research, writing, and conclusions, however, rests solely with the author.

Mark A. Stoler

THE POLITICS
OF THE SECOND FRONT

CHAPTER ONE

PRELUDE TO CONTROVERSY

JANUARY 1941 TO JANUARY 1942

On June 6, 1944, combined Anglo-American forces under the command of General Dwight D. Eisenhower landed on the beaches of Normandy, France, in an amphibious assault ranking as the greatest in the history of warfare and assuring the Grand Alliance victory over Germany. Behind this assault lay years not only of preparation and planning, but also of intense and often acrimonious debate within the individual capitals and the Alliance as a whole. From its very inception, in fact, the so-called second-front concept was both a military plan and a highly political issue involving a complex series of factors that transcended purely strategic considerations. Long before the culmination of the plan on the Normandy beaches, these factors had emerged and converged, forcing military and political leaders to recognize the inseparability of strategy and politics and to redefine their positions in these realms.

THE ANGLO-AMERICAN STRATEGIC DISPUTE

Despite the unprecedented military cooperation between the United States and Great Britain during World War II a major strategic dispute dominated their relationship from 1941 to 1944. In general terms, this argument pitted the British "indirect" or "peripheral" approach to victory in Europe via encirclement of Germany against the American "direct" approach through a massive invasion of northwestern France. The debate involved more than pure strategy, however, for the two approaches reflected the unique and often conflicting positions, interests, and histories of the powers involved.

After the fall of France in June 1940, British plans for victory hinged on the use of seapower to blockade the European coastline, thereby forcing upon Hitler an extended war of attrition, while strategic bombing and commando raids were to weaken Germany to the point of collapse. At that distant time, London would land small bodies of troops on the continent to foment and lead large-scale uprisings against the Germans by the subjugated European populations. The first step was to gain control of the areas surrounding Europe, and in late 1940 and early 1941, this meant military operations to secure the Middle East, North Africa, and the Mediterranean.

Such plans flowed logically from British defensive needs and the reality of the situation in 1940. Standing alone after the fall of France, Britain's survival hinged on retaining the critical Middle East oil reserves and the Mediterranean lifeline to the rest of her empire through Gibraltar and the Suez Canal. Defense of these positions logically led to the use of the entire Mediterranean basin as an offensive base; reconcentration in the home islands for a massive assault on Europe would be impractical, if not impossible. Moreover, the relatively small British army could not hope to defeat the unbeaten *Wehrmacht* in a direct confrontation. More promising would be an attack on Hitler's southern flank, an area controlled by his weak Italian ally.[1]

Further reinforcing such factors was Britain's traditional aversion to direct continental clashes. With the disastrous exception of World War I, London had for centuries refrained from placing large bodies of troops on the European continent, correctly perceiving that land power, in terms of population if nothing else, was its weak point. Seapower, on the other hand, was the island empire's strength, and such power could most effectively be used in a peripheral campaign. Furthermore, the scattered nature of the empire dictated defense through a wide dispersion of forces rather than massive concentration in Europe.

This traditional British strategy found its strongest exponent during the war in Prime Minister Winston S. Churchill, a man who had always favored the indirect, naval approach over the use of large armies. As first sea lord during World War I, he had planned the ill-fated Gallipoli expedition, a classic example of peripheral strategy, and had become convinced that tactical rather than strategic blundering had led to the operation's failure. Hitler's recent successes with relatively small and highly mobile ground and air forces had only reinforced Churchill's belief that a modified form of his earlier strategy could achieve victory without engendering the appalling casualties of the World War I trenches.

Further strengthening this conviction was the prime minister's personal identification with the military glory of the British Empire, a glory that had been badly compromised by the failures in Norway and France. Churchill passionately desired a military victory to erase these blots. He naturally turned to the Mediterranean for that victory, since it was an area where the British could achieve greater concentration of forces than the Axis as well as face its weakest link, Italy. His identification with this approach remained so close throughout the war that he personally coined the two phrases popularly associated with it—"closing the ring" and "soft underbelly."[2]

Peripheral strategy, however, had traditionally been used to achieve limited goals and had depended for its success upon the existence of a powerful continental ally to tie down the bulk of the enemy forces. No such ally existed from the fall of France to Hitler's attack on Russia a year later, and Britain's goals in the war were far from limited.[3] In effect, London had adopted a modified form of its traditional, limited-goal strategy to achieve total victory without the presence of the continental ally needed for even the limited goals.

While necessity may have dictated such an approach, it also invited the disaster that overtook the British in the spring of 1941. In the aftermath of its desert victory over the Italians, London had sent part of its victorious army into Greece to buttress local resistance to Hitler, a dispersion of forces that quickly resulted in defeats on two fronts. German General Erwin Rommel and his newly arrived *Afrika Korps* cracked the now weakened British lines in Africa, while a lightning German campaign in the Balkans smashed through the British-Greek defenses and threw the British off the continent for a second time. By May 1941, London's entire Mediterranean position was in mortal danger, and only Hitler's decision to limit his southern drive in order to attack Russia in June saved the British from a total and disastrous defeat.

Despite these failures, President Franklin D. Roosevelt of the United States backed the prime minister completely and even considered coming to his aid in May. As an ex-assistant secretary of the navy, Roosevelt

shared many of Churchill's strategic preconceptions and was strongly at-
tracted to the Mediterranean as a theater of operations. Furthermore, in
planning for hemispheric defense, both he and his military advisers had
become extremely worried over the possibility of a German thrust into
the western bulge of Africa, a move they perceived as a threat to Brazil,
and they had been discussing with London since September 1940 the possibility of a preemptive American occupation of Dakar or the Atlantic
Islands. Hitler's spring victories, combined with the subsequent rumors of
a German move into French Africa, gave new urgency to these fears and
plans. Equally important, Roosevelt was looking in the spring for a military operation capable of rousing the public and preparing it for the possibility of full hostilities against the Germans. A movement into Northwest
Africa or the Atlantic Islands seemed the perfect answer. On May 22 the
president therefore ordered the armed forces to begin preparations to occupy the Azores. Five days later, he prepared the public for action by de-
claring a state of unlimited national emergency.[4]

Within the armed forces, there was intense opposition to such an occupation on the basis that the units were unprepared for immediate action
outside the Western Hemisphere. A more limited operation involving Bra-
zilian bases, the military planners felt, would be safer and sounder.[5] Behind this rationale lay a host of military and political objections not only
to the proposed operation, but also to the entire peripheral strategy in the
Mediterranean. The planners felt that such a strategy was both indecisive
and a gross violation of a cardinal principle of warfare—concentration of
forces.

Accustomed to working with an abundance of manpower and material
on a continent with no other major land power, the American military was
firmly convinced of the validity of the "direct" approach to strategy; the
quickest and the most efficient way to win a war was to meet the enemy
in a massive confrontation. Continuing British insistence on a wasteful
Mediterranean alternative, the planners felt, could be explained and justified historically and in the present only by reference to its political implications; London's strategy always had been and was once again being ori-
entated not to winning a war as quickly as possible, but to preserving the
British Empire. American acquiescence in such a strategy, the Joint Army-
Navy Planning Committee (JPC) warned in January 1941, could hurt American interests and should therefore be avoided. "We cannot afford," it
bluntly stated, "nor do we need to entrust our national future to British

direction." London's proposals at the coming conference "will probably have been drawn up with chief regard for support of the British Commonwealth. Never absent from British minds are their postwar interests, commercial and military. We should likewise safeguard our own eventual interests."[6]

American military planners thus did not naively believe in following a strategy based solely on ideas of military efficiency. They were well aware of the fact that war is an instrument of policy and should be conducted so as to facilitate the accomplishment of national political goals. The definition of such goals, they further realized, was not their job but that of the civilian leadership of the country.[7]

For many years, however, the planners had been dissatisfied with the lack of clear guidance in this field from civilian superiors and had therefore undertaken their own definition of national interests. Prior to 1940, that definition had been in terms of continental and hemispheric defense, the Monroe Doctrine and the Open Door principle, defense of the Philippines, isolation from Europe, and the necessity for foreign markets.[8] In November 1940, Chief of Naval Operations (CNO) Admiral Harold E. Stark had replaced isolation with retention of European and Far Eastern balances of power and "prevention of the disruption of the British Empire."[9]

Although Army planners had agreed with this redefinition, they feared that the latter goal might negate the other, more important ones, especially in the Western Hemisphere, and might lead to a blind acceptance and defense of British interests throughout the world at the expense of American interests. To many, such a fear had become a reality with the decision to aid Britain before building up continental and hemispheric defense forces.[10] By May 11, 1941, it appeared that Roosevelt was willing to divert untrained troops as well as supplies to support British political interests in the Mediterranean.

These diversions had already caused Army Chief of Staff General George C. Marshall severe problems in his attempts to build a large, balanced ground force for continental and hemispheric defense, and now promised to do even more damage. Marshall's efforts were also being hampered by a key axiom of British strategy, the belief that large land forces would not be required in this war. Such a belief had many American adherents, including the president, who apparently felt that the United States could defeat Germany and still avoid direct participation in the war simply by occupying key defensive positions while sending planes and material to British forces operating along the periphery of Europe. Marshall and his advisers disagreed vehemently. Roosevelt's policies, they believed, would soon involve the United States in active hostilities, and Germany could not be defeated without the use of massive American ground forces.[11]

As early as November 1940, Stark had pointed out that victory over Germany would probably depend upon Britain's ability "ultimately to make a land offensive against the Axis powers," and that American troops would in all likelihood be needed for such an assault.[12] Army planners had agreed with his conclusions but had quickly realized the problems involved in the word *ultimately*. In the present situation, no Anglo-American force could successfully meet the full strength of the German war machine in Europe. Only "wishful thinking," the Army's War Plans Division (WPD) had stated in January 1941, could offer even a "50-50 chance of success" in such a venture, and the idea of a landing in northwestern Europe should therefore be "discarded" for the present time. German power would have to be gradually worn down and bases captured before such an offensive could be seriously considered.[13]

The British approach seemed the logical way to achieve these goals. American planners had therefore agreed during combined staff conversations in early 1941 to a peripheral campaign of encirclement centering on the Mediterranean in the event Washington became a full belligerent in the war. The "early elimination" of Italy would be a key goal of this campaign, and American forces were charged with occupation of the Atlantic Islands. An "eventual" land offensive against Europe would be launched only when bases had been captured and "decisive victory could be assured by a minimum employment of land forces."[14] While agreeing to this overall strategy, the WPD privately voiced opposition to any American occupation of Dakar or the Atlantic Islands as a "dispersion of force" which the United States could not presently afford. A sounder plan would be to build up hemispheric defense and a large expeditionary force for eventual use in a single theater.[15]

This idea quickly ran into Roosevelt's desire for immediate military action to achieve political goals, Britain's increasing demands for supplies, and Churchill's continuing reinforcement of Roosevelt's belief that large ground forces would not be necessary. When the Azores plan collapsed in June because of Portuguese refusal to grant permission for the landings, British preference for American troops in Iceland, and evidence that Hit-

ler was turning east rather than south or west, the president thus refused
to agree to a defensive stance. Instead, he ordered American occupation
of Iceland and shifted his sights from the Azores to North Africa and the
Cape Verde Islands. Marshall's efforts to inform him of the impossibility
of such operations apparently met with little success.[16]

By July, however, Marshall's warnings, combined with continuing German victories in the Mediterranean and Russia, had succeeded in raising
presidential doubts over the wisdom of building up British forces in the
Middle East while leaving the United States and the United Kingdom virtually defenseless. Harry Hopkins, Roosevelt's closest adviser, aired these
doubts during a July visit to London by warning the British that the president's chief military advisers thought London's Middle East strategy and
position unsound and indefensible. Sending further reinforcements into
the area would be "like dynamite" to Roosevelt and Marshall and would
be equivalent to "throwing snowballs into hell"; Washington would prefer
to keep such material for hemispheric defense. On the evening of July 24,
however, Hopkins informed the British that the president had a "somewhat
different attitude" from his advisers and was "more inclined to support
continuing the campaign in the Middle East," since that was where the
enemy could be met. American opposition to British plans, he concluded,
stemmed from a lack of information.[17]

While such reasoning may have correctly presented Roosevelt's and
Hopkins' positions, it certainly did not reflect the beliefs of the American
military. Nevertheless, Churchill and the British chiefs of staff (COS) took
advantage of the opening presented to them and proceeded to explain
their rationale both for the Middle East campaign and for American action
in North and West Africa. A convinced Hopkins quickly urged the president to bring Marshall and Army Air Forces (AAF) Chief General Henry
H. Arnold to the proposed summit conference with Churchill in order to
enlighten them on the British point of view. London, he cabled on the
evening of July 25, was "determined" to fight in the Middle East, and
its reasons for doing so seemed "very convincing."[18]

Churchill and the COS repeated those reasons during the August "Atlantic" Conference with Roosevelt and his military chiefs off the coast of
Newfoundland. While the prime minister expounded on the mobility of
modern warfare, the advantages of the indirect approach to Germany, and
the necessity for American action in the Atlantic Islands, his military advisers presented their American counterparts with a strategy paper which

detailed peripheral plans, defended the Middle East campaign, requested more American supplies, and stressed the urgent necessity of sending American troops into North Africa. Such a move, the British claimed, would "revolutionize" the entire situation and enable London to break the Germans through blockade, bombing, and subversion.[19]

Informed of the conference at the last minute, the disorganized and unprepared American chiefs of staff stated some of their disagreements with London's approach, but avoided any full strategic discussion with their British colleagues.[20] After the conference, however, the American planners blasted the British strategy paper mercilessly, labeling it disjointed and "groping for panaceas." WPD members insisted that it highly over-rated the effects of strategic bombing and American entry, and that it was actually a "propaganda effort to bring the United States into the war at the earliest possible date" in order to use American troops "to protect the British Empire while they take care of the United Kingdom with our material help." That empire, one planner maintained, had begun to "dis-integrate" before 1939, and the war was only postponing the process. The United States, WPD planners concluded, must look out for its own, not British, interests in determining whether to enter the war. Such interests definitely did not call for landings in North Africa at this time.[21]

These Army studies were combined with similar Navy WPD papers in late September to form a JPC report that the Joint Army-Navy Board accepted as its own. Thus, the signatures of Marshall and Stark were placed on a document that attacked every point of the British strategic concept except the belief in the mobility of forces and the desire to arm Europe to help defeat the Nazis. Stressing the importance of continued Russian resistance and the subsequent value of aid to Moscow, the report questioned London's material requests, insisted on the present impossibility of Amer-ican action in Africa, and claimed that Britain's Middle East position, while of "great importance," was not vital. Furthermore, it attacked the British emphasis on bombing and complained about London's lack of interest in a land invasion of the continent, pointing out "as an almost invariable rule that wars cannot be finally won without the use of land armies."[22]

At the same time, the Joint Board expounded on these and related ideas in a crucial group of documents delivered to Roosevelt in response to his July 9 request for an immediate exploration of the "over-all production requirements required to defeat our potential enemies."[23] Such explo-ration had to involve strategic and foreign policy evaluations. Since Roosevelt had given no further guidance in these fields, the planners found themselves discussing not only production goals, but also American aims and planned actions in the war. The resulting documents, entitled the "Joint Board Estimate of United States Over-All Production Requirements" and commonly known as the "Victory Program, " picked up where Stark had left off in November 1940 by outlining American policy objectives as

> preservation of the territorial, economic and ideological integrity of the United States and of the remainder of the Western Hemisphere; prevention of the disruption of the British Empire; prevention of the further extension of Japanese territorial dominion; eventual establishment in Europe and Asia of balances of power which will most nearly ensure political stability in those regions and the future security of the United States; and, so far as practicable, the establishment of regimes favorable to economic freedom and individual liberty.[24]

Stating that these goals could not be attained through defense of the Western Hemisphere alone, the estimate concluded that Germany and Japan would have to be defeated and that to accomplish such goals the United States would be forced to enter the war and concentrate on defeating Germany first. In explaining how this victory was to be accomplished, it admitted that air and naval power were presently the "principle" strengths of the Western Powers and were capable of preventing wars from being lost and of contributing "greatly" to victory by weakening enemy power. "By themselves, however," the estimate warned, "naval and air forces seldom, if ever, win important wars. It should be recognized as an almost invariable rule that only land armies can finally win wars."[25]

Since it was "out of the question" to expect the United States and Britain to undertake a land offensive in the near future, the Joint Board was forced to accept a peripheral approach for the time being. By recommending production goals to further Allied air and naval power, the Navy indicated an intent to continue permanently with such an approach. The Army, seeing such goals as contradictory to the basic strategic statement and capable of reinforcing a general trend to cut Army strength, informed Stark that his approach was "fundamentally unsound." In the estimate, it concluded that the peripheral strategy "may not accomplish the defeat of Germany and that it may be necessary to come to grips with the German armies on the continent of Europe."[26]

For this purpose, the WPD recommended, in a separate estimate, the building of an army of over eight million men, comprising a huge air force and 215 ground divisions, to be used for a massive assault on Germany no later than July 1943. These forces could be used, the WPD admitted, to wear down and encircle Germany first by action in Africa, the Near East, Iberia, and Scandinavia. Operations in those areas, however, "must be so conducted as to facilitate the decisive employment of allied forces in Central Europe," an area designated "our principle theater of war."[27]

With the United States still officially out of the war and Congress recently agreeing to a draft extension by only one vote after a bitter fight, Roosevelt was anything but pleased with such suggestions. In a "very frank" ninet minute discussion of the estimate with Secretary of War Henry L. Stimson on September 25, the president expressed his displeasure over the Army's assumption "that we must invade and crush Germany," an assumption he felt would elicit "a very bad reaction" from the American public. Stimson was forced to agree with this judgment. Roosevelt then returned to the subject of West Africa by asking the Army to prepare a study on possible action in the area. Two weeks later, Secretary of the Navy Frank Knox backed up this request by presenting Stimson with a plan drawn up by William C. Bullitt, former ambassador to the Soviet Union and France, to send an American expeditionary force to Casablanca.[28]

An alarmed Stimson immediately called upon Marshall and his highly respected senior military adviser, Lieutenant-General Stanley Embick, to convince Knox that such an operation would be an unworkable diversion while he pressed a similar position on Roosevelt. By October 9, Stimson had succeeded in convincing the president of the present impossibility of sending a force to West Africa, and the operation was temporarily shelved.[2]

Despite this success, the Army seemed to be fighting a hopeless, rear-guard action. Public opinion simply would not tolerate the massive build-up the planners envisioned as necessary, while the president continued to toy with some form of quick offensive action in West Africa with unprepared and inadequate forces. Further complicating matters was the Army's own admission in the Victory Program that a massive assault would require preliminary peripheral action to weaken Germany and to acquire bases for the eventual offensive. The problem was that such action could so disperse Allied forces as to preclude the possibility of concentration for the eventual assault.

As early as August, at least one Army planner had arrived at a possible solution which revolved around the unexpected continuation of Russian resistance on the Eastern front. Immediately after Hitler's June 22 attack on the Soviet Union, most British and American planners had concluded that the German Army would cut through the Soviet forces "like a hot knife through butter," thereby providing the West with only a temporary respite from the full force of German strength.[30] By August, however, Russia's ability to withstand the German onslaught had led to a massive revision of these estimates and a realization that the Eastern front might contain the key to eventual victory through its ability to hold and destroy large portions of the German Army. American planners had therefore concluded in that month that United States aid might be more useful in Russia than in the Middle East. In the Victory Program they rated such aid as "one of the most important moves that could be made by the Associated Powers."[31] In October, the WPD reinforced this conclusion by pointing out that decisive defeat of Russia would make Germany "practically invulnerable" against even the tightest sea blockade.[32]

Two months earlier, however, Lieutenant-Colonel Edwin E. Schwien of the Army's Intelligence (G-2) Division had concluded that material aid would be of insufficient help to keep Russia in the war. Her collapse, he stated in an August memorandum which echoed recent public statements by the Soviets, could only be avoided by the creation of an immediate "diversion front" in Europe to relieve the pressure on the Red armies. That front could then serve as the base for future operations on the continent, thereby negating the need to wear down Germany first and obtain bases along the European periphery.

Schwien dismissed Dakar, North Africa, the Iberian Peninsula, the Balkans, and the Mediterranean as possible sites for this front on the grounds that they were unsafe, too far from existing bases of operations, and without the "vital strategic objectives" necessary for offensive operations. Further consideration of these areas he therefore labeled "unquestionably a patent absurdity." Northwest France, on the other hand, fulfilled all preconditions as both a diversion front and an offensive base. Schwien therefore recommended invasion of the area as " the only possible method of approach to an ultimate victory by the Democracies." The forces needed would include thirty-five infantry divisions with full support and local air superiority.[33]

Schwien's memorandum had stated in essence what would become the Army's rationale for a 1942 second front. While members of the WPD studied the concept,[34] the Soviets made clear their insistence on the immediate launching of such an operation if the West desired continued Russian participation in the war.

THE RUSSIAN ALLY

Hitler's June 22 attack had relieved the immediate pressure on Britain and provided her with the continental ally so desperately needed in 1941. Hence, Churchill temporarily buried his long and deep hostility to communism by welcoming Soviet Premier Josef Stalin to the Allied fold and offering him all the material aid that "time, geography and our growing resources allow." By July 12, the two powers had agreed to render each other all possible aid and not to conclude a separate peace.[35]

This agreement might truly be described as a "scrap of paper." Forced into an alliance because of the immediate German threat, neither Britain nor Russia had truly lost the mutual hostility and suspicion that had long dominated their relations. Moreover, in the summer of 1941, it was not at all certain that the immediate menace outweighed these older feelings. The Russians, viewing the German attack as a possible result of a secret Anglo-German agreement reached through the recent and mysterious flight of Rudolf Hess to Britain, feared that London might now take advantage of the situation by sitting back and watching the two land powers bleed each other to death. London in turn feared that the Soviets might quickly make a separate peace, as they had in 1918 and in effect in 1939, thereby once again unleashing the full force of the German military machine against Great Britain.[36]

Churchill had hoped his promise of economic assistance would end Russian suspicions. The Soviets, perhaps perceiving this offer as nothing more than an attempt to prolong the mutual bleeding to the advantage of London, demanded two further actions: recognition of their 1939-1940 conquests in Eastern Europe and the creation of an immediate "second front" in Western Europe. British recognition of the expanded Soviet frontiers, besides fulfilling Moscow's consistent demand over the past two years, would be a sign of "good faith" and would erase a major area of contention between the two powers. Thus, it would lessen the chance of friction that could lead to a separate peace during the war or a breakup of the alliance after the war. A second front in Western Europe would

commit the British in blood for the duration of the war and would immediately relieve the hard-pressed Russian armies.

During the first week in July, the Soviet ambassadors in London and
Washington voiced their desire that the East European conquests be recognized.[37] At the same time, former Soviet Foreign Minister Maxim Litvinov
was taken out of obscurity to sound the call for an immediate second front,
while local communist parties in Britain and the United States pressed a
similar line.[38] On July 18, Stalin formally responded to two messages from
Churchill by requesting British fronts against Hitler in northern France and
the Arctic.[39]

Both sets of Soviet demands ran into strong British opposition, the second even more than the first. Recognition of the East European conquests
involved a major modification of policy, but one that the Foreign Office
had considered prior to the June 22 attack as a means of weaning Moscow
from its benevolent neutrality towards Germany.[40] An immediate second
front in France, on the other hand, violated British strategic doctrine and
asked London to risk everything on a new offensive, in the aftermath of
its devastating defeats, while it still did not believe the Eastern front would
survive another month. Stalin "might as well have demanded the moon,"
was the later comment of a member of the COS.[41] Churchill therefore responded to Stalin by explaining the impossibility of establishing such a
front and offering to send him more airplanes instead. Meanwhile, British
Foreign Secretary Anthony Eden kept the door open to future recognition of Soviet territorial conquests by informing the House of Commons
that his approval of the recently signed nonterritorial treaty between Moscow and the Polish government-in-exile "does not involve any guarantee
of frontiers by His Majesty's Government."[42]

In Washington, the reaction to Soviet demands was quite different.
Partially because of Stalin's East European conquests, official American
policy toward Russia had been, in Dean Acheson's later words, "one of
coolness to the point of hostility."[43] Throughout 1940 and 1941, the administration had consistently refused to consider recognition of those conquests as a means of improving relations, and it had warned London of
its opposition to any British move in that direction.[44] On the day before
Hitler's attack, the State Department's European Affairs Division had
stated bluntly its belief that a Russo-German war would not mean that
the Soviet Union would be "defending, struggling for, or adhering to the
principles of international relations which we are supporting." In the event

of such a war, it continued, the United States should make no advance promises of assistance to Moscow or any commitments on such possible future policies as recognition of a Soviet government-in-exile.[45] Hitler's attack on the following day did little to change these views. As career officer Charles Bohlen later stated, the specialists insisted that Moscow, "even though now an ally, had to be watched closely because its ultimate aims clashed with those of the United States."[46]

American military planners showed similar mistrust. Their estimates of the Soviet Union had long assumed that Moscow's basic foreign policy goal was to expand communism, and they had noted the possibility of increased Soviet influence in geographically adjacent areas.[47] In April 1941, Colonel Joseph McNarney had brought this danger closer to home by informing General Marshall that, if Britain fell and the United States was forced to face the Axis alone, "internal disturbances may bring on communism."[48] According to his later recollections, General Albert C. Wedemeyer, author of the Army's Victory Program and one of Marshall's chief strategic planners, freely informed his chief at this time and later both of his belief that communism was a greater menace than fascism, and of his hope that Germany and Russia would "chew each other up" so that the Western Powers could arrange a peace to their liking. The United States, he further warned Marshall, "should always be mindful of the conditions that would prevail in the areas of combat after all hostilities had ceased." Wedemeyer grafted these beliefs onto his already strong anti-British sentiments when he attacked London's August strategy paper. Groping for "panaceas," the British were turning "to any ally out of necessity. They have even risked the consequences of an alliance with Russia, a step which every European knows has dire implications."[49]

As early as July, Assistant Secretary of State Adolph Berle had stated what those "dire implications" could be for the United States. Seeing the present detente with the Soviets as a temporary phenomenon that Moscow might easily break via a separate peace, he pressed for continued FBI surveillance of Soviet and communist agencies in the United States and the Hemisphere. He also warned Hopkins and Under Secretary of State Sumner Welles against giving military secrets to the Russians.[50] On July 22, Berle informed diplomatic officers to be wary of commercial transactions with the USSR because the Soviets were likely to use such transactions "to lay aside substantial sums for themselves and for their future work in this hemisphere."[51]

Equally important to the State Department was the necessity to block any British recognition of Soviet conquests in Eastern Europe. Besides expanding Russian influence, such recognition would lead to the same nightmarish repercussions as had the World War I secret treaties, thereby threatening American postwar goals. Berle thus termed the issue "damned dangerous,"[52] while Welles made clear to London that American approval of the July 12 Anglo-Soviet treaty was based on the pact's not dealing with territorial questions.[53] On August 1, a group of high-ranking State Department officials concluded that the United States should definitely "take part in European reconstruction" at the end of the war, and they recommended that a note be sent to the British proposing no postwar territorial or governmental commitments prior to the peace conference.[54]

With the ghost of Woodrow Wilson constantly in his mind, Roosevelt needed no urging in this direction. Despite his insistence on promising aid to Stalin shortly after Hitler's attack, [55] the president shared many of his advisers' fears, especially in regard to territorial treaties during the war. As early as July 14, he had informed Churchill of his opposition to such "deals," and Hopkins brought a similar message to London a few days later.[56] In August, Welles returned to the issue during the Atlantic Conference and received British assurance that no territorial treaty had been signed.[57]

By that time, however, the hard-pressed Stalin had temporarily dropped the frontier issue in favor of more military aid. When Hopkins visited Moscow in late July, the Soviet leader made no mention of Eastern Europe, pressing instead for long-term material aid and an American army on the Russian front.[58] Ivan Maisky, the Soviet ambassador to London, reinforced this desperate request by informing the British a few days later that, unless the United States entered the war and helped to create a second front, the Russians could not and would not continue the struggle.[59]

Roosevelt ignored Stalin's request for direct military intervention but did move in early August to speed the flow of material aid.[60] With the West rejecting both a second front and a territorial treaty, such aid was the only effective way to keep Russia fighting. At the end of the Atlantic Conference on August 13, Churchill and Roosevelt sent Stalin a joint letter outlining the results of the conference and suggesting a meeting of representatives in Moscow to determine Soviet supply needs.[61] In the words of two historians of this era, aid to Russia "had ceased to be a temporary expedient and had become a long-term project."[62] It had also become, Churchill and Roosevelt hoped, a substitute for a second front and territorial recognition.

Stalin at first appeared willing to accept such a substitute, for on August 15 he agreed to the proposed conference, expressed "sincere thanks" for the offer of supplies, and even admitted to the Western ambassadors that it would be "difficult" for the British to create a new front.[63] His opinions changed sharply when the German Army renewed its offensive a few weeks later. On September 4, he warned Churchill in an urgent message that the Russian front had "considerably deteriorated" during the past three weeks and that Russia was now in "mortal danger" with

> only one means of egress from this situation—to establish in the present year a second front somewhere in the Balkans or France, capable of drawing away from the Eastern front thirty to forty divisions, and at the same time of ensuring to the Soviet Union thirty thousand tons of aluminum by the beginning of October next and a monthly minimum of aid amounting to four hundred aircraft and five hundred tanks. . . .
>
> Without these two forms of help the Soviet Union will either suffer defeat or be weakened to such an extent that it will lose for a long period any capacity to render assistance to its allies by its actual operations on the fronts of the struggle against Hitlerism.[64]

With Maisky and the British ambassador in Moscow repeating the implied warning of a collapse and/or separate peace, [65] Churchill responded by informing Stalin that supplies and troops for the southern Russian front would be available after the completion of the planned offensive against Rommel. Diversionary operations in the West or the Balkans, on the other hand, were presently impossible. When Stalin replied by asking for twenty-five to thirty divisions in either Archangel or on the southern Russian front, Churchill quickly pointed out the impossibility of honoring such a request. He again attempted to mollify the Soviet leader by stressing the substantial forces that would be available for the southern front after the Libyan battle. General Sir Hastings Ismay of the COS would accompany the Lend-Lease mission to Moscow in order to study "any plans for practical co-operation which may suggest themselves."[66] At the same time Churchill instructed Lord Max Beaverbrook, head of the British supply mission, to show Stalin that his present ideas had "no foundation of reality on which to rest."[67]

The Soviet leader was anything but pleased to receive such news when Beaverbrook arrived in Moscow on September 28. With the guns at the front audible and the Soviet capital in immediate danger, Stalin interpreted the message as a deliberate refusal to help a beleaguered ally. "There is no war in the Caucasus," he replied to the offer of aid after the Libyan battle, "but there is in the Ukraine."[68] As for possible British operations near Archangel, he sardonically remarked that the theater "at least has the advantage that Churchill knows the way there—and the way back again,"[69] a grim reminder of the prime minister's role in the 1918 Allied intervention and Stalin's continuing distrust of him.

That distrust was only increased by Churchill's October 12 offer to let British troops replace the Russians in northern Iran so that five or six Soviet divisions could be released for combat on the Eastern front. Seeing the offer as a further attempt to maximize Russian casualties, the Soviets pointedly asked why the British refused to go to the front and fight, while the British ambassador in Moscow warned of growing Russian suspicion and mistrust. Cooperation would occur, the Soviets had made clear to the ambassador, "as soon as we could do something on land to relieve the German pressure."[70]

Such warnings were not limited to diplomatic channels. Throughout the summer and fall, Moscow maintained a high-level propaganda campaign in Britain to force Churchill into action, and by September that effort had achieved startling results. A poll in the middle of the month found 17 percent of the British public rating invasion of the continent as the government's most important problem, the highest percentage for any problem listed.[71] A month later, 49 percent of those polled felt that Churchill had not taken full advantage of the new situation created by Russian entry into the war.[72] Upon his return from Moscow, Lord Beaverbrook and his powerful press joined the growing chorus of attack on British strategy. "It is nonsense," he wrote, "to say that we can do nothing for Russia. We can, as soon as we decide to sacrifice long-term projects and a general view of the war which, though still cherished, became completely obsolete on the day when Russia was attacked."[73] The American military estimates of August and September, stressing similar points, arrived in London at the same time.

While Churchill realized the necessity to respond to this combined assault, he insisted that British action in France or southern Russia was presently neither desirable nor possible and that his Mediterranean strategy remained valid. The way to silence his critics without violating his strat-

egic concepts was to offer immediate offensive action against Rommel in
Libya with a rapid Mediterranean followup. During October, the prime
minister therefore developed a grandiose strategic plan hinging upon the
destruction of Rommel (CRUSADER), which he hoped would bring French
North Africa voluntarily into the Allied fold, strengthen Turkey's neutrality, and pave the way for an attack on Sicily (WHIPCORD). That attack
would in turn provide Stalin with a "second front" of sorts, silence criticism at home and abroad, fulfill his old desire to knock Italy out of the
war and regain control of the Mediterranean, and set the stage for later
attacks along the European periphery in conjunction with revolts by the
subjugated European populations. On October 20, he fully explained these
plans to Roosevelt and requested American troops in Ireland (MAGNET)
in order to release more British forces for the planned offensive.[74]

Unfortunately, this plan contained major political and military difficulties. As Churchill himself had realized and made clear to Roosevelt, it
would provide no aid to Stalin for six crucial months.[75] Furthermore, his
military advisers and Middle East commanders thought WHIPCORD too
risky and preferred an attack on Tunis after CRUSADER in order to secure
control of North Africa. While they made this preference clear, Churchill
heard of Bullitt's proposal for an American move on Casablanca. Seizing
this opportunity to involve the United States directly in a major Mediterranean offensive, Churchill quickly acceded to the wishes of his military
advisers. On October 28 he agreed to replace WHIPCORD with GYM-
NAST, the plan for a North African exploitation of CRUSADER.[76]

Even this modified plan, however, ran into immediate difficulties.
CRUSADER was delayed until November 18, and on that very day German pressure forced the recall of General Maxime Weygand, commander
of French forces in North Africa and the man London had counted on to
bring his area into the Allied fold. To make matters worse, Rommel launche
a bold counterattack that upset British estimates, while Stalin exploded
over the lack of British action. On the evening of November 6, Stalin publicly attributed Russian military reverses to "the absence of a second front."
In a blistering letter to Churchill two days later, he warned that military
supplies in no way settled the issue of relations between the two powers.
The present lack of "clarity" and "mutual confidence," he stated, was the
result of lack of agreement not only on military assistance, but also on war
aims and "plans for the post-war organization of peace." Churchill's November 4 offer to send two generals to Moscow to "clear things up" would

therefore be accepted only if the officers arrived prepared to discuss such issues.[78]

Insulted at the tone of this message and extremely reluctant to discuss postwar boundary questions, Churchill at first refused to respond. Stalin's need for Britain, he bluntly told Eden, was "greater than our need for him."[79] Eden's contrary feelings, combined with continuing expressions of Soviet dissatisfaction, separate peace rumors, and an apology from Maisky for the rough tone of the November 8 message, quickly led Churchill to change his stance and agree in late November to send Eden to Moscow to discuss the issues Stalin had raised.[80]

Exactly what the British foreign secretary would do in Moscow remained unclear, for any postwar agreement would arouse a storm of protest from Washington. On December 4, the Foreign Office attempted to calm American fears by informing the State Department that Eden would attempt to allay Soviet suspicion and resentment and give Stalin "as much satisfaction as possible," but "without entering into commitments."[81] Washington, however, had received word in September that London had already given Moscow a "half promise" in regard to postwar Soviet domination of Eastern Europe,[82] and so remained unconvinced of British sincerity. On December 5, Roosevelt and Secretary of State Cordell Hull warned Eden against going beyond the Atlantic Charter in dealing with postwar problems and stated that the test of Western "good faith" should be the prompt deliverance of supplies. To make sure London did not go beyond this position, the Americans insisted upon being kept informed of all negotiations. Forced to agree, Eden could offer Stalin nothing on the diplomatic front.[83]

The situation in regard to military aid was not much better. Eden had originally been authorized to offer the Soviets ten air squadrons for the southern Russian front after Rommel's defeat, but the German General's counterattack, combined with the disaster at Pearl Harbor two weeks later, forced the cancellation of even this modest offer on December 13.[84] Eden thus arrived in Moscow three days later completely empty-handed.

With his armies having successfully defended the Soviet capital and launching a massive counterattack on Hitler's overextended lines, and Anglo-American forces under heavy Japanese pressure, Stalin did not press Eden for any second front.[85] On diplomatic issues, however, he now demanded a treaty of alliance for the duration of the war and a second treaty for the postwar era that would contain a secret protocol recognizing Soviet frontiers as of June 21, 1941, and Moscow's right to bases in Finland and

Rumania, and stating Allied agreement to divide Germany after the war. In
return, the Soviets would support postwar British bases in Western Europe,
European confederations, and a council of victorious powers. These agreements, Stalin informed Eden, would make the Alliance stronger by making
the war aims of the two powers "identical"; if war aims differed, he warned
"there would be no alliance."[86]

Eden agreed, but made clear his powerlessness to act in the face of the
positions of Washington and London and his own inability to sign any
treaty without prior approval from both capitals. After two days of deadlock, Stalin was forced to agree on December 20 that the United States be
consulted before any treaty was signed. Eden wired Churchill that his mission had been a success but warned that London must expect "continued
badgering" from the Soviets on the frontier issue.[87]

THE ARCADIA CONFERENCE

Churchill received this disturbing warning while on his way to Washington by sea. Viewing the Baltic States as "the outpost of Europe against
Bolshevism,"[88] he personally opposed recognition of Stalin's territorial
demands, and, further, he wished to avoid any discussion of an issue capable of alienating the United States at this crucial juncture in the war. In
the wake of Pearl Harbor, he feared that the Americans might turn against
not only his Mediterranean strategy, but also the entire Germany-first
concept in an attempt to gain immediate revenge for the Japanese attack.
He was traveling to Washington to avoid just such a calamity.[89]

By the time Eden's message arrived, in fact, Churchill had completed a
long strategic memorandum for Roosevelt that meshed British Mediterranean plans with the Russian military and political situation without violating
either his strategic ideas or American political sensibilities. He had accomplished this extraordinary feat by admitting that Hitler's failure and losses
in Russia were "the prime fact in the war at this time," but concluding
that neither the United States nor Britain had "any part to play" on this
front except to send "without fail and punctually, the supplies we have
promised. In this way alone shall we hold our influence over Stalin and be
able to weave the mighty Russian effort into the general texture of the
war."[90]

Such a statement enabled Churchill to avoid Soviet demands for a second
front and to return to the Mediterranean. At the same time, it was also an
indirect acceptance of Washington's December 5 position that prompt de-

liverance of supplies to the USSR would be the Western sign of "good faith" and the way to exert influence on Russia without territorial concessions.[91] The prime minister dismissed Stalin's earlier warning that such aid was an insufficient sign on the grounds that the Russians "have got to go on fighting for their lives anyway" and were dependent upon the supplies. He therefore informed London on December 20 that Soviet demands were contrary to the Atlantic Charter and that territorial issues should be saved for the postwar peace conference. On the same day, he reminded Eden that Britain was pledged not to enter into any secret pacts and that to approach Roosevelt with Stalin's proposals "would be to court a blank refusal, and might cause lasting trouble on both sides." Even to raise such issues "informally" with the president would be "inexpedient."[92]

Now was the time, however, to approach Roosevelt on combined action in North Africa, for as he told the COS before departure, the "cautious" approach used while "wooing" the United States had ended; "now that she is in this harem, we talk to her quite differently!"[93] In his memorandum, Churchill expanded on his October plans by bluntly requesting not only MAGNET, but 150,000 American troops to join 55,000 British troops for GYMNAST to be launched in conjunction with a revived CRUSADER against Rommel. Successful completion of these operations would enable the West to occupy and control the entire North African shore in 1942, thus closing the ring around Germany and setting the stage for a 1943 move into Sicily or Italy as well as a bombing offensive against Germany. In turn, small armored and mechanized forces would be able to land in three or four European countries with arms and material for the rebelling European populations; these combined forces could then advance on Germany.[94]

When Churchill and his advisers arrived in Washington on December 22 to begin the ARCADIA Conference, they quickly discovered that their fears had been groundless. Not only did the Americans seem determined to continue with the Germany-first concept, but Roosevelt had retained his intense interest in an African landing. A version of that operation still maintained a high priority in American hemispheric defense plans as well as in Roosevelt's own mind. On December 21, he and his advisers had therefore agreed to make West Africa the "foremost" area to be considered for an American expeditionary force after defense efforts had been completed in the Atlantic, Pacific, and British Isles.[95] On the following evening, the president and prime minister discussed GYMNAST and, according to Churchill's later recollections, "the discussion was not *whether*, but *how*."[96]

Contrary to Churchill's expectations, Roosevelt was also apparently interested in discussing Stalin's territorial demands. While no formal discussion of the issue took place during the conference, strong evidence exists that numerous informal talks between the two leaders culminated in an agreement to postpone all territorial settlements until the peace conference.[97]

Beneath these military and political agreements lay severe problems. The decision to postpone territorial settlements conveniently ignored the fact that Stalin would not tolerate such postponement, and the military situation in December 1941 in no way guaranteed that he would be forced to accept it. Equally insoluble problems surrounded the decision to invade North Africa. British and American planners soon concluded that launching GYMNAST would adversely affect all other troop movements and convoys to Russia, and that no expeditionary force could be assembled and transported until May 1942. Even then, the West would not have the power to land and hold North Africa unless French forces refused to fight, Madrid remained neutral and held up any German countermove through Spain, and Russia continued to engage the bulk of the *Wehrmacht* on the Eastern front.[98]

Nor were the Americans unified in support of the ARCADIA decisions. For a group within the State Department, postponing territorial settlements with Russia would be a severe mistake. American influence over Moscow, this group claimed, was now at its height and could only decrease as the war progressed. That influence should therefore be used immediately, through the lever of Lend-Lease aid, to force Stalin to drop his demands.[99]

The American joint chiefs of staff (JCS) disapproved of such an aggressive policy. Extremely apprehensive over Stalin's September 4 warning of collapse and/or separate peace, they wished to avoid any serious dispute with Russia while the military situation was so precarious. Roosevelt apparently agreed with such reasoning. Furthermore, both he and Hull continued to insist that the mistakes of World War I not be repeated. The postwar peace conference would have to have a free hand in settling territorial disputes, and any discussion of Soviet frontiers beforehand could lead to compromises that would be binding on the delegates. Such compromises might also alienate ethnic voting blocs in the United States at a time when internal unity was of paramount importance.[100]

Also of importance was the fact that not all parties agreed that Western influence over Russia was at its height in December 1941. Such influence

might not reach its zenith until the end of the war, when American and
British power would be fully mobilized while Russia was desperately seek-
ing reconstruction aid. As Churchill stated in a January 8 letter informing
Eden of the president's position on postponement,

> No one can forsee how the balance of power will lie or where the
> winning armies will stand at the end of the war. It seems probable
> however that the United States and the British Empire, far from
> being exhausted, will be the most powerfully armed and economic
> *bloc* the world has ever seen, and that the Soviet Union will then
> need our aid in reconstruction far more than we shall need theirs.[101]

Internal American divisions over proper strategic policy were even more
intense than those over territorial issues. While the JCS formally agreed to
the British approach during the conference,[102] Army planners continued
to express strong suspicions regarding its viability and motivations. In the
aftermath of Pearl Harbor and the Navy's and the public's subsequent desire for immediate revenge in the Far East, these planners were more than
ever convinced of the necessity to limit present efforts to defense while
building up forces for an eventual concentrated assault on Germany via
Western Europe.[103] London's approach, they insisted, involved a poten-
tially disastrous dispersion of forces and was motivated, in General Embick's
words, "more largely by political than by sound strategic purposes." Occupation of North Africa, Embick informed Marshall during the conference,
would not restore Mediterranean communications as the COS had claimed,
and any belief that the Allies could launch an invasion of Europe from the
area was so "irrational" as to be "fantastic." Undertaking GYMNAST, he
concluded, would be "a mistake of the first magnitude."[104]

Other Army planners stated that GYMNAST would adversely affect
their desperate defense efforts in the Far East [105] and would be an extremely
risky operation. By early January, many had concluded that the odds were
about four to one against success in what they were referring to as a "cock-
eyed" and "crazy gamble." One infuriated planner wanted to send Roosevelt a one-page memorandum listing "65 reasons why we should *not* do
GYMNAST."[106]

Efforts by Marshall and Stimson to warn Roosevelt of the problems involved in GYMNAST and Army opposition to the project met with very
limited success.[107] Reinforced by reports of an imminent German move

through Spain or Portugal and positive recommendations from his civilian advisers as well as Churchill, and anxious in the wake of Pearl Harbor to shift public attention away from the Pacific while boosting morale through offensive action, the president continued to insist upon the operation in some form for 1942.[108]

From the Army's point of view, such insistence only showed the dangerous influences of the Navy and Churchill on Roosevelt's rather naive strategic thinking and its own inability to influence that thinking. "The Navy is the apple of his eye and the Army is the stepchild," complained Major-General Joseph Stilwell in the privacy of his diary. Roosevelt, an "amateur" in military affairs likely to "act on sudden impulses," had been "completely hypnotized by the British," who had "sold him a bill of goods" and had "his ear, while we have the hind tit." Events in the world and the "tremendous pressure to do something," Stilwell concluded, were "crowding us into ill-advised and ill-considered projects."[109]

As the official British military history of this period has stated, the ARCADIA agreements were thus "more formal than real."[110] In both political and military spheres, those agreements rested upon unwarranted assumptions and masked deep divisions beneath the surface. During the next few months, disasters in both spheres would reveal those divisions and would lead to a new American initiative within the Alliance.

CHAPTER TWO

THE AMERICAN INITIATIVE
JANUARY TO APRIL 1942

The ARCADIA Conference was followed by a series of Allied military reverses that quickly negated most of the planning done in Washington. While Rommel launched another counterattack in the desert, the British suffered a series of naval disasters in the Mediterranean which temporarily gave the Axis control of that sea. Malta was under heavy air attack and expecting invasion daily, and London found itself unable to reinforce its desert army or prevent supplies from reaching Rommel. Churchill's grandiose Mediterranean plans had failed miserably, and on January 31, the COS concluded that supplies could no longer be set aside for GYMNAST. By March 3, the combined chiefs of staff (CCS) had indefinitely postponed the operation, and Churchill and Roosevelt were forced to concur a few days later.[1]

In the Atlantic, German U-boats were having their best season against Allied shipping. In addition, three German capital ships escaped from Brest to the North Sea on February 12, thereby endangering future northern convoys to Russia as well as insulting British naval and air prowess. On the Eastern front, the Soviet counteroffensive ground to an inconclusive halt in the same month, and the Germans began preparations for a massive spring assault.

In the Pacific, disaster followed disaster as the Japanese wrecked Allied defense efforts and advanced virtually at will. By mid-February, they had effectively isolated the Philippines and had taken the "unconquerable" British bastion of Singapore. The conquest of Australia, New Zealand, Hawaii, Burma, and India all appeared to be within Japanese capabilities, and on the horizon loomed the nightmare of a triple juncture between Rommel, the German Army in southern Russia, and the Japanese. Allied troops and supplies were rushed in every direction and usually arrived too late to do much good anywhere.

The political outlook mirrored the somber military situation. Australia and New Zealand now demanded the return of their troops from the Middle East. In the United States, public opinion, reinforced by the Navy and General Douglas MacArthur, insisted upon immediate offensive action in the Pacific against what it considered the "real" enemy—Japan. Roosevelt's inability to provide such action led to severe attacks on his war leadership.

Even more ominous was Russia's continued pressure for more aid, a second front, and recognition of her conquests in Eastern Europe. Rumors of a separate peace again filled the air, and in February, London reversed its position and decided to sign a territorial treaty in order to mollify the Soviet. Washington remained adamantly opposed to such a move, and the three-way argument threatened to critically weaken the Grand Alliance in this moment of crisis.

From the American point of view, Britain's approach to the war had resulted in complete failure. On both military and political levels, it was time for an American initiative within the Alliance. That initiative emerged in the spring of 1942 in the form of a military plan for immediate concentration of forces in Britain for a cross-Channel assault to be launched as soon as possible.

THE ARMY PLAN

Army planners developed this second-front concept in late February as the best method of dealing with what they had concluded were the two basic military problems facing the West in 1942: the worldwide dispersion of forces and the need to aid the crucial Russian front as quickly as possible. Both problems and the proposed solution were obviously military in nature, but they were also political and were recognized as such by the planner.

The Army had long viewed dispersion as an integral part of a strategy designed by London to protect its political interests. Such dispersion, they had argued, was militarily unsound and was capable of leading to disastrous repercussions. The events of early 1942 only served to support such beliefs. Furthermore, American ability to determine strategy within the Alliance was based on the growing productivity of the United States. Continued dispersion of American resources could easily weaken that ability to the point of placing American men and material at the mercy of present and future British plans.[2]

Roosevelt's continuing agreement with those plans in the face of Army opposition seemed to show the dangerous degree to which the president was under Churchill's influence. It also suggested the low esteem in which he held his military advisers. Such a situation was not only dangerous to American interests, but was also a direct assault upon the Army's pride and position. If continued, it could easily lead to unsound military operations, American defense of British political interests, and an undermining of General Marshall's position as chief military adviser to the president. These in turn would adversely affect Army staff morale and Marshall's effectiveness as the staff chief. Roosevelt's insistent desire for quick offensive action at ARCADIA had been a prime factor in his agreement with Churchill's plans. The Army realized that it would have to substitute a concentration-oriented offensive for its defensive plans in order to regain its position with the president.[3] The obvious answer was a cross-Channel attack.

Equally important to the Army was its deteriorating position in relation to the Navy. Despite the ARCADIA decisions, American public opinion, General MacArthur, and Navy planners all viewed Japan as the primary enemy; Pearl Harbor, they felt, had to be avenged and losses in the Pacific stopped.[4] In line with such reasoning, Admiral Ernest J. King, the new CNO, was already pressing for Army troops to garrison islands in the Pacific.[5] If King's request was honored, it could easily prove to be the first step in destroying the Germany-first concept, a decision the Army viewed as imperilling final victory in the war. Interestingly, such a decision would also raise naval influence at the expense of the Army by dispersing the Army's forces to the whims of a Pacific-oriented naval strategy, as well as cripple General Arnold's efforts to establish a separate air arm by continuing the trend toward treating his forces as the "step child" of the other services.[6] Concentration in one theater meant concentration of air power, and subsequently greater control by the AAF over its own destiny.

Such concentration for the defeat of Germany would have to be accomplished, however, before public and naval pressure for Pacific action became overwhelming, and the quickest method was via a cross-Channel attack. A peripheral approach through the Mediterranean would probably involve fewer casualties than such a direct confrontation with German power, but would be so time-consuming as to endanger the Germany-first approach and, with it, the Army's entire position. Continued dispersion in the European theater would thus lead to further dispersion in the Pacific, with disastrous consequences for the Army and the country as a whole in both military and political spheres.

The Army, in short, viewed its own future to be intricately interwoven with its concept of the correct way to defeat the Axis. It had, in fact, equated its own interests with those of the United States in the war. Concentration of forces in the United Kingdom for a cross-Channel attack may have been the only way to achieve victory, but in the context of early 1942 it was also the only way to counter the growing influence of Britain and the Navy. While the principle of concentration is a cardinal tenet of military thought, adherence to it in this case was as political as it was military in nature.

The Army also recognized the political aspect of aiding Russia and the relationship of this issue to the entire dispersion debate. The planners had kept themselves informed of Soviet demands regarding frontiers, supplies, and a second front, as well as the veiled threats of a separate peace if these demands were not met.[7] Such a peace would be catastrophic to the war effort and would either end the chance of victory or delay it indefinitely. It would certainly destroy any hopes of a cross-Channel attack, since such an operation depended upon the bulk of the German Army being tied down in the East. Thus it would probably lead to American acceptance of dispersion and a Pacific-first strategy.

Ironically, Moscow had made clear that Russia's continued participation in the war against Germany and her eventual participation in the war against Japan depended on the establishment of a second front in France.[8] As at least one Army planner realized, the logic was circular; continued Russian participation was necessary to launch the cross-Channel attack, and the launching of that operation was necessary to keep Russia in the war.[9] Furthermore, both the attack and continued Russian participation were needed to save the principles of concentration and Germany-first, and with them the entire Army position.

As an added point, Soviet propaganda for a second front was proving dangerously effective in the West. By late March, the Joint Psychological Warfare Committee (JPWC) was warning that public demand for cross-Channel operations could prove "embarrassing to the actual conduct of the war," and if not satisfied could result in a lowering of public morale.[10] On all levels, the Russian demand thus strengthened the Army's insistence on immediate concentration for a cross-Channel attack.

As in August 1941, the Russian situation provided the immediate stimulus for second-front plans in Washington. On February 12, G-2 circulated a somber report on that situation to Hopkins and to the Army and Navy. Because of the Soviets' great distrust of the Western Allies, G-2 warned, there was a "distinct possibility" of a separate peace on the Eastern front "which should be kept constantly in mind." That distrust and danger, it admitted, was partially a function of the Soviet system and therefore could not be completely negated. A large portion of it, however, was caused by American reliance on Britain in all relations with Moscow, general Allied military weakness, and the small amount of Lend-Lease aid being sent to the USSR. To keep Russia in the war, G-2 recommended direct contact with the Russians on high policy matters, more aid, and decisive action capable of convincing the Soviets "of our strength and determination" as well as "our desire and ability to fight a war vigorously and victoriously."[11]

Whether this memorandum profoundly affected the planners and policy-makers or simply supported and coalesced thoughts already prevalent remains unclear. In any event, American military and political leaders soon acted to implement these recommendations. On February 28, the WPD's new chief, Brigadier-General Dwight D. Eisenhower, summed up two months of divisional discussions and private musings in a memorandum to Marshall which stressed the urgent need for a second front to aid the Soviets. In the present situation, Eisenhower maintained, only three objectives beyond continental and Hawaiian defense were "necessary" as opposed to "desirable": maintenance of the United Kingdom and her sea lanes, prevention of a German-Japanese junction in the India-Middle East area, and retention of Russia as an active participant in the war. Of the three, retention of Russia was the most pressing. It required "immediate and definite" action by the West consisting of Lend-Lease aid and "the early initiation of operations" to divert "sizable portions of the German army" from the Eastern front.

Such operations, Eisenhower noted, were of both a political and a military nature; they had to prevent a Russian willingness to end the war as well as make it militarily possible for Moscow to continue fighting. The operations therefore had to be *"so conceived and so presented to the Rus-*

sians," he emphasized, "that they will recognize the importance of the support rendered." Since only a cross-Channel assault fulfilled these requirements, Eisenhower recommended that the United States and Britain immediately develop a "definite plan" for such an offensive capable of engaging German air and ground forces by the late summer.[12]

Other planners and officials were thinking along similar lines. As early as February 24, Stimson had reached the same conclusions without even knowing of Eisenhower's memorandum.[13] On March 3, Arnold pressed Marshall for immediate concentration of air and ground forces for an invasion of the continent "at the earliest possible moment."[14] At a meeting with the president on March 5, Marshall, Arnold, and Stimson all argued for an end to dispersion and an immediate buildup in Britain for a cross-Channel attack to aid Russia. King objected, writing on the same day to Roosevelt that the United States could not allow Japan to overrun the "white man's countries" of Australia and New Zealand "because of the repercussion among the non-white races of the world." He therefore recommended a Pacific offensive as an alternative to any cross-Channel assault.[15] But the president, according to Stimson, "seemed strongly and favorably impressed" by the Army idea, as was Hopkins, who felt his chief "would come to it."[16]

While Stimson worked on Roosevelt, Marshall attempted to convince King of the necessity for a cross-Channel assault. At a March 7 JCS meeting, Marshall informed the CNO that he had received a warning from one of his military observers that the Russians would consider a separate peace "justified" if the Allies "do not initiate an offensive on a large scale in the West."[17]

That warning was also sent to the president, and along with Stimson's urgings and word of the indefinite postponement of GYMNAST, succeeded in convincing Roosevelt of the necessity for such an operation. On March 6, the secretary of war found Roosevelt "keenly interested" in a second front and desirous of further discussion of the issue on the following day. After that discussion, Stimson noted that "the matter is working along in the direction which I had hoped. The President seems to have accepted it into making it his own."[18] On March 8 and 9, Roosevelt agreed to Churchill's recent request for shipping dispersions in the Pacific on condition that GYMNAST was now out of the question. Roosevelt then suggested a redivision of Allied areas of responsibility to give the JCS complete control over the Pacific and the creation of an Atlantic-European theater of combined responsibility with "definite plans for establishment of a new front on the European continent. . . . I am becoming more and more interested," he explained, in "the establishment of a new front this summer."[19] Stimson joyfully noted that with this message the president had "accomplished what I have been hoping and working for, namely, he took the initiative out of the hands of Churchill, where I am sure it would have degenerated into a simple defensive operation to stop up urgent rat holes most of which I fear are hopeless."[20]

During the next two weeks, the second-front concept picked up increasing momentum. Arnold promoted the idea in letters to friends in England.[21] On March 14, Hopkins wrote Roosevelt that the plan "should be pressed home. There is nothing to lose. . . . I doubt if any single thing is as important as getting some sort of a front this summer against Germany."[22] Further support came the next day when Ambassador William D. Leahy in France reported that any Allied force landing in that country would have the immediate support of 100,000 ex-soldiers in the unoccupied zone.[23] Ambassador to Britain John G. Winant, temporarily home for consultation on the Russian frontiers issue, also backed the Army plan,[24] and on March 18, Roosevelt informed Churchill that he expected to send in a few days "a more definite plan for a joint attack in Europe itself."[25] On March 20, the president's feelings on the proposed operation were so strong that Stimson rated their discussion "one of the best talks I ever had with him."[26]

The Navy proved a good deal more difficult to convince. During February, the Joint U.S. Strategic Committee (JUSSC) and the Joint Planning Staff (JPS) had been discussing the second-front issue in depth but had been unable to reach agreement. While the AAF representatives proposed accepting the possible loss of the Southwest Pacific to permit the launching of a 1942 cross-Channel assault to keep Russia in the war, the Navy pressed for a Pacific-first strategy. Taking a middle position, Army planners called for a defensive effort to hold the Southwest Pacific in conjunction with a buildup in the United Kingdom for 1942.[27]

Unable to reconcile these differing approaches, the JPS on March 14 forwarded the individual JUSSC studies to its superiors with the recommendation that the JCS choose one definite course of action. King, of course, refused to accept the loss of the Southwest Pacific, while Marshall and Arnold were equally opposed to any Pacific-first strategy. The Army plan was thus the only effective compromise. On March 16, the JCS with little debate agreed to a modified version of that plan by calling for a United Kingdom buildup coupled with reinforcements to the Southwest Pacific "in accordance with current commitments."[28]

Unfortunately, this JCS agreement avoided the crucial question of when the cross-Channel attack could be launched. A 1942 assault was necessary to keep Russia in the war and to force an early concentration in Britain. Because of shipping shortages, however, few American troops could arrive in England in time to take part in such an assault, and the decision to defend the Southwest Pacific only compounded the problem. A revised annex to the JUSSC studies had highlighted the difficulties by pointing out that, because of present shipping commitments, there might be no American ground forces in England for an assault "at the time deemed essential from strategic considerations." To solve this dilemma, it stated that Britain would have to provide the bulk of the forces for any 1942 attack; if London refused to agree, then the American strategic concept should be reevaluated "and the possibility of concentrating U.S. offensive effort in the Pacific area considered."[29] In a March 25 memorandum, the WPD's successor, the Operations Division (OPD), partially backed away from this extreme position by refusing to mention a 1942 target date. The OPD insisted, however, that if London refused to accept the principle of immediate concentration for an attack to be launched as soon as possible, then "we must turn our *backs* upon the Eastern Atlantic and go, full out, as quickly as possible, against Japan!"[30]

Marshall presented the reasoning and conclusions contained in this memorandum to Roosevelt later that day in a White House meeting, and the president suggested that the matter be turned over to the CCS. Marshall, Stimson, and Hopkins all realized that such a move meant certain emasculation of the Army proposal. As a result of their knowledge of American plans and the work of British planners, the COS had by this time presented their own cross-Channel concept to the Americans. That concept differed drastically from the American plan, seeing invasion as a possibility only in 1943 and then on condition that the ring strategy had succeeded in severely weakening the Germans.[31]

As Marshall had succinctly observed, the two plans "represented widely divergent views," and on his suggestion the CCS had directed the Combined Planning Staff (CPS) on March 24 to reconcile the two approaches.[32] Chance of a successful compromise were obviously quite slim. Hopkins therefore suggested at the March 25 meeting that the president bypass the entire combined machinery by sending the plan with "a most trusted messenger" directly to Churchill and the COS once it had been perfected. Roosevelt agreed and told his advisers to put the plan into shape as soon as possible.[33]

The OPD was given the task and by March 27 had completed its work. Officially entitled "Operations in Western Europe" and commonly known as the "Marshall Memorandum," the proposal called for an immediate concentration of forces in Britain (BOLERO) for a cross-Channel attack in the spring of 1943 (ROUNDUP) comprising thirty American and eighteen British divisions as well as 5,800 airplanes. In addition to its military merits, the OPD pointed out that such an operation might provide the Allies with an "active sector" across the Channel during the summer of 1942, thereby making veterans of raw troops, raising morale, giving "immediate satisfaction to the public," and aiding Russia. In this regard, it also proposed launching a limited "emergency" operation of five divisions in the fall of 1942 (SLEDGE-HAMMER) if the Germans were "critically weakened" in Western Europe or if the Eastern front became desperate. Since continued Russian participation was "essential" to defeat Germany, launching the assault in such a situation "should be considered a sacrifice for the common good."[34]

Army planners had labeled the 1942 operation a "sacrifice" with good reason. Although the CPS was still working on the American and British plans, the OPD had been informed in advance of the staff's probable conclusions that a successful 1942 assault was not feasible and that even an early 1943 attack was only a "possibility" contingent upon continued Russian resistance and an early decision to concentrate forces in the United Kingdom.[35] While these conclusions meant that no 1942 attack could sustain itself, they also highlighted the paradoxical necessity of such an attack to assure the prerequisites for a 1943 assault—continued Russian resistance and early concentration in Britain.

For the time being, Roosevelt and his advisers ignored this dilemma. On the afternoon of April 1, Marshall presented the OPD's memorandum at a White House meeting and received full presidential approval. Plans were also made for Hopkins and the chief of staff to fly to London to win British support. King, however, had recently appealed to Marshall for further Pacific reinforcements at the expense of the European theater,[36] and before the meeting ended Hopkins moved to insure American unity by asking for the CNO's personal approval of the Army plan. Realizing that he could never get full concentration against Japan as long as Germany remained undefeated, King acceded to Hopkins' request.[37]

The Army had thus been successful in the first phase of its second-front plan. Both the Navy and the president had been won over; now it was time for the prime minister. Or so it seemed at this time. Closer examination shows that, while Roosevelt had approved the plan, his reasons for doing so were quite different from those of his military advisers.

ROOSEVELT AND THE SECOND FRONT

Roosevelt shared his military advisers' beliefs regarding the Germany-first concept and, in theory at least, the necessity of preventing further dispersions.[38] Like them, he also realized that public pressure for a Pacific-first approach was reaching dangerous proportions and necessitated adoption of a decisive plan for quick victory in Europe.

From Roosevelt's point of view, however, such a plan had to include early and successful offensive action. The previously apathetic public was now clamoring for such action, but in the Pacific, and the press had begun to attack Roosevelt for not properly assuming his military functions and ordering an assault. Moreover, Soviet propaganda had had its desired effect; the public was also screaming for a second front to relieve the hard-pressed Russian armies. From the president's viewpoint, these rather contradictory public feelings all led to one conclusion—the necessity for an immediate offensive in the European theater. Such a move would satisfy demands for an offensive to aid the Russians, fulfill the public's psychological need for aggressive action, and take the American people's minds off the Pacific theater.[39] But GYMNAST, the only European offensive planned for 1942, had been indefinitely postponed in early March, and Roosevelt knew that for domestic reasons he would have to find a new one. The Army provided him with just such an offensive at the very moment the North African assault was being shelved.

While this public opinion issue was critical in the president's acceptance of the Army plan, fear of a separate peace in the East and Britain's February decision to accede to renewed Soviet demands for recognition of the absorption of the Baltic States were equally important. Reversing Churchill' earlier logic, Eden had decided as early as January 28 that the possibility of increased and uncontrolled Soviet power and prestige by war's end necessitated such recognition.[40] On February 18, the Foreign Office informed Washington that Russian military action might defeat Germany "before our own and American war potentiality is fully developed." In such a situation, Moscow could establish communist governments in Europe and denude German factories for Soviet reconstruction, thereby enabling the Russians to become independent of Western assistance and influence. This possibility was

> in itself a powerful reason for establishing close relations with Russia while her policy is still in a fluid state in order to exercise as much influence as possible on her future course of action. It would be unsafe to gamble on Russia emerging so exhausted from the war that she will be forced to collaborate with us without our having to make any concessions to her. On the contrary common prudence requires us to lay our plans on the assumption that, if we want Russia's collaboration after the war, we shall have to be prepared to make such a policy advantageous to her. The application of this policy will be [a] laborious and lengthy process. If we are to adopt it we must start now and not wait until the war is over.[41]

The State Department, warned in January by reports from London of extensive Soviet postwar goals in Eastern Europe,[42] objected vehemently. After intensive study, it informed Roosevelt on February 4 that any territorial treaty would not only violate the Atlantic Charter and prejudice the peace conference, but would also encourage the Soviets to make further demands, have dire implications for the American image with the rest of the world, give Axis propaganda a field day, and make Russia "the dominating power of Eastern Europe if not of the whole continent."[43] Roosevelt apparently agreed with such logic, for on February 20, Welles informed Lord Halifax, the British ambassador, that the president thought London's position "provincial" and remained opposed to any Anglo-Russian frontier treaty.[44]

American opposition, however, was no longer capable of stopping London. In his February 23 Order of the Day, Stalin made no mention of his allies or their material aid, and blamed the war on the Hitler clique rather than the German people. This order was widely interpreted as a sign of a possible separate peace unless major Allied support of the Red Army developed soon.[45] Seeing such support as impossible in the immediate future and pressed by public opinion to do something for Russia, London informed Washington of its decision to conclude a frontier treaty, despite American opposition, "as a political substitute for material military assistance."[46]

In early March, Winant returned to press the British position on Roosevelt,[47] and on March 7, Churchill bluntly asked the president for a "free hand" in signing a territorial treaty on the basis of the "increasing gravity" of the situation.[48]

With the Army's second-front plan, Roosevelt realized that he could reverse British logic by offering a cross-Channel assault as a substitute for the political treaty.[49] Even before the Army had presented its plan to him, the president had moved to block the treaty by implementing the February 12 G-2 recommendations regarding direct contact with Moscow on high policy matters and greater Lend-Lease aid to Russia. During their February 20 conversation, Welles informed Halifax that the president intended to discuss the frontier issue directly with Stalin. London protested that the United States had no right to such an active role in the discussions since it would not be a signatory to the proposed treaty, but the protest was ignored. On March 12, Roosevelt communicated his views to Stalin through Soviet Ambassador Litvinov.[50] In his March 18 telegram to Churchill stating that he hoped soon to send a more definite plan for an attack on Europe, the president explained his recent diplomatic move in terms of his ability to "personally handle Stalin better than either your Foreign Office or my State Department. Stalin hates the guts of all your top people. He thinks he likes me better, and I hope he will continue to do so."[51]

Roosevelt tied this reasoning to G-2's second point—greater Lend-Lease aid. On March 11, he informed Secretary of the Treasury Henry Morgenthau that the United States must get such aid moving rapidly to the Soviets. Arguing that it would be better to lose Australia and New Zealand than to have Russia collapse, the president stressed the crucial importance of the aid and stated that Washington must avoid the British error of failing to keep its word. The only reason the United States stood so well in Russian eyes, he maintained, was because it kept its promises.[52]

The key to Roosevelt's initiative was G-2's third point, decisive action, and the new second-front plan for such action. Combined with the other two points, the Army concept could be used to talk Stalin out of his territorial demands, convince him of American desire and ability to fight, and gain the initiative within the Alliance on American terms. On March 7, the very day Churchill requested a "free hand" to sign a territorial treaty, Stimson found the president accepting the cross-Channel plan and "making it his own." Two days later, Halifax found Roosevelt adamant about direct negotiations with Stalin, and on that same date the president suggested to Churchill the redivision of areas of responsibility and mentioned his interest in a "new front this summer." Stimson was correct when he stated that this message took the initiative out of Churchill's hands, but in more ways than he realized.[53]

Roosevelt's reasoning was further reinforced at this time by visiting Polish Premier General Wladyslaw Sikorski, who had come to the United States partially to strengthen Washington's opposition to the proposed treaty and who also favored the early establishment of a second front. In a February 19 memorandum to the president, Sikorski stressed the "urgent necessity" of such an operation in 1942,[54] and on March 21, he told Stimson that this offensive "was by all means the most important thing in his mind in the whole war."[55] At the same time, his colleagues in London impressed upon Anthony J. Drexel Biddle, Jr., the American ambassador to the European governments-in-exile, the necessity of such a front not only to defeat the Germans, but also to enable the Allies to drive on Berlin as quickly as the Soviets. The move on Berlin would "ensure an Allied, not a Russian, victory," which was "essential in order to ensure an Allied and not a Russian peace."[56] Biddle's messages were forwarded to the White House and the War Department, where Wedemeyer had been thinking along similar lines. According to Wedemeyer's later recollections, such logic had entered into the JUSSC discussions of the second front and had been crucial in his decision to support the concept. It would become more and more important as the war progressed.[57]

On the surface, Roosevelt's acceptance and use of the Army's plan were nothing short of brilliant. With one military operation, he would be able to solve all the major problems of the Grand Alliance on American terms, take the initiative within that Alliance, end his chief domestic problems, and silence his critics all at the same time. But Roosevelt's approach ignored two crucial problems. In the first place, the 1942 assault was highly problematical. Yet, this assault, not the major one for 1943, was the key to all his plans, and failure in the operation would only deepen his problems. Worse still, the 1942 assault depended almost entirely on British willingness to risk their troops in what could easily be another Dunkirk.

Such problems would in time prove impossible to overcome. For the time being, however, the president and his military advisers were united in their concept of the strategy needed to achieve victory and accomplish their multiple and differing political goals, a fact clearly indicated by the choice of Hopkins and Marshall, representatives of the president and the Army respectively, as emissaries to London. Now it was time to win British approval.

CHAPTER THREE

SECOND FRONT
DIPLOMACY
APRIL TO JUNE 1942

On April 2 and 3, Roosevelt cabled Churchill that he was sending Hopkins and Marshall to London to present "certain conclusions" he had reache The president pointed out the political importance of those conclusions by informing the prime minister that he hoped the Soviets would greet them with "great enthusiasm" and that "on word" from Churchill, he would ask Stalin to send two representatives to Washington. Furthermore, he added, the conclusions would "work out in full accord with [the] trend of public opinion," which demanded "the establishment of a front to draw off pressure on the Russians" and was "wise enough" to see that the Soviets were "killing more Germans and destroying more equipment than you and I put together. Even if full success is not attained," he noted, "the *big* objective will be."[1]

LONDON

Hopkins and Marshall arrived in London on April 8 and immediately began to hammer away at the same points by stressing the effect of their proposals on keeping Russia in the war and warning that the American people were demanding action in the Pacific. The president and his military advisers, Hopkins admitted, still felt that the main effort should be against Germany, but everyone in the United States agreed that American troops would have to fight soon.[2] On the diplomatic level, he informed Eden of

Roosevelt's continuing opposition to any frontier treaty and "impressed" upon the foreign secretary "as strongly as I could the President's belief that our main proposals here should take the heat off Russia's diplomatic demands."[3] These efforts met with quick success, for on April 12 Churchill cabled Roosevelt that he and the COS were in "entire agreement in principle with all you propose," and that SLEDGEHAMMER "met the difficulties and uncertainties [of 1942] in an absolutely sound manner." Two days later, the War Cabinet concurred.[4]

Churchill's quick agreement surprised many, including his personal physician, Sir Charles Wilson, Lord Moran, who felt that this surrender, "almost, as it were, without a fight," was not normal behavior for his patient.[5] Nor was it normal for General Sir Alan Brooke, chief of the Imperial General Staff (CIGS), who had been opposed to the idea of cross-Channel operations before the Americans arrived.[6] But British leaders were as subject as their American counterparts to the dictates of public opinion, and in Britain that opinion was also demanding immediate offensive action to aid the Russians.

Such public pressure had probably led Churchill on March 7, in the wake of the cancellation of GYMNAST and his decision to sign a territorial treaty with Moscow, to inform Roosevelt that he was "by no means excluding an effort to take the weight off Russia once Hitler is definitely committed to an attack." At the time, the prime minister had wished to keep the idea "a secret between us,"[7] but by April that was no longer possible. Fifty percent of the British public had recently expressed dissatisfaction with the government's conduct of the war, and members of the Cabinet were echoing the cries for action.[8] Hopkins had correctly concluded on April 1 that because of public opinion, Churchill "wouldn't dare do anything but go along with us."[9] Furthermore, London still feared an all-out American effort against Japan, and Hopkins' warnings struck home. Acceptance of the second-front plan, however, would bind the United States to a Germany-first approach by concentrating American forces in the United Kingdom.[10]

Brooke bitterly noted in his diary that these factors had forced him to agree to a plan in which he had little faith. Pessimistic over the possibility of launching a successful invasion even in 1943, the CIGS was adamantly opposed to any "sacrifice" landing in 1942 to aid the Russians. Mirroring the American mistrust of British strategy because of its alleged political motives, he saw the American plan as Marshall's attempt to counter the Pacific "drain" being proposed by King and MacArthur. Brooke rated it a "clever move," fitting in "with present political opinion and the desire to help Russia," and "popular with all military men who are fretting for an offensive policy." Militarily, however, it was nothing more than "castles in the air." The fact that Marshall had not even begun to think about what to do after the landings took place only strengthened Brooke's belief that the plan was merely a political ploy and the American chief of staff a strategic fool. In retrospect, Marshall's memorandum seemed "fantastic" and, according to one British planner, "almost childish in its simplicity."[11]

Brooke expressed enough of his doubts to make Marshall realize that all was not well beneath the surface of the agreement.[12] On April 13, the chief of staff warned the War Department that British acceptance of the American plan would have to be "considerably and continuously bolstered by firmness,"[13] and a week later he informed his CCS colleagues that agreement was limited to 1943.[14] But the CIGS never fully expressed his total opposition to SLEDGEHAMMER. Nor did Eden, who shared many of Brooke's views on the 1942 assault, or Churchill, who preferred either an invasion of northern Norway (JUPITER) or a revival of GYMNAST in 1942 to the cross-Channel attack. For the sake of the entire American proposal, the prime minister agreed to SLEDGEHAMMER,[15] and his April 12 message to Roosevelt was thus a good deal less than honest.

Roosevelt proved to be no more straightforward in his dealings with Churchill. On April 4, eight days before the prime minister endorsed the American plan, Roosevelt unilaterally raised the priority on the building of landing craft needed for a cross-Channel assault. On April 9, the War Department began preparations for amphibious training programs geared to such an operation.[16] As early as April 1, the president and his military advisers had seriously considered the possibility of informing Stalin of the American plan "without letting Churchill know anything about it." After "considerable discussions," they had decided that "perhaps it would be better" to talk over the matter with London first.[17] On April 11, however, Roosevelt reverted to his previous plan by writing to Stalin, without Churchill's knowledge or consent and before his approval of the American plan, to suggest a private meeting between the two of them that summer. In the meantime, the president added, "an exchange of views" was critically needed and the Soviet leader should therefore send Foreign Minister Vaycheslav Molotov and "a reliable general" to Washington "in the immediate future" to discuss "a very important military proposal involving the utilization of our armed forces in a manner to relieve your critical western front."[18]

The president's haste was due to the total failure by April 11 of his diplomatic initiative. Moscow had simply "taken note" of his opposition to a frontier treaty while continuing to press the British, and on April 8, the same day Hopkins and Marshall arrived, London requested a visit from Molotov to work out difficulties and sign a treaty.[19] In order to block such a settlement, Roosevelt returned to his earlier idea of dealing directly with the Russians behind Churchill's back.

Stalin agreed to send Molotov to Washington, but at the same time insisted that his foreign minister go to London first, thereby reversing his earlier position that Maisky could handle all the details of the treaty alone. Furthermore, the Soviet leader now increased his territorial demands so as to include eastern Poland, and he delayed Molotov's departure until mid-May.[20]

Despite such confusing signs, Roosevelt's initiative had not failed. Stalin was apparently willing to consider the president's implied bargain, but only if he was convinced he could get a second front and would still need one for 1942. Molotov was to go to London first because the Soviets knew that the British, who would have to supply the bulk of the troops for any 1942 assault, were opposed to such an operation.[21] If the foreign minister went to Washington first and gave up Russian territorial demands for a second front, London might still refuse to honor the American pledge, thus leaving the Soviets with nothing; the British therefore had to be sounded out beforehand. Perhaps as a way of making the British more amenable to a second front, Stalin correspondingly raised the price of the alternative treaty. If London still refused to agree to the operation, Russia might at least gain British recognition of its full 1941 frontiers.

Furthermore, the Soviet winter offensive may have created some doubts in Moscow as to whether the Russians needed a second front badly enough to sacrifice recognition of their 1941 frontiers. During early and mid-May, however, the Germans launched an offensive that destroyed the Russian bridgehead at Kerch, thereby sealing the fate of Sebastopol and the entire Crimean peninsula, stopped the Russian offensive at Kharkov, and launched a powerful counteroffensive of their own. Although the main German attack was still a month away, the urgent need for a second front in 1942 was quite visible when Molotov arrived in London on May 20. By that time, in fact, the Russian situation was so desperate that, according to popular anecdote, the Soviet foreign minister's English was limited to four words—"yes," "no," and "second front."[22]

As far as London was concerned, this anecdote contained a kernel of truth. Molotov was well known for his adamancy and bluntness, but he apparently outdid himself at this conference. After less than two days of negotiations, Sir Alexander Cadogan, Britain's permanent under-secretary for foreign affairs, wrote in his diary that the Soviet foreign minister "had all the grace and conciliation of a totem pole."[23] In his first meeting with the British on May 21, Molotov stated that the second-front issue was more important than the treaty and that the treaty should be postponed if London would not agree to the minimum Soviet demands. The second-front question, he added, "was primarily a political one, and discussion of it should be conducted on political lines with Great Britain and the United States."[24] On the following day, he pressed Churchill for British views on a cross-Channel operation capable of drawing forty German divisions from the Eastern front in 1942, correctly pointing out that, although the United States had brought up the topic, "it was upon Great Britain that the main task of organizing the second front would initially fall."[25]

Churchill replied by stressing the military problems involved in a cross-Channel assault. He stated it was "unlikely" that any 1942 attack, even if successful, would draw a large number of German troops from the Eastern front. The Western Allies could and would divert German air power in 1942, he added, and they were already diverting forty-four German divisions through actions in Libya and threats of action in Norway, France, and the Low Countries. If any "sound and sensible" plan for further action could be devised, he would "not hesitate to put it into effect," but disaster "for the sake of action at any price" would not aid anyone except the Germans. When Molotov pointedly asked if Washington shared these views, Churchill correctly responded that, although the Americans were anxious "to take their share in any operations carried out this year," their contribution in the near future would be small.[26]

Facing such opposition to a 1942 second front, Molotov returned to the frontier issue but soon found mounting problems on that topic as well. Saddled with the 1939 treaty with the Poles as well as American and Polish threats to oppose and publicize the proposed accord, Eden had backed away from territorial recognition and on May 23 proposed a draft treaty that made no reference to frontiers. Molotov responded by dropping his demand for eastern Poland, but he continued to insist on British recognition of the absorption of the Baltic States. On May 25, he dropped this demand too, and he signed the nonterritorial treaty on the following afternoon.[27]

The motive for Molotov's sudden shift lay in a discussion he had had with Winant on the evening of May 24 during which the American ambassador had stated that Roosevelt was interested in a second front, a new Lend-Lease agreement with the Soviet Union, and a postwar Russian relief program, but was opposed to any territorial treaty. The president's position, Molotov had replied, was a matter for "serious consideration," and he promised to reconsider Eden's treaty.[28] On the following morning, he informed the British foreign secretary that statements made by the British and Winant had convinced him that any territorial treaty would raise "serious objections" in the United States, and that he had therefore asked Stalin for permission to work out an agreement based on the British draft. That permission arrived on the next day and was followed by the foreign minister's signature.[29]

Molotov's stated reason for changing his stance was about as sound as the Italian Army, for the Soviets had known for many months about the "serious objections" of the United States and those objections had not deflected them in the least. More important was Winant's offer, which had previously been implied by Roosevelt but had never before been stated in such blunt and total terms. Combined with the continuing deterioration on the Russian front, the American offer was simply too good to refuse.

Nevertheless, Molotov knew by May 24 that even if the United States favored a second front, Britain did not, and that the operation was not possible without London's cooperation. Molotov may have felt that a joint Russian-American insistence on crossing the Channel would force the British to agree. On the other hand, he may have realized that London could not be budged but, with total diplomatic failure staring him in the face, decided to accept Winant's offer anyway. An American promise, even if it failed to materialize, was worth more than a half-baked treaty, American enmity, and worldwide publicity of a split in the Alliance. At the very least, such a promise would give a boost to the war-weary Russian people at this critical juncture. Furthermore, a broken pledge could always be used as a bargaining tool in future diplomatic negotiations. In the absence of documentation, it is impossible to make any definitive statements about Molotov's motives. Whatever they were, he was soon on his way to Washington to collect his reward.

THE SECOND-FRONT "PROMISE"

By the time Molotov arrived in Washington, Roosevelt was aware of Britain's growing opposition to SLEDGEHAMMER. On May 27, British military leaders informed Churchill that securing a permanent bridgehead in France during 1942 was impossible because of the landing-craft shortage. Responding that he would definitely not give way "to popular clamour for such a disastrous operation, the prime minister asked the COS to examine once again his pet project, JUPITER.[30] On the following day, he forwarded to Roosevelt the minutes of his meeting with Molotov and took the opportunity to explain the difficulties with SLEDGEHAMMER. Lord Louis Mountbatten, he informed the president, would soon arrive in Washington to explain those difficulties in greater depth. As an alternative to the 1942 cross-Channel assault, Churchill pushed JUPITER and reminded Roosevelt, "We must never let 'Gymnast' pass from our minds."[31]

The impact of this message on the president became clear during his May 29 discussions with Molotov. In their pre-dinner conversation, Roosevelt dwelt on political rather than military problems by explaining his "Four Policemen" concept as a postwar alternative to the balance of power, approving the Anglo-Soviet treaty, and restating his position that the time was not ripe for frontier discussions. Molotov brought the president back to military issues during dinner by painting a bleak picture of the Eastern front and warning that the Russians might lose Moscow and Rostov and be forced to withdraw to the Volga. Such a "catastrophe," he stated, would mean Soviet inability "to pull anything like their present weight in the war and the whole brunt of carrying it on against an appreciably strengthened Hitler would fall on the British Empire and the United States." What Moscow needed now was Western action to divert forty German divisions.[32]

Roosevelt took his reply straight out of Churchill's May 28 message by suggesting JUPITER, but Molotov bluntly replied that he "did not ascribe any merit to British notions about an invasion of Norway." Roosevelt then brought up SLEDGEHAMMER by asking whether a landing of ten divisions with the possibility of withdrawal *a la* Dunkirk would be a sufficient diversion. American morale, according to the president and Hopkins, could support "even such an effort in the general cause." Molotov, dubious about the effect of such an operation, reiterated an earlier judgment that thirty regular and five armored divisions constituted the minimum force necessary to do the job with some prospect of success.[33]

Molotov was in effect asking for ROUNDUP in 1942 while rejecting both SLEDGEHAMMER and JUPITER as insufficient to accomplish the necessary diversion of German forces. A 1942 ROUNDUP, however, was militarily impossible. SLEDGEHAMMER was the largest operation the West could undertake that year, something that had never been explained to Molotov.

Roosevelt did not explain it at this or any other meeting with the foreign minister. The president commented later in the evening that he had to reckon with military advisers who preferred sure success in 1943 to a risky 1942 venture, but this partial warning had no followup.

To the contrary, with clear evidence that the British were backing out of SLEDGEHAMMER and that the Soviets rejected the operation, Roosevelt returned to the 1942 concept on the following morning. He informed his military chiefs, in Molotov's presence, that although the Russians had received no positive second-front commitment from the British, the precariousness of the Eastern front necessitated asking "what we can do even if the prospects for permanent success might not be especially rosy." Molotov then restated his belief that the second-front problem was "predominantly political," as well as his arguments and warnings of the previous evening. Stressing the necessity of diverting forty German divisions from the Eastern front, he concluded by requesting a "straight answer" on the question of a 1942 second front. According to the interpreter's minutes, Roosevelt responded by asking Marshall "whether developments were clear enough so that we could say to Mr. Stalin that we are preparing a second front. 'Yes,' replied the general. The President then authorized Mr. Molotov to inform Mr. Stalin that we expect the formation of a second front this year."[34] Later that day, Marshall backed up this "pledge" by a public statement at West Point that American troops were landing in England and "will land in France."[35]

Despite these statements, Roosevelt called a special meeting on May 31 and informed Hopkins, Marshall, and King that the military decisions of May 30 were "a little vague and the dangerous situation on the Russian front required that he . . . make a more specific answer to Molotov in regard to a second front."[36] The problem revolved around a previous decision that convoy losses, shipping and aircraft shortages, and the second-front buildup all necessitated a cut in Soviet Lend-Lease supplies.[37] That decision was reaffirmed at this May 31 meeting. Unfortunately, on the previous day the president had sought to reassure Molotov by offering him an unreduced Lend-Lease protocol. Revised estimates now indicated that the Soviets would have to accept a cut of close to 40 percent,[38] and since the second front was the stated reason for the cut, absolute clarity on the proposed operation became a necessity.

Roosevelt therefore read his advisers the draft of a proposed telegram to Churchill that stressed the "precariousness" of the Russian front and Roosevelt's subsequent desire for a second front in August. "I am especially anxious," he wrote, "that Molotov shall carry back some real results of his mission and give a favourable report to Stalin," for the Russians were "a bit down in the mouth at present." Marshall and Hopkins both voiced objections to the August reference and informed the president that London would resist the setting of a definite date. While Roosevelt agreed to drop this "unfortunate" reference, his final substitution indicated that the operation would have to be launched by the fall of 1942.[39] On June 1, he pressed Molotov for a reduction of Lend-Lease aid in order to launch it earlier.

The Soviet foreign minister remained noncommittal, for he knew that there would be no 1942 second front without British agreement. When Roosevelt stated that the Russians "could not eat their cake and have it too," Molotov shot back "that the second front would be stronger if the first front still stood fast, and inquired with what seemed deliberate sarcasm what would happen if the Soviets cut down their requirements and then no second front eventuated." Reminding the president that Russia had fulfilled her end of the bargain by emphasizing the Anglo-Soviet treaty he then pressed for a direct reply to the question of a 1942 second front. Roosevelt stated that British military leaders were on their way to the United States to discuss this very issue, and that "we expected to establish a second front" but could move faster if the Soviets would make it possible for the Allies to use more ships. He concluded by telling Molotov to discuss "further arrangements" with Marshall, and on that note the meeting ended.[40]

Roosevelt's remarks defused what had verged on an explosive session, but Molotov remained dissatisfied with the vagueness of the second-front pledge. On June 3, he therefore requested the addition of certain phrases to the planned public communique on the conference, including the statement that "full understanding was reached with regard to the urgent tasks of creating a Second Front in Europe in 1942."[41]

Marshall now objected vehemently. On the same date that Molotov made this request, Eisenhower reported after returning from a trip to London that planning for the cross-Channel attack was progressing so poorly that even the 1943 operation was now in doubt. At the same time, the British, the Navy, and General MacArthur were all continuing their dispersion requests, and with the battle of Midway approaching, the Pacific theater promised to make even further demands in the future.[42] Complicating the situation was Churchill's May 28 message to Roosevelt which had revived the GYMNAST nightmare. In short, by June 3 Marshall found himself squeezed between the demands of the Russians, the British, the Navy, and MacArthur, as well as mounting logistical and planning difficulties. In such a situation, he probably became convinced that he could no longer promise SLEDGEHAMMER. Accordingly, he informed Hopkins that the public communique should make no mention of a 1942 date.[43]

Hopkins brought Marshall's fears to Roosevelt's attention, but the president insisted that the 1942 phrase be included in the public announcement.[44] He apparently felt, in Charles Bohlen's words, that "encouragement, even when based on false premises, would stiffen the Soviet will."[45] As a result of such reasoning, Molotov left for London and Moscow with a public American pledge for a 1942 second front.

As Molotov departed, Mountbatten arrived to explain the problems of SLEDGEHAMMER. On June 6, a worried Hopkins informed Churchill that Washington was "disturbed" about the Eastern front as well as "what appears to be a lack of clear understanding between us as to the precise military move that shall be made in the event the Russians get pushed around badly on their front." This and other "matters of high policy" required a meeting of Roosevelt and the prime minister, Hopkins concluded, and the president was therefore hopeful Churchill could make a "quick trip" to the United States.[46]

In a five-hour meeting on the evening of June 9, Mountbatten informed Roosevelt that because of the landing craft shortage, not enough troops could be landed in France in 1942 to divert German forces from the East. The president remained insistent, however, upon putting American troops into action in 1942. He informed Mountbatten that he had been very much struck by the prime minister's May 28 reference to a revival of GYMNAST, and if SLEDGEHAMMER was now out of the question, six American divisions should be sent to North Africa.[47]

While Mountbatten was working on Roosevelt, Churchill and Brooke were continuing their efforts to have SLEDGEHAMMER dropped. The CIGS spelled out his objections to the operation in a June 4 all-night discussion with the prime minister, and on June 5, the COS stated that SLEDGEHAMMER could not be launched so as to divert German divisions from the Eastern front. Churchill responded by pushing for JUPITER or GYMNAST, and on June 8, he suggested that the British undertake no landing in France "unless we are going to stay" and the Germans were "demoralized by another failure against Russia." With SLEDGEHAMMER failing rapidly, the COS then approved an offer of six air squadrons to Russia and agreed to restudy the prime minister's Norway project.[48]

Thus, when Molotov returned to London, SLEDGEHAMMER was as good as dead. Nevertheless, he brought with him the public communique stating that full understanding had been reached in regard to a 1942 second front. Feeling that they could not give a conflicting statement and that this announcement might succeed in deceiving the Germans and creating apprehension in the *Reich,* the British agreed to the communique.[49]

Informed of such logic, Molotov warned Eden that there should be "no deception between friends,"[50] and demanded clarification of London's position. He had agreed to consider a reduction in Lend-Lease aid for the sake of a second front, he informed the British on the evening of June 9, and Roosevelt was willing to risk 100,000 to 120,000 men in what "might lead to a second Dunkirk," although the foreign minister himself "thought a mere six to ten divisions would be ineffective."[51]

Churchill was in complete accord with Molotov on this point, but he too did not bother to explain that "a mere six to ten divisions" was the absolute maximum the Allies could offer for 1942. Instead, he told Molotov that landing craft, not shipping used for Lend-Lease, was the main problem, and he discussed JUPITER as a possible substitute for a 1942 second front. Reminding Molotov of Western plans for a forty- to fifty-division assault for 1943, the prime minister stated that "he would be very glad if it were possible to do in 1942 what was planned to do in 1943," but that the British could give no promise in the matter. On the following day, June 10, he formalized these conclusions in an *aide-memoire* which stated that a disastrous operation would not further the Russian or Allied cause as a whole and that, therefore, "we can give no promise in the matter" of a second front in 1942. The British were prepared, on the other hand, to send air squadrons to Russia, invade northern Norway, and launch a full-scale cross Channel attack in 1943.[52]

With the Soviets warned of British thoughts, Churchill proceeded in his attempt to get SLEDGEHAMMER shelved once and for all. On June 11, the day of the public communique, he and the War Cabinet agreed that no landing should be attempted in France unless the Allies intended to stay and prospects of success were good. On the following day, he received Mountbatten's report on his visit with Roosevelt and the president's insistence on some sort of action in 1942. At the same time, Field-Marshall Sir John Dill, head of the British Joint Staff mission in Washington, informed

London after a conversation with Hopkins that SLEDGEHAMMER was "losing ground" in Roosevelt's mind. Churchill needed no further urging; on June 13, he cabled the president that he was coming to the United States to discuss problems with the second-front plan.[53]

The Russians, meanwhile, proceeded to ignore Churchill's warning. Upon publication of the communique on June 11 and Molotov's return to Moscow shortly thereafter, the Soviets began to treat the public statement as a "promise" of a second front for 1942, and on that basis, relations between the Soviet Union and her allies began to improve.[54] At the same time, Churchill and his advisers set off for Washington with the firm purpose of negating what they refused to consider a "promise."

In retrospect, it is clear that there was no "misunderstanding" over the June 11 communique. Each member of the Grand Alliance agreed to that announcement as a result of a series of deceptions designed to achieve differing short-term political goals. Fearing public opinion and an American Pacific-first strategy, British leaders agreed to an operation they had no intention of undertaking. They did explain their opposition to SLEDGE-HAMMER to the Russians but were still willing to reap the benefits of the American plan—a nonterritorial treaty of alliance. Aware of London's unwillingness to launch a 1942 second front as well as the fact that such a front was impossible without British support, the Russians then pressured Roosevelt into a "promise" they knew he could not keep so that they could offer something to their war-weary people and gain a future bargaining point.

The president, in turn, offered the Soviets a second front before London agreed to the operation in order to mollify public opinion, block a proposed frontier treaty, and gain the initiative in relations with his allies. He then promised the Russians a 1942 assault in return for a nonterritorial treaty. He used that operation to justify a decrease in Lend-Lease aid, while knowing that the British were backing out of the proposed attack and that the Soviets did not approve of its small size. He did not even inform Moscow that the operation it considered inadequate was the most the West could possibly offer in 1942.

Although all parties appeared satisfied with the short-term results of this series of deceptions, in the next few months the "promise" would be broken, as it had to be. The long-term results of this period of "second-front diplomacy" would prove disastrous for later Allied unity.

CHAPTER FOUR

THE POLITICS OF TORCH

JUNE TO SEPTEMBER 1942

By the time Churchill and his advisers arrived in Washington on June 18, the military situation was reaching a crisis stage in the Libyan desert and on the Russian front. With Rommel's rapid advance threatening British positions, the prime minister absolutely refused to sanction any "sacrifice" operation across the Channel to aid the Soviets. More important from his point of view would be action to aid the desert army, and he was thus determined to replace SLEDGEHAMMER with a revised form of GYMNAST.

HYDE PARK, WASHINGTON, AND LONDON

Churchill's May 28 telegram and Mountbatten's gloomy predictions had succeeded even before the British arrived in reviving Roosevelt's interest in North Africa and shaking his resolve to launch SLEDGEHAMMER. Stimson and Marshall quickly responded by pointing out to the president that GYMNAST would be an indecisive and dangerous dispersion of forces that would not help the Russians in the least and would so damage the BOLERO buildup as to endanger the 1943 as well as the 1942 cross-Channel assault plan.[1] On June 19 and 20, Churchill countered these warnings in a series of private conversations with Roosevelt at Hyde Park. London, the prime minister pointed out, had been unable to come up with any cross-Channel plan for 1942 that could work; had the Americans been more successful? If so, he would support such a plan, but if not, "what else are we going to do? Can we afford to stand idle in the Atlantic theater during the whole of 1942?" With the recent "promise" to Molotov and continuing public pressure for action, the answer was obviously no, and Churchill pressed for GYMNAST as the best alternative.[2]

Marshall responded to Churchill's attack in a memorandum which insisted that the 1942 cross-Channel operation was still viable and should remain the core of Allied planning. GYMNAST, he reiterated, was a "poor substitute" for SLEDGEHAMMER and would prove a meaningless diversion incapable of aiding Russia.[3] Much to his surprise, the chief of staff found Brooke in complete agreement. Fearing the consequences of Rommel's recent advance, the CIGS wished to avoid any offensive action until the Middle East stabilized. Continuing with BOLERO-SLEDGEHAMMER planning would enable him to postpone any attack decision for a few months while building up forces in the United Kingdom for future contingencies.[4] As a result of such reasoning, the CCS were able to agree while Churchill and Roosevelt were at Hyde Park that action in 1942 should be undertaken only "in case of necessity" or "an exceptionally favorable opportunity," and that in this eventuality, SLEDGEHAMMER, JUPITER, or an attack on the Channel islands were all preferable to GYMNAST.[5]

While militarily sound, this conclusion ignored the public opinion and Russian factors, both of which necessitated an offensive in 1942. A "very upset" Churchill thus returned to Washington on June 20 intent upon reversing the CCS judgment and replacing SLEDGEHAMMER with GYMNAST. News of the fall of Tobruk arrived on the following afternoon and only hardened the prime minister's resolve to rescue his desert army rather than risk another Dunkirk in 1942.[6]

After a day of stormy debate, Roosevelt and Churchill agreed with their military advisers to continue with the BOLERO buildup until September 1, at which time plans would be reexamined in light of the existing situation. However, the two leaders then added clauses to the agreement stating that it was "essential" for the United States and Britain to "be prepared to act offensively in 1942," and stressing GYMNAST as an alternative if a successful SLEDGEHAMMER proved to be "improbable."[7] With good reason the official British military history of this period labeled June 21 the "Day of Dupes,"[8] for the added clause actually negated the basic CCS conclusion that no action in 1942 was preferable to GYMNAST. Churchill and Roosevelt had in effect decided to invade North Africa if they could not get a successful SLEDGEHAMMER.

Even worse, the two leaders decided later that evening that the critical Middle East situation might necessitate the sending of American troops to bolster the British. They called upon Marshall to offer his opinion of the proposed operation. The chief of staff, who opposed such a move even more than GYMNAST, angrily informed the president that it would be "an overthrow of everything they had been planning for." He then walked out of the room with the comment that he would not even discuss the issue "at that time of night."[9]

Such unprecedented bluntness, combined with hard reasoning and extra American supplies for the Middle East, apparently convinced Churchill and Roosevelt to drop their plan. Marshall concluded on June 29 that these material "concessions" to the British had, in fact, saved the second-front concept.[10] The prime minister, feeling that he had failed in his mission, bitterly agreed.[11] In reality, the final decision had merely been postponed, and Roosevelt's insistence on offensive action in 1942 meant that time was on Churchill's side.

Continued defeats during the next two weeks made this fact clear. By early July, the Germans had conquered Sebastopol on the Eastern front, advanced to El Alamein in the Middle East, destroyed the June convoy to Russia, and taken their heaviest toll of Allied shipping in the Atlantic. Because of the fall of Tobruk, Churchill was forced to ask Commons for a vote of confidence and, although he received it, it was obvious the British public would not tolerate continued defeats. During the first week in July, the COS and the British War Cabinet therefore agreed that chances of mounting SLEDGEHAMMER were "remote."[12] On July 8, Churchill informed Roosevelt of this conclusion and suggested GYMNAST as the best alternative to aid the Russians. "This has all along been in harmony with your ideas," he commented. "In fact, it is your commanding idea. Here is the true second front of 1942."[13]

The American planners disagreed vehemently. In the aftermath of the Washington Conference, they had already expressed extreme bitterness over what they considered Churchill's misinterpretation of the facts and influence over Roosevelt. Since SLEDGEHAMMER's main purpose was to create a diversion to aid Russia, Wedemeyer complained, the prime minister's insistence on a permanent bridgehead was a complete distortion of the operation and "beside the point."[14] Churchill had taken up GYMNAST according to Stimson, "knowing full well I am sure that it was the President's great secret baby."[15] Marshall felt that the British, motivated by "political considerations," had been after "face-saving diversions" to make up for the Tobruk fiasco,[16] and that such diversions would in no way aid the Russians. To the contrary, they would so disperse Allied forces as to rule out a cross-Channel assault until 1944, and a decision to launch GYM-NAST was thus equivalent to giving up on the Eastern front. In that case, the Germany-first strategy would no longer make any sense.

As early as July 2, Marshall had agreed to a modification of that strategy by sanctioning limited Pacific offensives to take advantage of the Midway victory.[17] A week later, a "very stirred up" chief of staff decided that Churchill's July 8 telegram called for a "showdown," a conclusion Stimson heartily endorsed.[18] Returning to the OPD's February reasoning, Marshall proposed at the July 10 JCS meeting that, if forced to accept GYM-NAST, the United States "should turn to the Pacific for decisive action against Japan." Such a move, he advised, would concentrate American forces and be "highly popular" in the country. Second only to BOLERO, it would also "have the greatest effect towards relieving the pressure on Russia."[19]

Marshall never explained this rather odd conclusion, but King nevertheless agreed "completely" with the Army chief's reasoning. The British, according to the CNO, "had never been in wholehearted accord" with the cross-Channel plan[20] and would not invade Europe "except behind a Scotch bagpipe band."[21] Furthermore, GYMNAST would require diverting large American naval forces from the Pacific. King therefore agreed with Marshall to send Roosevelt a memorandum warning that the indecisive North African invasion would destroy the cross-Channel attack for 1942 and probably 1943, have no effect on the Eastern front, void United States commitments to Russia, heavily drain American resources, and jeopardize Washington's naval position in the Pacific. If the United States engaged "in any other operation rather than forceful, unswerving adherence to full BOLERO plans," they concluded, "we should turn to the Pacific and strike decisively against Japan; in other words, assume a defensive attitude against Germany. . . ; and use all available means in the Pacific."[22]

While this memorandum may have been a bluff to force London into acceptance of American plans, it is equally possible that Marshall and Stimson seriously considered the Pacific approach less of an evil than GYM-NAST.[23] King certainly did, but Roosevelt disagreed completely. On July 14, he informed Marshall that he had decided instead to send the chief of staff with the CNO and Hopkins to London "immediately."[24] The JCS quickly grasped the significance of this message, agreeing on the same date that, although they still preferred the Pacific alternative, both the president and "our political system would require operations this year in Africa."[25]

This prediction was proven accurate on July 15. In separate meetings with Stimson and Marshall on that day, Roosevelt blasted the Pacific proposal as equivalent to "taking up your dishes and going away,"[26] and he referred to it as "something of a red herring, the purpose for which he thoroughly understood."[27] Not only did he refuse to consider using the alternative, but he even suggested altering the record so that later historians would not conclude that Washington had considered abandoning London.[28] For the present, he insisted that the trip to London be made and that his representatives closely examine the possibilities of mounting SLEDGEHAMMER. If the operation was out of the question, however, they would have to agree to an alternative in either North Africa or the Middle East capable of bringing American troops into action against Germany in 1942.[29] On the evening of July 15, Roosevelt stated these conclusions and his complete disagreement with those of the JCS more clearly by bluntly informing Hopkins that if SLEDGEHAMMER was out of the question, he wanted GYMNAST in 1942 and ROUNDUP in 1943.[30] The JCS warnings of the impossibility of mounting both operations apparently held little weight with him.

Still hoping to save SLEDGEHAMMER, Marshall now ordered Eisenhower in London to have a "searching analysis" of the operation ready for him on arrival.[31] Agreeing totally with JCS reasoning, Eisenhower and his staff concluded that, although chances of landing successfully in 1942 were only one in five, the "prize" sought, keeping Russia in the war, justified the risk. In answer to the British critique that SLEDGEHAMMER would fail and would not divert any German forces in the east, Eisenhower returned to his February 28 argument that the psychological effect on the Russians was the critical factor. Even if the operation failed, this effect would still make the effort worthwhile. Mounting GYMNAST, on the other hand, would in no way aid Russia and would mean no ROUNDUP in 1943. It was thus logical only as an alternative to ROUNDUP and should be undertaken if the West believed "*that the Russian Army is certain to be defeated*" and wished to take advantage of the present situation to improve its defensive position. If Russia was defeated, Eisenhower concluded, then the United States should turn its major effort towards the Pacific.[32]

Marshall and King made use of such reasoning in their conversations with the British on July 20 and 22, but to no avail. Churchill countered that a 1942 assault would not aid the Russians and would hinder rather than help ROUNDUP by eating up "the seed corn of the larger operation." GYMNAST, he insisted, was the proper move for 1942; coupled with a successful offensive against Rommel, it would open possibilities for action against Sicily and Italy. Such a prospect only hardened the American opposition. King bluntly informed the British that their arguments could also be used against ROUNDUP and that he felt the 1943 assault "would never take place." Churchill replied that he was an "ardent believer" in ROUNDUP, but he stood fast on SLEDGEHAMMER.[33] On July 22, a date Eisenhower felt might go down as the "blackest day in history,"[34] the Americans were forced to inform Roosevelt of the deadlock.

Replying that he was not surprised, the president insisted that his envoys agree to some 1942 operation against the Germans, preferably GYMNAST, as soon as possible.[35] Marshall and King were thus forced to give in and accept the North African invasion, now rechristened TORCH. Nevertheless, neither American was as yet willing to give up completely. They proposed a compromise whereby preparations would continue for both SLEDGEHAMMER and TORCH until September 15, when a final decision would be made in accordance with the situation on the Eastern front. A decision to invade North Africa would mean that the West had given up hope on the Russian front and had accepted a defensive European strategy that would allow the Americans to concentrate on the Pacific. As stated in CCS 94, the final conference document, the mounting of TORCH "renders ROUNDUP in all probability impracticable of successful execution in 1943 and therefore we have definitely accepted a defensive, encircling line of action for the Continental European Theater, except as to air operations and blockade."[36]

The British objected strenuously, for their concept of Mediterranean operations was anything but defensive. Furthermore, Churchill refused to believe that TORCH ruled out ROUNDUP, even though his planners agreed with this American conclusion. From the prime minister's viewpoint, a successful North African invasion would open the possibility of simultaneous attacks across the Channel and from the South in 1943, with the major effort in the latter theater. Refusing to admit that such a strategy differed

drastically from the American massive assault concept, Churchill concluded
that his form of ROUNDUP was indeed possible and that he was in no way
opposed to a 1943 cross-Channel attack.[37]

Marshall and King were adamant, however, and the COS, fearing that
they might be pushing the Americans too far, agreed to CCS 94 and convinced their doubting superiors to do likewise.[38] Once again, British agreement was somewhat less than honest.

Roosevelt did not approve of CCS 94 either. He had previously refused
to accept the idea that TORCH would cancel ROUNDUP, and he reiterated
this viewpoint on July 25.[39] On the same date, he also effectively negated
the rest of CCS 94 by informing his envoys, in response to a plea from Hopkins, that TORCH should be launched no later than October 30.[40] On the
evening of July 30, he reinforced this decision by informing General Arnold
and Admiral William D. Leahy, the new chief of staff to the commander-in-
chief, that TORCH now took precedence over all other operations, BOLERO
included.[41]

In effect, Roosevelt had decided to launch TORCH long before the September 15 date set down in CCS 94. Political factors, and not the Russian
military situation, governed this decision. With the British refusing to launch
SLEDGEHAMMER, Roosevelt apparently felt that he could fulfill his promise to Molotov by offering TORCH as a substitute. Equally, if not more important, public demands for offensive action and press attacks on the president's war leadership had continued, and congressional elections were
fast approaching. Marshall later stated that the great lesson he had learned
in 1942 was that in wartime "the politicians must do *something* every year."

In short, British refusal to launch SLEDGEHAMMER led Roosevelt to
return to the project he had originally supported to achieve his political
goals—the North African invasion. Unfortunately, Roosevelt conveniently
ignored the serious implications of such a move. From the point of view
of his military advisers, TORCH would destroy ROUNDUP and with it the
entire American strategy. In the aftermath of the decision, they blamed
the British as much as the president. Churchill, they felt, had violated a
written agreement and used his influence to talk the naive Roosevelt into
an unsound operation for the sake of defending British political interests.
Their response to this breach of faith was extremely bitter. British plans
and operations, Wedemeyer informed Marshall, "have been designed to maintain the integrity of the British Empire," were "absolutely unsound," and
would lead to defeat in both Europe and the Far East.[43] At the July 28 JCS

meeting, Leahy drew dire parallels between TORCH and the Salonika landings of World War I.[44] Two weeks later, Arnold implied in a letter to Marshall that perhaps the Americans should begin treating the British as the Germans treated their Italian allies.[45]

The debate also left serious splits within the American ranks, for Roosevelt had clearly overruled his advisers and ignored their warnings. Stimson, who credited Roosevelt's refusal to accept this fact to his "happy faculty of fooling himself," continued to fight the decision "to the limits prescribed by loyalty" and even offered to bet the president on the eventual wisdom of TORCH.[46] The argument became so heated that the secratary of war lost favor in the White House and dropped out of the strategic picture for the next nine months. The weight of sustaining the BOLERO concept now fell squarely on Marshall's shoulders.

CCS 94 did not make the Army chief's task any easier, for, on paper at least, the Germany-first strategy was no longer valid. In the aftermath of the August 7 launching of the Guadalcanal offensive, King felt justified in calling for further Pacific offensives, and Marshall found it quite difficult to object. Arnold, however, refused to accept such dispersion of his air forces, and he argued vehemently with King over the future of fifteen air groups CCS 94 had transferred from BOLERO to the Pacific. By August 11, the ensuing JCS split had convinced the air chief that his colleagues, Marshall included, favored a Pacific-first strategy.[47]

Even more ominous, despite the claims of the president and prime minister to the contrary,[48] TORCH violated the promise to Molotov and would now have to be explained to the Russians. As early as July 17, Churchill had cryptically warned Stalin of the probable fate of SLEDGEHAMMER by justifying cancellation of JUPITER and the July northern convoy on the basis of recent shipping losses and the need to create "a really strong second front in 1943."[49] The Soviet leader had been greatly displeased. With the Germans about to take Rostov and Maisky reinforcing the prime minister's warning,[50] Stalin bitterly objected on July 23 to the lack of a July convoy. He stated that the second front was "not being treated with the seriousness it deserves" and warned "in the most emphatic manner that the Soviet Government cannot acquiesce in the postponement of a second front in Europe until 1943."[51]

Thus, on July 24 instead of feeling exhilarated by his victory over the Americans, Churchill, according to King, was "extremely morose and unpleasant" over the thought of having to see Maisky on the following day.[52]

Further compounding the problem were renewed Soviet public pleas for an immediate second front and veiled warnings that, without it, Russia would be forced to make a separate peace.[53] Churchill therefore decided to go to Moscow so that he could personally explain the change in Allied plans, a task, he later admitted, equivalent to "carrying a large lump of ice to the North Pole."[54]

TORCH AND THE RUSSIANS

By the time Churchill arrived in Moscow on August 12, that conclusion was an understatement. With the Germans at the Maikop oilfields and driving on Stalingrad, Stalin was in no mood to accept the prime minister's statement that evening that a 1942 second front was now out of the question but that the West was preparing "a very great operation" for 1943. The fact that the Guadalcanal offensive had been launched five days earlier only served to strengthen the Soviet leader's conviction that the delay was deliberate. According to W. Averell Harriman, who had accompanied Churchill to Moscow, Stalin responded "with bluntness almost to the point of insult" regarding what he considered British fear of the Germans and refusal to take risks.[55]

Churchill attempted to warm this frigid atmosphere by discussing the bombing of Germany, and the tactic worked brilliantly. According to Harriman, the two leaders "soon destroyed most of the important industrial cities of Germany."[56] Sensing the great change in atmosphere, Churchill then introduced TORCH by drawing a crocodile and explaining his famous analogy of attacking the "soft underbelly" as well as the hard snout of Europe. Sitting up and breaking into a grin, Stalin showed "great interest" in the North African plan as well as a strategic understanding of its objectives which astonished the Westerners present. In response to his specific queries, Churchill stated that the operation would be launched no later than October 30 and hopefully before October 7. Harriman added that Roosevelt was in "full agreement" with all the prime minister had said. "May God help this enterprise to succeed," the Soviet premier exclaimed to his startled guests. Discussion of a proposed Anglo-American air force in the Caucasus was equally pleasant, and at 10:40 P.M., the meeting broke up in what Churchill referred to as "an atmosphere of good will."[57]

Churchill left the meeting quite pleased with the results. Stalin, he told his advisers afterward, was "just a peasant" whom he "knew exactly how to tackle."[58] Brooke was far less sanguine, and later stated that the Soviet leader's physical and mental demeanor had given him "the creeps."[59] By the following evening, that judgment seemed more valid than Churchill's. Continuing the precedent set at earlier meetings with his allies, Stalin returned to the conference table on the second night in a bitter and hostile mood. He began the meeting by handing Churchill an *aide-memoire* highly critical of Western refusal to launch a 1942 second front and followed this up with a series of insults culminating in charges of bad faith and cowardice. An angry Churchill retorted that he pardoned such remarks only because of the bravery of the Red armies, and promised Stalin a written reply on the following day. Abruptly shifting gears, the Soviet leader then stated that he must accept the Western decision, and he invited the British to a banquet on the following evening.[60]

Churchill accepted the invitation but informed Stalin that he would depart immediately afterwards. When the Soviet premier asked him to stay longer, Churchill's pent-up emotions finally exploded. Pounding his fist on the table, he launched into a five-minute oratorical and emotional response to the insults. The interpreters sat stunned and silent. Stalin, however, seemed pleased by the outburst. "I do not understand what you are saying," he exclaimed, "but by God, I like your sentiment!"[61]

Churchill remained infuriated. "I am not sure it wouldn't be better to leave him to fight his own battles," the prime minister muttered that evening to Lord Moran.[62] On August 14, he sent the Russians a counter *aide-memoire* stating that no promise had been broken and that TORCH was both the best and only possible second front for 1942.[63] Nor did the banquet that evening calm his aroused feelings. Cadogan was stunned by the "violence and depth" of Churchill's resentment. He told Lord Moran that the prime minister "was like a bull in the ring maddened by the pricks of the picadors" and determined to return to London without seeing Stalin again.[64]

Ambassador Sir Archibald Clark-Kerr managed to convince Churchill to remain for another session, and so the two leaders met again on the evening of August 15. Perhaps sensing that he had pushed his ally too far, Stalin ended the short meeting by inviting the prime minister to his apartment for "drinks." Churchill accepted, and the two men adjourned to what turned out to be a pleasant, informal, and rambling six-hour conversation that did not end until 2:30 A.M. A few hours later, Churchill departed Moscow with his optimism restored, for after having heard "the worst," Stalin had accepted TORCH and taken him "into the family." The two of them, Churchill concluded, had "ended friends."[65]

But Churchill was being too optimistic. Stalin had had no choice but to accept TORCH in place of a 1942 second front, and after the conference ended the Soviet press was strangely quiet regarding its outcome.[66] Nor had Churchill really told Stalin "the worst," for he had never mentioned the planners' conclusion that TORCH ruled out ROUNDUP in 1943 or the implied Pacific-first strategy contained in CCS 94.

To make matters worse, the promised North African invasion was by no means assured, for British and American military leaders had not reconciled their differing concepts of TORCH. The ensuing argument, known as the "transatlantic essay contest," threatened by August to cancel the landings completely. The British saw the invasion as a full-scale offensive designed to conquer Tunisia in three- to- four weeks and, in conjunction with the Eighth Army, drive Rommel completely out of North Africa and the Mediterranean. Such a plan required a large operation with landings as far east as Algiers or Bone. Fearing French resistance and a German move through Spain to cut Allied communications, the Americans concluded that such a plan was militarily unsound. Furthermore, in line with CCS 94 and their original North African plans, they insisted that TORCH be a limited and purely defensive operation. On August 25, the JCS therefore proposed formally that the landings go no farther east than Oran but include Casablanca in the west in order to insure communications.[67]

Churchill returned to London just in time to receive this "bombshell," although, according to his physician, "the epithet he used at the time was even more descriptive." The prime minister felt he had made a bargain with Stalin by promising him a large operation by October 30 and could not now "fob him off with a simplified version."[68] Eisenhower reported that, as a result of the conversations in Moscow, Churchill was "completely committed to launching TORCH at the earliest possible date, on as grand a scale as possible and with ambitious objectives," and was ready to fly to Washington immediately to clear things up.[69] Churchill was also motivated by the fact that the limited American concept would accomplish nothing offensively in the Mediterranean, and his eyes were already on the Italian horizon. As he later explained, he wanted North Africa as "a springboard, not a sofa."[70]

Citing CCS 94, the JCS countered that TORCH had nothing to do with the Russian front and was intended simply to clear shipping routes in the Mediterranean. Equally important, a large assault would require naval support needed in the Pacific. Moreover, success in the North African plan was critical. The American public, Marshall pointed out, had been prepared for failure in a cross-Channel attack, but TORCH was different. For psychological and political reasons, this first American effort had to succeed, and the way to guarantee success was to launch a small operation that included a Casablanca landing.[71]

Roosevelt, of course, agreed with such reasoning. His support for the JCS position was also influenced by the fact that a limited operation involving less manpower, shipping, and material could be launched earlier than a large operation. Speed was essential in order to show the Russians and the public offensive action, hopefully before the November elections. Unknown to Churchill, Roosevelt had even considered cutting the original forces required by one-third so that the date of the landings could be advanced.[72]

The British soon turned such arguments against the Americans. London agreed that TORCH was an unsound operation that risked failure, but only because of the limits insisted upon by the Americans; a larger operation would guarantee success.[73] Regarding the necessity for speed, the Guadalcanal landings and the unsuccessful Dieppe raid had succeeded by late August in calming public pressure for immediate action,[74] and Churchill's promises to Stalin now dictated that the size of TORCH was more important than launching it quickly. Citing those promises as well as the possibility of future action against Italy, the prime minister pressed Roosevelt in late August to cancel the defensively- oriented Casablanca landing in favor of a more offensive one at Algiers. Now willing to compromise, Roosevelt suggested keeping the Casablanca landing, but reducing it in size and launching a third assault at Algiers. He somehow found the extra shipping for such an attack, and full agreement was reached by September 5.[75]

Churchill's victory was now complete. In less than three months he had successfully reversed Allied strategy and convinced the Russians to acquiesce in that reversal. Like Roosevelt's similar victory a few months earlier, however, Churchill's success left many unresolved contradictions. Caused to a great extent by the political factors involved in strategy-making, these contradictions would emerge fully within the next few months and reveal insoluble problems.

CHAPTER FIVE

THE CONSEQUENCES OF TORCH

SEPTEMBER 1942 TO JANUARY 1943

In the autumn of 1942, the Allies reached what is usually considered the "turning point" in their war against Germany by successfully counterattacking on three separate fronts—Egypt, North Africa, and Russia. On October 23, the British began their long-awaited Alamein offensive against the overextended *Afrika Korps* in Egypt; two weeks later, combined Anglo-American forces landed in North Africa and soon began to close in on Rommel's rear. On the Eastern front, the Stalingrad "meatgrinder" bled the Germans white through October, and on November 19 the Soviets launched a massive counterattack that isolated the German Sixth Army within three days and forced its surrender on January 31, 1943.

While these great victories spelled eventual victory for the Allies, they also led to a strategic paradox. The Soviet triumph at Stalingrad, evident long before the final German surrender, meant that CCS 94 was no longer valid, for Russia had not collapsed and Europe was still open to offensive operations. Therefore, the logical offensive for the West in 1943 was a cross Channel assault. The obvious followup to the victories in Egypt and North Africa, on the other hand, consisted of further Mediterranean offensives. Such offensives, however, would end all hope for a 1943 second front, there by negating Western promises to Stalin at a time when the West could ill afford Russian anger. During the remainder of 1942, British and American leaders attempted unsuccessfully to deal with this paradox.

DILEMMAS OF VICTORY

On September 21, Eisenhower informed Marshall that Churchill had finally become "acutely conscious of the inescapable costs of TORCH" which the chief of staff had forecast in July. Now forced to admit that the North African operation could only give "indirect support" to the Russian front while its logistical requirements meant cancellation of the northern convoys in 1942 and perhaps ROUNDUP in 1943,[1] Churchill warned Roosevelt on the following day that he feared "the most grave consequences" from this failure to make good on previous pledges to Stalin. He suggested three compensatory moves: launch JUPITER to reopen the convoy routes and show Moscow some action, even if such an attack meant abandoning future assaults on Sicily, Sardinia, and Italy; send an Anglo-American Air Force to the Caucasus (VELVET) after Rommel was defeated; and continue the BOLERO buildup in order to take advantage of any sudden German weakening or collapse. Russia, he concluded, was "my persisting anxiety. . . and I do not see how we can reconcile it with our consciences or with our interests to have no more PQ's [northern convoys] till 1943, no offer to make joint plans for JUPITER, and no signs of a spring or even autumn offensive in Europe."[2]

Such peripheral solutions left Stimson "aghast" and convinced that Churchill was attempting to rectify his "first false step," TORCH, by laying out a diversionary strategy for the next two years.[3] This the Army refused to sanction. Future Mediterranean operations, coupled with a United Kingdom buildup to take advantage of any German weakening, meant tying down American ships and men in two separate European theaters with subsequent loss to the Pacific effort. The American planners rated JUPITER a meaningless and dangerous diversion.[4] VELVET, they concluded after a month's study under presidential directive, was diversionary, impractical, and motivated by British political goals,[5] a fact Churchill had admitted on two separate occasions. On August 30, he had informed Roosevelt that the proposed air force would "form the advance shield of all our interests in Persia and Abadan" and would have tremendous "moral effect" on the Russians. On September 14, he added that a firm offer to send the force could be coupled with asking "for some favors for the Poles," and thus "help two birds with one piece of sugar."[6]

Considering the areas involved, "our interests" seemed to refer to British interests. As for the "moral effect" argument, Marshall responded on September 18 by informing Roosevelt that the American Lend-Lease policy to Russia "would seem to obviate the necessity for our sending combat troops for political or ideological reasons."[7]

Such reasoning ignored Stalin's stated position on aid as well as the fact that Lend-Lease shipments were way behind schedule[8] and would fall even further behind if the northern convoys were canceled. As early as August, Roosevelt had realized that postponement of the second front meant that relations with Russia hinged entirely on Lend-Lease aid, and that the northern convoys were therefor a "must" operation on par with TORCH and justifying continuation on schedule, even at the expense of American coast convoys.[9] On October 5, he thus responded to Churchill by suggesting the launching of VELVET before Rommel was defeated and sending another convoy in small groups of ships, rather than informing Stalin of cancellation. With his ambassador in Moscow asking to return in order to deliver "a very important message" and with "some fears as to what that message might be," Roosevelt felt it was far better to take such a risk "than to endanger our whole relations with Russia at this time."[10]

Churchill maintained that VELVET had to await the outcome of the desert battle and that the president's convoy plan was impractical. He did agree to let ten ships sail separately for Russia but insisted that Stalin be immediately informed of the true situation, as it was always best to tell the Soviet leader the "blunt truth." Roosevelt was forced to agree. On October 9, the two men informed Stalin of the bad news regarding the northern convoys. They attempted to soften the blow by mentioning VELVET and JUPITER and giving the dates for the planned offensives in Egypt and North Africa. The Soviet leader's two-sentence reply was a chilly "I receive your message of October 9. Thank you."[11]

Such a response represented perfectly the state of Allied relations, which had been deteriorating since Churchill's August visit to Moscow and which by October consisted largely of public Soviet complaints over the lack of a second front and rumors of a separate peace. As the battle of Stalingrad reached its most critical stage, those complaints and rumors increased, reaching a crescendo with Stalin's November 6 claims that German successes were solely the result of the lack of a second front and that Moscow did not aim to destroy all military forces in Germany. To his allies the Soviet leader continued to send curt, two-line telegrams. Although discussion of VELVET took place, the project eventually came to nothing. As Churchill later stated, "The atmosphere was heavily charged with suspicion."[12]

The assaults on El Alamein and North Africa eased the situation somewhat but had a much greater effect on Western public opinion than on Stalin. Despite Roosevelt's efforts, TORCH could not be launched before the congressional elections, during which the Democrats suffered heavy losses. Nevertheless, the landings did relieve much of the public pressure on Roosevelt and Churchill to launch a second front.[13] Continuing his earlier logic, Roosevelt represented those landings as "effective second-front assistance to our heroic allies in Russia."[14] On November 10 he wrote to former Secretary of the Navy Josephus Daniels that he was "happy today in the fact that for three months I have been taking it on the chin in regard to the Second Front and that this is now over."[15]

On the diplomatic front, it was far from over. Stalin sent congratulations after the landings but indicated that he looked upon TORCH as only a prerequisite for a true second front in 1943.[16] At the same time, British planners recommended that no second front be launched until bombing and Mediterranean action had virtually destroyed German military power.[17] Churchill responded by bluntly informing the COS on November 9 that operations limited to Sicily and Sardinia would be equivalent to "lying down" in 1943 and would not be tolerated by the Russians or himself. "However alarming the prospect may seem," he insisted, "we must make an attempt to get on the mainland of Europe and fight . . . in 1943."[18]

The prime minister's "mainland," however, was southern Europe, not northern France. BOLERO, he told the COS, should be continued as a deception to tie down German forces across the Channel so that the West could invade through Italy or southern France in conjunction with a grand linkup of British, American, Turkish, and Soviet troops in the Balkans.[19] According to Eisenhower's chief of staff, Walter Bedell Smith, bringing Turkey into the war in order to accomplish such a goal had by November 9 replaced JUPITER as Churchill's dominating idea, while he had cooled on ROUNDUP "except as a final stroke against a tottering opponent."[20] On November 12, Roosevelt indicated interest in this southern approach, and on the following day Churchill expressed his pleasure over "what you have to say about bringing Turkey in. Our minds have indeed moved together in this, as in so much else."[21] On November 17, he spelled out his ideas in detail to the president, and on November 20, the COS ordered the CPS to examine the grandiose scheme.[22]

While Churchill's plan fitted in perfectly with his traditional strategic approach and desire to vindicate his World War I ideas, postwar political issues may have also entered his calculations. As early as October 21, he had written to Eden of the "measureless disaster" that would occur "if Russian barbarism overlaid the culture and independence of the ancient States of Europe."[23] It is conceivable that Churchill was already thinking in terms not only of linking up with the Russians, but also of blocking their expansion into the Balkans.

As Churchill noted in his letter to Eden, however, "Unhappily the war has prior claims on your attention and on mine,"[24] and the war demanded continued Russian resistance. That continued resistance was in turn dependent upon the establishment of a second front in 1943. Churchill may have felt that he could convince Stalin to accept the Balkan approach, but another problem now arose to change his position drastically. In line with CCS 94, the JCS were continuing with Pacific offensives, and word soon reached Churchill that the Americans were considering abandoning BOLERO-ROUND-UP altogether and turning to the Far East for 1943.[25] Coupled with Stalin's position on a second front, this fact led Churchill to suggest a 180-degree shift in strategy.

On November 18, the prime minister informed the COS that TORCH was no substitute for ROUNDUP and suggested closing down the Mediterranean theater in order to launch a cross-Channel assault in August 1943. "We have," he warned his military chiefs, "pulled in our horns to an almost extraordinary extent, and I cannot imagine what the Russians will say or do when they realize it." Six days later, he again cited the fact that TORCH was no substitute for ROUNDUP as well as his August promises to Stalin in pleading with Roosevelt not to abandon the cross-Channel project. A 1943 ROUNDUP, he admitted, was possible only if the Germans collapsed, but the buildup in the United Kingdom had to be continued in order to "be ready to profit from any opportunity which offers" in 1943 or to launch a full assault in 1944. It was "absolutely necessary" that Hopkins, Marshall, and King return to London for another conference; if they could not come, he was willing to return to Washington.[26]

Recent correspondence with Stalin only served to increase Churchill's urgency. In describing his Mediterranean plans to Stalin on November 24, Churchill had stated that the West was building up forces along the Channel coast and would be ready "to take advantage of any favourable opportunity." Three days later, Stalin replied that he hoped this phrase "does not imply renunciation of your Moscow promise to open a second front in Europe

in the spring of 1943." When the prime minister ignored this reference,
Stalin directly requested a reply on December 6.[27]

A worried Churchill brought both messages to Roosevelt's attention and
pleaded for a London meeting as soon as possible on the grounds that "every
day counts."[28] At the same time, he again spurred his staff on ROUNDUP.
Citing recent Russian victories, his promises to Stalin, and the possibility
of severe German weakening or collapse in 1943, he informed the COS on
December 3 that CCS 94 was no longer valid, that Allied offensive plans
for 1943 were insufficient, and that the situation called for a complete
strategic reevaluation, including the possibility of closing down the Mediterranean theater during the summer so that ROUNDUP could be launched
in August or September.[29]

One stunned British planner felt that Churchill could only be playing
devil's advocate as a means of strengthening British Mediterranean arguments for the coming conference with the Americans.[30] Brooke, however, realized that Churchill was quite serious, and concluded that exagger-
ated warnings of a separate peace if no second front materialized in 1943
had forced the prime minister to call for this drastic strategic shift. Such
a shift, the CIGS insisted, was militarily unsound. ROUNDUP could not
possibly be launched in 1943, and extensive Mediterranean operations would
be needed during that year to disperse the Germans if the West hoped to
successfully cross the Channel in 1944.[31]

Brooke's logic was only strengthened by Hitler's decision to reinforce
Tunisia and by the subsequent German counterattack on December 1.
That counterattack also effectively ended Churchill's grandiose 1943 plans
by destroying their basic precondition—conquest of Tunisia within a month
of TORCH so that Mediterranean forces could be shifted rapidly. On December 15, the COS recommended a full Mediterranean strategy for 1943,
and Churchill was forced to agree on the following day. He still insisted,
however, that the 1943 United Kingdom buildup continue in case "conditions hold out a good prospect of success" for a cross-Channel assault in
August or September.[32]

Roosevelt, meanwhile, agreed with Churchill that a meeting was necessary to determine future strategy, and for the next month, the two leaders
tried to convince Stalin to join them in North Africa.[33] For Roosevelt, such
a meeting would deal not only with strategic issues, but with future occupation policy for Germany and Russian entry into the war against Japan.[34]
But Stalin insisted that he could not leave the USSR at that crucial time
for any meeting, and on December 14 he reiterated his warning regarding a

1943 second front.[35] In effect, the Soviet leader was linking any future
political collaboration to that front at a time when its establishment was
more questionable than ever.

THE AMERICAN QUANDARY

Disunity over proper strategic policy for 1943 pervaded not only British
but also American circles in late 1942. Within the Army, some members
of the OPD felt that further Mediterranean operations would be completely
indecisive and would indefinitely postpone ROUNDUP. They therefore
concluded that the JCS should insist on a maximum buildup in the United
Kingdom so that the cross-Channel attack could be launched in 1943 or
1944; if the British insisted on further Mediterranean operations, the United
States should turn to the Pacific.[36] Others in the OPD countered that a
1943 ROUNDUP was now impossible and that giving up the hard-won Mediterranean initiative in order to amass forces for a 1944 assault would be
senseless. The ensuing inaction, OPD's Policy Committee further pointed
out on December 19, might "adversely" affect the Russians to such an extent "that Stalin may make a separate peace." Such "political" factors, som
staff members insisted, necessitated "limited offensives" in Sicily and/or
Sardinia for 1943.[37]

The JCS were just as badly split as the OPD planners. Backed by Leahy
and the force of public opinion, King continued to insist on adherence to
CCS 94 and further Pacific action,[38] while Arnold maintained his opposition to such dispersion of air power and pressed for concentration against
Germany. From the air-power point of view, however, Britain, North Africa, and the Mediterranean were all complementary theaters. Hence, the
air chief was lukewarm to any complete closing of the Mediterranean theate
in order to launch ROUNDUP in 1943.[39]

Marshall, on the other hand, had no such qualms. Planning and logistical
difficulties in late 1942 led the Army chief to dismiss both his temporary
flirtation with the Pacific alternative and the split within his own staff, and
to become once again the main proponent of immediate concentration for
a cross-Channel attack. While the lack of any clearcut offensive policy for
Europe made it impossible to estimate future Army needs, shortages of
supplies and men, together with postponement of the second front, had
led to attempts to severely limit the size of the armed forces, especially the

Army, on the grounds that Britain and Russia could handle Germany while the United States Navy fought the Japanese. Marshall believed that the Egyptian and North African campaigns strengthened what he referred to as this "fallacious and humiliating proposition" and "fatal psychology."[40] A return to the cross-Channel concept would obviously bolster his arguments regarding the need for massive ground forces, as well as make it possible for the planners to match logistics and strategy. He therefore pressed for an end to Mediterranean "dabbling" and a return to BOLERO-ROUNDUP in both JCS meetings and conferences with the president.[41] But Marshall could hardly speak for a united Army staff, let alone a united JCS.

The depth of the JCS split emerged fully during a December 12 discussion of a Joint Strategic Survey Committee (JSSC) report. The paper had totally rejected the Mediterranean approach and called for a 1943 buildup and cross-Channel attack in order to assist Russia and make sure that the primary American effort would be against Germany rather than her satellites. Insisting that the Germany-first approach was now "considered uncertain," Leahy attacked the entire report while Marshall and General Embick of the JSSC defended the basic Allied concept. King stated that he was willing to agree to the Army position, but objected to the "offhand" treatment the JSSC had given the Pacific and wondered why the planners assumed that Britain would "continue to assist us after [the] defeat of Germany." He concluded that the Pacific theater required at least 25 percent of total American resources and immediate offensive action to avoid "indefinitely" postponing Japanese defeat.[42]

During the next two weeks, the JCS grappled with their differences. By December 26, they reached a compromise whereby all members backed Marshall's plan to consolidate in North Africa after Rommel's defeat and concentrate in Britain for a 1943 cross-Channel attack. In return, Arnold received support for continued air offensives against Germany from Britain and North Africa, while King was won over by JCS advocacy of Pacific offensives to maintain the initiative over the Japanese and a Burma campaign to reopen the supply route to China.[43] Unfortunately, this compromise shared the weakness of Churchill's plan by attempting to do too much with too few resources. Furthermore, it had been reached at the top level only; the planners still disagreed sharply.

The COS responded to the American plan with two strategy papers that pressed for a vigorous followup to TORCH in the Mediterranean on the grounds that a 1943 ROUNDUP sufficient to relieve the Russians and be successful was now impossible. Instead of attempting such a project, the West should continue the pressure in the Mediterranean via a bombing campaign against Germany and Italy, operations against Sicily or Sardinia to knock Italy out of the war, material assistance to bring Turkey in, and possible Balkan operations to rally guerrilla forces in the area. Such actions, the COS felt, would aid the Russians in 1943 more than any disastrous attempt to launch a cross-Channel attack, and would so disperse the German that either a collapse would follow or the path would be clear for a 1944 invasion from Britain. The BOLERO buildup should therefore continue within the limits imposed by Mediterranean operations so that the Allies would be ready to reenter the continent in 1943 "if conditions hold out a good prospect of success" (i.e., German disintegration), or in 1944. In the Far East, only "limited" offensives to "contain" the Japanese rather than take the initiative should be launched, with Burma operations taking place "as soon as resources permit."[44]

To the Americans, this program meant total subordination of the Pacific to an indecisive, wasteful Mediterranean strategy coupled with a useless tying down of American forces in the United Kingdom. In light of Churchill's famous November 9 statement that he had "not become the King's First Minister to preside over the liquidation of the British Empire" and the belief by General Staff members that Brest or Cherbourg could have been taken with the equipment and supplies already allocated to TORCH, the COS plan seemed a blatant attempt to preserve and expand the empire at the expense of quick victory over Germany and subsequent defeat of Japan.

On January 4, Generals Embick and Muir S. Fairchild of the JSSC explained such a possibility to Marshall by quoting a Washington correspondent who had written on the previous day that London's desire to control North Africa was an "open secret." Some Britishers, according to that correspondent, saw the area as "the answer to the United Kingdom's crying need for British-controlled raw materials and markets." If this was true, Embick and Fairchild stated, then the British would want islands in the Mediterannean as

> fortified outposts of the empire guarding the mandated territory of North Africa. . . . If these islands have been seized from the enemy and are firmly in British possession at the time of the peace settlement, Great Britain might be able to maintain her claim to their

permanent possession. Hence the necessity from the British viewpoint, of undertaking these operations *prior* to undertaking decisive operations directly against Germany.

Furthermore, British foreign policy, according to the two generals, had attempted for "the past century or more" to maintain a balance of power on
the European continent, and

> A defeated and prostrate Germany leaving a strong and triumphant
> Russia dominating Europe, is not in accord with that unchanging
> policy. It would be in strict accord with that policy, however, to
> delay Germany's defeat until military attrition and civilian famine
> had materially reduced Russia's potential toward dominance in
> Europe.

The purpose behind the British strategy, Embick and Fairchild concluded,
was thus "not primarily military, but . . . political."[47]

Such a strategy, the JSSC warned in a series of papers written at this
time, tended "to repeat the unsuccessful efforts to win the last war from
the south and southeast of Europe," and by its negative effect on ROUND-
UP invited a long war culminating in stalemate or defeat. Furthermore, Mediterranean operations would require heavy American naval support needed
for operations in the Pacific and Burma. Hence, they placed British political interests in the Mediterranean in direct collision with those of the United
States in the Far East. The JSSC bluntly stated in this regard that the basic
Allied disagreement was not over the proper followup to TORCH, but over
the relation of the Pacific war to the war as a whole. In conclusion, it felt
that with the turning point of the European war at hand, the West "should
forego indirect and eccentric concepts and strike hard and straight at Germany."[48] On January 5, the JCS concluded that resolution of this strategic
conflict "must rest on the highest level," and they immediately directed
the JPS to prepare a letter for the president outlining the problem and recommending that he discuss it with the prime minister.[49]

Roosevelt needed no urging in this direction, for he was very concerned
over Stalin's refusal to attend a conference and was more than ever interested in mollifying the Soviet leader with the military operation he demanded. But such an operation was only one of numerous possible ways to reassure the Soviets of the West's good faith. Picking up on an earlier idea of

Major-General James H. Burns of the Lend-Lease Administration,[50] Roose
velt suggested at a January 7 meeting with the JCS that General Marshall
go to Moscow to bolster Soviet morale and reassure Stalin, who "probably
felt out of the picture" and had "a feeling of loneliness." Marshall could ac
complish these goals by informing the Soviet leader of the results of the
coming conference with Churchill. At that meeting, Roosevelt intended
to discuss postwar disarmament, a possible summit conference during the
summer, and "the advisability of informing Mr. Stalin that the United Nations were to continue on until they reach Berlin, and that their only term
would be unconditional surrender."[51]

Since Stalin would be most concerned with the second front, Roosevelt
then asked the JCS if they were "agreed that we should meet the British
united in advocating a cross-Channel operation." Marshall was forced to
respond "that there was not a united front on that subject, particularly
among our Planners." The JCS, he continued, favored a second front over
Mediterranean operations, "but the question was still an open one." He
explained the "very decided difference of opinion" between the American
and British on future strategy, and pressed his own position in the most
direct manner possible: ". . . to state it cruelly, we could replace troops
whereas a heavy loss in shipping, which would result from BRIMSTONE
Operation [Sardinia], might completely destroy any opportunity for successful operations against the enemy in the near future."[52]

After questioning Marshall, Roosevelt pointedly warned his chiefs that
at the coming conference "the British will have a plan and stick to it." See
ing that the same could not be said of his advisers, he suggested a buildup
in both the Mediterranean and Britain, with deferral of a final decision for
a few months. The proper course of action to follow at the conference,
he concluded, would be up to the JCS.[53]

Roosevelt had thus thrown the issue back into the laps of his advisers.
Aware of their own disagreement and the solid British stance, they had as
the president to take the initiative. He in turn had insisted on remaining
noncommittal because of the lack of a united front and had told them to
take the initiative. In such a situation, strategic decisions would obviously
rest in British hands.

THE CASABLANCA CONFERENCE

This fact became clear during the first two days of discussion at Casablanca. While the massive British planning staff dominated and outargued

its tiny American counterpart and the COS enunciated their refusal to cross the Channel in 1943 without prior German weakening, Churchill and his advisers carefully noted and exploited the split within the JCS and Roosevelt's continuing inclination for Mediterranean action.[54] To compound the problem, Eisenhower informed Marshall that ROUNDUP would require twice the assault force and landing craft originally anticipated and could not be launched before August.[55]

The JCS thus had to admit on January 16 that a massive cross-Channel assault was impossible in 1943 and that Mediterranean operations would be, in Arnold's words, "a necessity to keep the Russian's encouraged." Moreover, the excess of troops soon to be available in North Africa made the conquest of Sicily a logical and attractive followup to TORCH in order to reopen the Mediterranean shipping route and release vessels for operations in other theaters.[56]

As a precondition for American acceptance of the Sicilian invasion, however, King insisted on British agreement to his Pacific offensives with an allocation of 30 percent of the Allied war effort to that theater.[57] The COS balked at this demand, and the result was a series of bitter exchanges during the CCS meetings of January 17 and 18. Arguing for definite Pacific action over a "dormant" force in the United Kingdom "awaiting an opportunity," Marshall warned that British refusal to agree to a Burma campaign could lead to a situation in the Pacific "that would necessitate the United States regretfully withdrawing from the commitments in the European theater." Interpreting such comments as an attempt to overthrow the Germany-first concept, Brooke retorted sharply that such a decision would make victory impossible.[58] On January 17 he noted in his diary that the CCS were "further from obtaining agreement than we ever were."[59]

Brooke's colleagues disagreed. The COS, according to Air Chief Sir Charles Portal, were "in the position of a testator who wishes to leave the bulk of his fortune to his mistress. He must, however, leave something to his wife, and his problem is to decide how little he can in decency leave apart for her." As Marshall's biographer has pointed out, the fortune belonged to the wife from the beginning, and the real question was how little she would be willing to accept. The answer was a clause sanctioning offensives on the Pacific and Burma, but with the distinct proviso that that these operations be within limits set by the CCS so as not to jeopardize the capacity of the Allies to defeat Germany in 1943.[60]

With all parties accepting this rather contradictory clause, the CCS quickly reached preliminary agreement and reported to Roosevelt and Churchill on

January 18. First priority, they stated, would be given to defeat of the U-boat menace and to the continued sending of the greatest possible volume of supplies to the Soviet Union "without prohibitive cost in shipping. Operations in Europe aimed at further dispersing German forces, diverting them from Russia, and defeating Hitler in 1943 would include an invasion of Sicily (HUSKY) and the mounting of the heaviest possible bomber offensive from the United Kingdom. Limited ground operations across the Channel would be conducted if they appeared possible, with BOLERO continuing so as to enable reentry of the continent at the first signs of German weakening or collapse.[61]

Churchill and Roosevelt were only partially satisfied with these conclusions. At the January 18 meeting, Churchill requested inclusion of clauses in the final CCS document giving the British a "free hand" to deal with the Turks and mentioning the possibility of operations in the Dodecanese Islands. Roosevelt agreed.[62] Both men were upset, moreover, by the pessimistic CCS position regarding a 1943 cross-Channel assault, for Stalin was now complaining over the fact that North African operations had come to a "standstill" and were not diverting any German divisions from the Eastern front.[63] A worried Churchill had informed the COS on the evening of January 13 that only a cross-Channel assault, combined with Mediterranean offensives and the recapture of Burma, "would be worthy of two great Powers and their obligations to Russia."[64] At the January 18 meeting, he stated that the 1943 SLEDGEHAMMER operation should be given "a sharper point," and he called for the designation of a planning commander and a target date for the assault.[65]

Roosevelt concurred and on the following evening told his son Elliot that he was worried about the effect of the CCS decisions on Stalin.[66] On January 20, he informed the JCS that he was "reluctant to accept the status of SLEDGEHAMMER in 1943," since it appeared that the West was designating the operation "as the last one to be accomplished and this would be done only if the estimated requirements of all other theaters of operations are met."[67]

The CCS quickly complied with their superiors' wishes by including provisions in their final report for a British lead in bringing Turkey into the war, possible ground operations in the Dodecanese and the Balkans. An August 1943, cross-Channel assault (HADRIAN), and the formation of a combined staff under a British commander to plan cross-Channel operations (COS-SAC).[68] Marshall made clear to both leaders, however, that any 1943 second front would be "difficult if not impossible" once the West was committed to HUSKY and would be "extremely limited" in size unless there was a "complete crack in German morale."[69]

Stalin would not be pleased by this news. Nor would he welcome the possible temporary cessation of northern convoys in order to launch HUSKY—a fact that both Churchill and Roosevelt had rebelled against but been forced to accept by the CCS.[70] The two Allied leaders sought a temporary escape from these harsh realities by refusing to inform Stalin of the convoy cancellation while telling him that the bomber offensive and United Kingdom buildup would enable the West to reenter the continent "as soon as practicable." Such vagueness could not, and did not, pacify the Soviet premier.[71]

Roosevelt's solution to the problem was a statement that would reassure Stalin that his allies were not going to let Germany and Russia bleed each other to death. In other words, he proposed a verbal pledge that would serve as a political and psychological substitute for a second front. Returning to his January 7 idea, the president announced such a statement at his January 24 press conference—unconditional surrender for the Axis Powers. It was, he told Elliot Roosevelt beforehand, "just the thing for the Russians."[72] Furthermore, it could serve as a substitute for the war-aims statement Roosevelt had hoped to work out in the meeting Stalin had refused to attend. The president was soon to discover, however, that Stalin did not consider words a valid substitute for action.

With the military discussions concluded, Roosevelt and Churchill both congratulated the CCS on January 23 for their work. The conference had been, according to Churchill, "the first instance he knew of when military leaders had remained together so long, free from political considerations, and had devoted their full thought to the strategic aspects of the war."[73] To the Americans, it must have seemed that Churchill either had tongue in cheek or an ability to fool himself exceeding the president's. Certainly the full British victory regarding future plans was anything but nonpolitical to Wedemeyer, who informed OPD Chief General Thomas Handy on January 22 that "we lost our shirts and are now committed to a subterranean umbilicus operation in mid-summer. One might say we came, we listened and we were conquered."[74]

In fact, while the British viewed the CCS decisions as a great triumph,[75] the Americans found the entire conference worthless and frustrating. Disappointed and depressed over its results, Hopkins rated the planned Mediterranean efforts "feeble" for two great powers in 1943.[76] Leahy, who had been prevented from attending because of illness, concluded in his diary, after talking with the JCS and Roosevelt, that the meetings had accomplished "little of value to ending the war."[77] Marshall, according to one British source, had vented his frustrations by informing Eisenhower that "in my discussions with our politicians, I have found that there are more brass hea among them than brass hats among the soldiers," and had warned the CCS that if HUSKY was replaced by an even lesser operation, "someone else would have to be found to sit in his chair."[78] Feelings against the British were so intense that Eisenhower thought it necessary to warn Handy again the dangers toward which the planners seemed headed:

> I am not so incredibly naive that I do not realize that Britishers
> instinctively approach every military problem from the viewpoint
> of the Empire, just as we approach them from the viewpoint of
> American interests. But one of the constant sources of danger to
> us in this war is the temptation to regard as our first enemy the
> partner that must work with us in defeating the real enemy.[79]

Nor were the politics of the Casablanca Conference limited to matters of strategy. Considering the probable lack of a second front in 1943, the CCS decision to maintain a high priority on convoys to northern Russia appeared to Hopkins to be a "political expedient," despite Marshall's January 18 statement that it was not necessary "to take excessive punishmen in running these convoys simply to keep Mr. Stalin placated." On January 23, the presidential adviser suggested dropping the convoys entirely on m: itary grounds, but with Western relations with Russia still based solely on supplies, Roosevelt and Churchill refused to agree.[80] The final conference decisions also reflected the political intervention of the two heads of state in their attempts to placate Stalin. Both Operation HADRIAN and the un conditional surrender announcement were attempts by Roosevelt and Churchill to reassure the Soviet leader in the absence of a firm commitme to launch a 1943 second front.

In total, the military decisions of the Casablanca Conference were high political and reflected an attempt to satisfy all three partners in the Gran Alliance. These paper decisions, however, had very little to do with realit for in their attempts to satisfy everyone, the conferees had planned too many operations with too few resources available. The results would be f ther recriminations, further politicization of strategy-making, and a near rupture in the Grand Alliance. In effect, the Western Allies were now fac with the full consequences of their July decision to mount TORCH.

CHAPTER SIX

___THE MERGING OF___
OLD AND NEW ISSUES
JANUARY TO MAY 1943

The JCS and their planners returned from Casablanca determined to avoid any repetition of their failure. They quickly realized, however, that future victory would depend upon the ability to achieve better organization and full unity within American ranks before meeting the British again. As Wedemeyer succinctly stated, London's ability in this regard had kept the Americans "on the defensive practically all the time" at Casablanca, and winning COS approval in the future for a major cross-Channel assault would be impossible "without the full weight of national policy as opposed to that of the British."[1]

The armed forces thus moved in early 1943 to improve contacts with the White House and the State Department, while the joint committee system was completely revamped in April to insure agreement between the different services. At the same time, the planners began intensive military and political studies on future operations, realizing, in the words of one Army historian, that they "could not keep foreign and political affairs out of . . . military calculations."[2] The events of early 1943 only served to reinforce this conclusion.

THE ELUCIDATION OF OLD IDEAS

Between February and April, the excessive commitments made at Casablanca continually drained resources set aside for HADRIAN. In addition, fear of German reinforcement in Sicily led to pessimistic estimates regarding the possibility of a successful HUSKY as well as further demands for BO-

LERO forces. In late March, the Americans responded by requesting a re-examination of the Sicilian assault and the Casablanca commitments as a whole, including the possibility of abandoning HUSKY altogether and placing more emphasis on the Far East.[3]

The British, of course, objected to any such reexamination. To the contrary, they now interpreted the Casablanca decisions as justifying an invasion of Italy and landings in the eastern Mediterranean. As Churchill explained to Roosevelt on April 5, HUSKY was "only a stepping stone" to greater prizes.[4] As a result of such plans and the sad state of BOLERO, the COS not only refused the American request, but also suggested completely dropping HADRIAN and the spring 1944 target date from the planning directive being prepared for COSSAC.[5] At the same time, Churchill requested that London be considered the "senior partner" in any military administration of conquered Italian territory.[6]

To the Americans, such moves were clear evidence of British intent to reap political benefits in the Mediterranean at the expense of winning the war. The JCS responded by refusing to drop HADRIAN or the 1944 target date, as well as informing the president of their opposition to further Mediterranean operations after HUSKY.[7] An aroused Stimson, who decided in late April to reenter the strategic debate in order to convince Roosevelt to "crush" Britain's "stupid opposition" to a cross-Channel assault, backed up their warnings by informing the president on May 3 that action in the eastern Mediterranean could resurrect the historic Anglo-Russian clash in the area.[8] Arnold and General Frank Andrews, commander of the European Theater of Operations, voiced their belief that the British had absolutely no intention of crossing the Channel because London did not want to see Germany totally defeated and Russia dominant on the continent.[9]

The State Department was equally vociferous in opposing British control of military administration in occupied territories. While one department official quoted the old motto that an Englishman's idea of cooperation was "to persuade someone to do what he wants him to do,"[10] Welles insisted that Washington must maintain control of territory occupied by troops under American command so as not to be "at a disadvantage in peace negotiations."[11] On April 13, Hull and Stimson informed Roosevelt of their joint opposition to Britain's military administration plans.[12]

With the British pressing those plans as well as further Mediterranean action and with another conference approaching, the joint planners recommended in late April, "as a matter of urgency," that the JCS order a study prepared "relating to current British Empire policy and grand strategy in its relation to that of the United States." The JCS quickly concurred.[13] Even before their decision, however, the Strategy and Policy Group of the OPD had delved into this highly political issue. They concluded that Britain's Mediterranean approach was part of a slow strategy of attrition designed to weaken Germany and Russia in order to preserve a European balance of power, and to strengthen and consolidate the remnants of the British Empire in the India-Middle East-Africa area by controlling Iraq and Iran. Since the main routes to those countries ran through Turkey, getting her into the war and mounting major operations in the eastern Mediterranean would protect the empire from any European incursion.[14]

On May 3, the JSSC reached similar conclusions. The divergence in strategic viewpoint between Washington and London, the committee felt, sprang not simply from differing strategic estimates but "from such fundamental causes as the differences in geographic situation vis-a-vis the several enemies, and in the marked contrast between the two nations in respect to their territorial structures and their bases of power." For Britain, occupation of the Mediterranean was a national policy objective "essential" to both the maintenance and improvement of its present imperial power. Thus the British placed operations in this area above those in the Pacific or across the Channel. In the Far East, London was apparently convinced that it would regain its prewar position no matter how long it took to defeat Japan. As for ROUND-UP, the massive casualties involved in such an operation would result in a decline in imperial strength. Furthermore, Britain had traditionally opposed the development of a dominant military power on the continent, and in line with such reasoning might have mental reservations about both the unconditional surrender formula and any strategy that would end the European war quickly. London could not entirely overlook the possibility that, in a long war, Germany and Russia would exhaust each other.[15]

Such an approach, the planners pointed out, posed serious problems for the United States. In the first place, operations in the eastern Mediterranean invited a resurrection of the old Anglo-Russian clash over the Dardanelles. Echoing Stimson's warning to the president, the JSSC pointed out in its May 3 report and again on May 5 that Aegean operations, if not checked with the Russians first, would arouse Soviet suspicion and resentment. Moscow would then "become more susceptible to subsequent proposals by Germany which, following the pattern of 1870, would grant Russia control of the Straits."[16]

British strategy also involved a further dispersion of American forces and a lengthening of the European war, both of which would continue to hamper proper mobilization and production planning. Moreover, with 54 percent of the American people still rating Japan as the chief enemy,[17] the public would not tolerate a long war in Europe and would probably demand a Pacific-first strategy instead. As a special Army committee pointed out on April 28, mobilization and production had to be linked to national policy and strategic planning, and a long-range plan for the quick and decisive defeat of the Axis was now needed. Any dispersion of American forces should "be avoided," it warned, for the American public wearied quickly of war and would not tolerate a slow strategy of attrition.[18]

The Joint War Plans Committee (JWPC) reached similar conclusions on May 7 but used even blunter language than the previous studies, labeling the foremost aims of British national policy as

> the maintenance of the integrity of the British Empire and of her supremacy in world trade. She dominates her empire by controlling the economic destiny of her dominions and crown colonies. She maintains her position in the European area by preserving the balance of power on the Continent. She exploits the resources and people of other nations to insure her position of dominance. British war policy is influenced by these national policies and her post-war economic, territorial and political ambitions. She would, therefore, prefer that the conduct of the war be such that neither Germany nor Russia can emerge in a dominating position in Europe, and that the balance of power in Europe can rest in British hands. She would prefer that operations be so conducted and troops so disposed as to enable her to attain and retain areas which are vital to the maintenance of her empire or which might be used for bargaining purposes at the peace table.[19]

The JWPC saw the foremost American aims, on the other hand, as hemispheric security and "improvement of her world economic position by reciprocal trade pacts." Since neither aim presently required a balance of power policy, the committee concluded that current American military policy "is not strongly influenced by post-war aims." In the same report, however, it modified and then contradicted this conclusion. The conflicting national aims of the two powers, it warned, led not only to differing strategic concepts, but also to the possibility of economic warfare between the two countries, for the United States had achieved supremacy in commercial air transport "wherever her companies have operated" and recent indications showed that Britain was "using war necessity as a means of undermining the United States supremacy." Moreover, the American people would "not countenance a long war of attrition" in Europe, and Washington could not tolerate the loss of Chinese cooperation and the collapse of Chiang Kai-shek's regime which might result from abandonment of the Burma campaign. Everything should be done, the planners concluded in supporting that campaign, "to maintain the prestige and influence of the United States in China."

In assessing the British position at the coming conference, the JWPC concluded that London would probably argue for operations in the eastern Mediterranean on the grounds that ROUNDUP was impracticable, "if not impossible," before late 1944 unless Germany collapsed, and that further operations before the assault would be necessary to keep Russia in the war. Such operations, the JWPC noted, would also tend to increase British influence in Turkey and enable London to block any Soviet move toward the Dardanelles. Equally important, they would contribute to the "possible" British aim of recommending one limited operation after another in the Mediterranean with a view to building up forces in that theater so that an invasion of Europe from the south rather than the United Kingdom "will inevitably develop into a commitment." This approach, the committee stated, was neither "feasible nor acceptable."[20]

Such analyses obviously pointed to American insistence on concentration for a cross-Channel assault. The planners had been forced to agree, however, to the validity of at least one British point—ROUNDUP was highly unlikely for 1943, and some action would be needed between HUSKY and the 1944 cross-Channel assault to keep Russia in the war. While some planners concluded from this point that limited Mediterranean offensives were necessary, others pointed out that such offensives could divert even more forces from BOLERO and thereby destroy the already diminished 1944 plan. A closing down of the Mediterranean theater combined with a massive bombing offensive from the United Kingdom, they concluded, would help Russia more than any further Mediterranean attacks and would also insure a 1944 ROUNDUP.[21]

Wishing to avoid another unhealed schism, the JCS ordered the JWPC and JPS to reconcile these conflicting ideas into one position. As approved by the JCS on May 8, that final position sanctioned limited Mediterranean offensives to keep Russia in the war but insisted that those offensives be subordinated to a planned thirty-six division ROUNDUP in the spring of 1944. To insure such subordination, six divisions would be transferred in late 1943 from the Mediterranean to the United Kingdom, and no American troops would be used in Italy or east of Sicily. Operations in those areas, the planners warned, would lead to political conflicts with Russia, outcries from the Pacific-minded American public, and a wasteful and indecisive dispersion of forces that could be put to better use in Britain or the Pacific. London should therefore be warned that refusal to agree to the primacy of BOLERO-ROUNDUP would lead the Americans to turn their major effort to the Far East, and that in any event the United States would insist on Pacific and Burma offensives.[22]

With position papers approved, the JCS turned their attention on May 8 to proper tactics at the coming conference. Approaching the meeting much as if it were a battle, they agreed to present their position papers immediately in order to "get the jump" on the British. But such maneuvers, Leahy pointed out, would be worthless without presidential agreement to the JCS position. He had therefore already sent Roosevelt the "most useful and forceful" May 3 JSSC report on British politics and strategy. The JCS now officially approved this report, sent a copy of their basic position paper to the president, and prepared to meet him on May 9.[23]

Roosevelt's position at that session remains shrouded in mystery. On the one hand, he filled his copy of the JCS position paper with derogatory notations and question marks, referring to their fear that eastern Mediterranean operations would arouse Russian suspicions and accomplish British political goals as "conversation," describing their warning of adverse public reaction to such operations as "Spinach," and warning against "closed minds."[24]

Yet, Roosevelt had previously shown intense interest in the public's reaction to planned operations, and within the next three months would voice agreement with every JCS judgment he attacked on May 9.[25] It may thus be concluded that his comments reflected nothing more than anger at the JCS for dealing with political issues. Furthermore, according to Leahy, Roosevelt agreed at the meeting that the "principle objective" of the United States at the coming conference "would be to pin down the British to a cross-Channel invasion of Europe at the earliest practicable date and to make full preparations for such an operation by the spring of 1944."[26] Such agreement was, according to Marshall, "only in principle," and both the chief of staff and Stimson had doubts about the strength of the president's stand.[27] Yet, it was a definite advance from the Casablanca episode, and it clearly showed the impact of the united JCS front on Roosevelt's thinking.

As in 1942, however, the position of the president and his military advisers can be fully explained only by referring to the diplomatic situation with Russia. Stalin's actions were again having a tremendous influence on strategic planning, although in a way quite different from 1942.

THE EMERGING FEAR OF RUSSIA

Neither the British nor the Americans had expected Stalin to be happy with the results of the Casablanca Conference. Churchill informed his Cabinet upon returning to London that the Soviet leader would be "disappointed and furious" with the message he and Roosevelt had sent outlining those results,[28] while Army G-2 warned on January 28 that Soviet pressure for a second front would shortly resume.[29] Two days later, Stalin responded to the lack of a clear second-front pledge in the Churchill-Roosevelt message by asking for specific information regarding Western plans and timing for 1943.[30]

Churchill quickly composed a draft reply that represented his own desires much more than it did the Casablanca decisions. In addition to explaining plans for North Africa and Sicily, he stated that the West would attack Italy in July and launch a seventeen- to twenty-division assault across the Channel in August or September.[31] While Roosevelt was apparently willing to agree to such a grandiose statement of aims and abilities, Western military leaders were not. The COS objected that the draft was "too optimistic,"[32] while Marshall informed Roosevelt that some of its statements were "misleading and may result in a misunderstanding of our intentions on the part of Mr. Stalin." Pointing out that the JCS had carefully avoided a commitment to invade Italy proper and that the cross-Channel assault was only possible if the Germans collapsed in 1943, Marshall suggested modifications in the proposed message that Roosevelt and Churchill were forced to accept.[33] The prime minister's message to Stalin on February 9 thus made no mention of an Italian invasion and stated that the exact timing of the cross-Channel attack had to "be dependent upon the condition of German defensive possibilities across the Channel at the time."[34]

Missing this cryptic warning, Stalin responded by complaining bitterly over the lack of action in Tunisia and the fact that the Germans had been able to transfer numerous divisions to the East since September. The cross-

Channel assault, he insisted, must be launched in the spring to ease the pres sure on his forces. With the CCS already shifting forces from BOLERO to HUSKY, Churchill replied on March 11 by explaining Western plans in grea detail, but warning that a "premature attack" across the Channel could onl result in a "bloody repulse" and Nazi vengeance against the local populatio Now realizing that "premature" might include all of 1943, Stalin warned both Allied leaders that HUSKY would not be considered a substitute for a second front in France, and he gave "a most emphatic warning . . . of the grave danger with which further delay. . . is fraught." The "vagueness" of their second-front statements, he concluded, "causes apprehension which I cannot conceal from you."[35]

Washington was equally apprehensive, for Stalin's warning was accom- panied by Russian victories in the East, a bitter argument between London and Moscow over northern convoy protection, and a public statement by Stalin that made no mention of Western aid and concluded that the lack of a second front meant that the Red Army was virtually fighting alone. Simul- taneously, the Soviets undertook a diplomatic offensive in Eastern Europe which included demands for their 1941 frontiers, a severe deterioration in relations with the Polish government-in-exile, postwar alliance talks with the Czechs, and support for the de Gaulle movement and the communist- led Yugoslav partisans in their civil war with the Chetniks. While separate peace rumors subsequently filled the air, warnings flooded Washington that Stalin aimed to communize at least part and perhaps all of Europe.[36]

This combination of Russian victories and diplomatic truculence had lec Stimson to conclude as early as December 18, 1942, that the best hope for the postwar world would be a peace settlement "based on the mutual rela- tions between the two English speaking nations."[37] On December 20, a State Department official warned that "the European civil war between the adherents or clients of the Anglo-Saxon powers on one hand and Russia on the other has already begun," and that the Yugoslav pattern would be re- peated all over Europe and cause the Grand Alliance to collapse before Ger many was defeated.[38] In early March, an Office of Strategic Services (OSS) memorandum warned that Charles de Gaulle had become "a trump card in Moscow's political game" and that his Free French movement "threatens to become simply an auxiliary of Russian grand strategy."[39] Later that month, fears were expressed that American communists were planning a huge campaign to discredit the State Department so that it would not oppose socialism in Europe after the war.[40]

Military planners also expressed concern over the growing crisis and suggested some basic changes in American policy toward the Soviets. On January 23, the OPD's Policy Committee concluded that the United States should continue to furnish Russia with Lend-Lease aid

> provided—and provided only—that Russia cooperates with us and takes us into her confidence. As we grow more powerful . . . we can afford to, and in simple self-interest must start exercising the dominant influence which such power properly entitles us. The time is appropriate for us to start some straight-from-the-shoulder talks, especially with Mr. Joseph Stalin.[41]

Such feelings were widespread enough in the War Department for Arnold to inform Marshall on February 23 of opposition to sending heavy bombers to Russia on the grounds of a "growing uncertainty" within the armed forces "as to where Russian successes might lead." Aid to the Soviets, the air chief further pointed out, was "based upon the necessity of hurting Germany, and not any desire to help Russia."[42] Handy heartily concurred in these judgments. He even suggested decreasing American aid inasmuch as it had already served its purpose and continuance could easily hurt postwar American interests:

> Victory in this war will be meaningless unless we also win the peace. We must be strong enough at the peace table to cause our demands to be respected. With this in mind, we should give only such equipment to our Allies that they can put to better and quicker use than we can.[43]

Such strength at the peace table required not only a change in Lend-Lease policy, but also the presence of American troops on the European continent, a fact both Wedemeyer and Sikorski had realized during the spring of 1942.[44] Sikorski had repeated his warnings in this regard during June 1942 when he stated that a second front was necessary "in order to establish a United Nations, rather than a chiefly Russian peace.[45] On December 22, he warned Welles and Marshall that communist propaganda could cause a German collapse and a "Bolshevist Europe" unless the Western Allies established themselves on the continent as soon as possible.[46] An official within the State Department dismissed most of Sikorski's fears as part of the "Polish phobia" about Russia. Even so, he emphasized that the possibility of a communized Germany "should never be lost sight of," since such a situation would negate the Soviet need for postwar American assistance and be "disastrous for any hope of a stable world after the war." The United States could thus agree with Sikorski's point, the official concluded, that it was in America's interest to hasten Allied operations in Europe

> so that peace would not find the Soviet armies alone on the continent. If Germany collapses before the Democracies have been able to make an important military contribution on the continent of Europe, the peoples of Europe will with reason believe that the war was won by the Russians alone. Under such conditions the prestige of the Soviet Union will be so great that it will be difficult for Great Britain and the United States to oppose successfully any line of policy which the Kremlin may choose to adopt.[47]

King echoed similar sentiments on January 16, informing his JCS colleagues that, unless the United States and Britain made "some definite move toward the defeat of Germany, Russia will dominate the peace table."[48] Still in desperate need of a second front, the Soviets had ironically been stressing the same point, warning in a December newspaper article noted by the OSS that if left to "win alone, they would ignore the Anglo-Saxons in establishing the peace."[49] In pressing upon Eden the necessity for a second front, Maisky repeated this warning in February.[50]

At the same time, William C. Bullitt brought the matter to Roosevelt's attention in a long memorandum dealing with the danger of postwar Soviet expansion. Stalin, he wrote the president on January 29, had not changed since the German invasion. He was still intent upon imperialistic expansion "perhaps as far west as the Rhine, perhaps even beyond," and would withdraw all annexed countries "from the area of normal trade which it is our policy to extend." His tactics, Bullitt pointed out in phrases quite similar to those George F. Kennan would use in his famous 1947 "Containment" article, were intelligent and realistic: "He moves where opposition is weak. He stops where opposition is strong. He puts out pseudopodia like an amoeba rather than leaping like a tiger. If the pseudopodia meet no obstacle the Soviet Union flows on."[51]

Like Welles, Bullitt concluded that American ability to block such expansion was now at its zenith and could only decrease as the war continued

Roosevelt should therefore act immediately to prevent the Russians "from replacing the Nazis as the masters of Europe" by setting up American administration in occupied territories to promote strong democratic governments, reorganizing the State Department to deal with the postwar world, forming a united front with Britain against Soviet demands, and pressing Stalin to dissolve the Comintern, enter the war against Japan, and renounce his claims in Eastern Europe. Even if Stalin agreed to such American demands, an "adequate force should stand behind the eastern frontier of Europe ready to resist the Red Army," for Europe "cannot be made a military vacuum for the Soviet Union to flow into." That force, the former ambassador made clear, could only arrive as a Balkan alternative to the cross-Channel assault.[52]

Such an invasion, however, would do nothing to forestall Soviet expansion in Western Europe, an area of much greater importance to the United States. Furthermore, as Wedemeyer had realized, the Balkan approach not only invited a long European war, but was also militarily unfeasible.[53] Equally important, it would increase Russian suspicion and hostility at a time when Moscow's future plans were still unclear and subject to numerous interpretations. Roosevelt thus balked at Bullitt's strategy and at any attempt to use Lend-Lease to wring concessions from Stalin, informing Bullitt that the Soviet leader would be impressed by his "*noblesse oblige*" of aid without strings attached. Roosevelt refused to believe Bullitt's retort that Stalin was "a Caucasian bandit whose only thought when he got something for nothing was that the other fellow was an ass."[54]

Nevertheless, Bullitt's arguments had a strong impact on Roosevelt and underscored the necessity for getting American troops into Europe as quickly as possible as a means of blocking any attempt at postwar Soviet domination. In March, Roosevelt asked the visiting Eden if he thought there was any validity to the "Bullitt thesis" that the Soviets were "determined to dominate all of Europe." The president also insisted that China have an important postwar role on the grounds that "in any serious conflict with Russia" Chiang Kai-shek "would undoubtedly line up on our side," and he discussed "at some length" with the foreign secretary the "political effect" of having troops in Italy and/or France at the time of Germany's collapse.[55] On March 17, Hopkins warned the two men and Hull that unless the West acted "promptly and surely" in regard to military occupation and administration plans,

> either Germany will go Communist or an out and out anarchic
> state would set in; that, indeed, the same kind of thing might

happen in any of the countries in Europe. . . . I said I thought
it required some kind of formal agreement and that the State
Department should work out the plan with the British and the
one agreed upon between the two of us should then be discussed
with the Russians. The President agreed that this procedure
should be followed. It will, obviously, be a much simpler matter
if the British and American armies are heavily in France or
Germany at the time of the collapse but we should work out a
plan in case Germany collapses before we get to France.[56]

While Roosevelt moved quickly to implement this decision,[57] American
military leaders expressed similar ideas. Arnold warned Eden that "if we
did not watch our step we could still be discussing ways and means for operating BOLERO while the Russians were marching into Berlin."[58] On
March 30, Marshall told Roosevelt that it was

> highly important for us to have at least a strong Army Corps in
> England because if events did suddenly culminate in an abrupt
> weakness of German resistance it was very important that there
> should be a sizeable American representation on the ground
> wherever a landing on the continent of Europe was made. I also
> gave him as my personal opinion the fear that if we were involved
> at the last in Western Europe and the Russian Army was ap-
> proaching German soil, there would be a most unfortunate dip-
> lomatic situation immediately involved with the possibility of
> a chaotic condition quickly following.[59]

In line with such thinking, the JCS at this time refused the COS request
to drop HADRIAN from the COSSAC directive. The combined planning
staff was therefore soon ordered to prepare not only a 1944 cross-Channel
assault plan, but also one for an immediate crossing in the event of German
weakening before the 1944 target date. Out of this latter directive would
emerge Operation RANKIN as the military successor to SLEDGEHAM-
MER and HADRIAN. In the context of Allied relations in early 1943,
however, RANKIN was also a political plan designed to keep alive the 1943

promise to Stalin, force a continuation of BOLERO for the 1944 assault, hamper British Mediterranean plans, and place American forces in Europe in the event Germany weakened or collapsed before the 1944 target date. Thus it would be possible to block Soviet domination of Europe and to give the West a powerful voice at the peace conference without arousing Soviet suspicions. No Balkan alternative could achieve all these goals.[60]

While COSSAC formulated its plans, the diplomatic situation continued to deteriorate. In late March, Churchill had been forced to inform Stalin of the cancellation of the March convoy and the suspension of further northern sailings until September because of HUSKY, a move the Soviet leader called "catastrophic" to the Russian war effort.[61] A few weeks later, the European diplomatic front exploded, with the Katyn forest incident providing the necessary catalyst. Russia suspended relations with the Polish government in late April, while the Moscow-controlled Union of Polish Patriots denounced the London-based Poles and began preparations to make itself their successor. The Czechs moved closer to the Soviets, and rumors began to spread that Russia was organizing special forces to conquer and communize Eastern and Central Europe.[62] An April 1 CCS Russian Combat Estimate reinforced these dire predictions by noting that Soviet victory or participation in Allied victory would mean "certain" Russian domination of Eastern Europe, Iran, Afghanistan, Outer Mongolia, Manchuria, and Far Eastern islands.[63]

Hoping to reach agreement with Stalin before the situation declined further, Roosevelt in early May sent former Ambassador Joseph E. Davies to Moscow with a personal message for Stalin suggesting a summer meeting between the two of them. Such a conference, Roosevelt stated, was necessary to get a "meeting of the minds" and make plans "for the many next steps" to be taken if Germany collapsed, for "we are none of us prepared today."[64]

Roosevelt knew, however, that Stalin would demand a second front before sitting down at the conference table, and that if the Soviets refused postwar cooperation, only the presence of Western troops in Europe could prevent the Red Army from overrunning the continent and dictating the peace settlement. On May 9, four days after sending his message to Stalin, the president met with the JCS and agreed to support a cross-Channel assault "at the earliest practicable date."[65] Once again, the Russian situation had influenced his decision heavily. The difference this time was that fear of Russian success was as strong a motive as fear of defeat or a separate peace.

THE TRIDENT CONFERENCE

On the morning of May 10, two days before the opening of the TRI-
DENT Conference in Washington, Marshall bluntly informed a Senate sub-
committee "that the thought of political matters was necessarily always in
the minds" of the JCS, that they were "not naive" regarding British "united
front methods and ideas," and that they were "now trying to get organized
to be in a proper position to meet the British Chiefs of Staff."[66] In the
afternoon, the JCS put the finishing touches on that "proper position" by
carefully going over their papers and the proposed line of attack in the presence of a huge supporting staff. While Leahy and Marshall both stressed
the necessity of cross-Channel and Burma operations to keep Russia and
China respectively in the war, the JCS decided for tactical reasons to stress
the speed and decisive nature of these operations during the coming CCS
sessions. Following Wedemeyer's suggestion, they then agreed to "take the
offensive" at the meetings by presenting four of their position papers in
advance. Other papers would be held back in order to be used, in Leahy's
words, "as background material . . . with a view to breaking down British
arguments."[67]

Churchill summed up those arguments during the first plenary session
of the conference on May 12. Drawing parallels to the Bulgarian surrender
of 1918, the prime minister claimed that Italian collapse, the "great prize"
awaiting the Allies in the Mediterranean, could "cause a chill of loneliness
over the German people, and might be the beginning of their doom." Even
if its effects were not so drastic, such a collapse would mean the surrender
of the Italian fleet and armies, the entrance of Turkey into the war, and the
opening of the Dardanelles. Hitler would then be forced either to give up
the Balkans or to reinforce the area by withdrawing troops from the Eastern
front. "In no other way," Churchill emphasized, "could relief be given to
the Russian front on so large a scale this year." In addition, the West had
to do something between HUSKY and a ROUNDUP that could not be
launched before the spring of 1944, for the Russian war effort "was pro-
digious and placed us in their debt—a position from which he would like to
emerge," and idleness after the Sicilian assault "would have a serious effect
on relations with Russia." Knocking Italy out of the war should therefore
be the "first objective" of the West; the road would then be open to Europe
and the Balkans.[68]

Roosevelt agreed that the West should stay on the offensive in the Mediterranean, and he showed great interest in the eastern portion of that sea.

He shied away, however, from the idea of placing large armies in Italy, and insisted that plans and preparations for a spring 1944 cross-Channel assault, whether a ROUNDUP or a SLEDGEHAMMER, be decided upon and begun immediately.[69] Such openness on the size of the assault, combined with the interest in the Mediterranean, seemed to show a clear split between Roosevelt and his advisers. But even the JCS had admitted that only Mediterranean action could offer the Soviets immediate assistance. Moreover, logistical difficulties had already forced the planners to substitute a thirty-six division assault for the original forty-eight division ROUNDUP plan. The thirty-six figure would be further cut to twenty-nine divisions before the conference ended, thereby placing the 1944 plan midway in size between the original ROUNDUP and SLEDGEHAMMER proposals.[70] Roosevelt's comments were thus not a break with the JCS. In fact, his insistence on the 1944 assault disturbed Churchill and convinced Hopkins that his chief could now "be safely left alone with the Prime Minister."[71]

Nevertheless, Stimson remained worried, and his fears were only heightened by a May 12 memorandum Bullitt sent Roosevelt pleading again for an invasion of Eastern Europe and claiming that this assault could link up with the Far Eastern theater.[72] To Stimson, such an idea was militarily absurd, and with public opinion clamoring for action against Japan, further Mediterranean operations would lead to "a widespread loss of support for the war among our people." The secretary realized, however, the importance of the Russian issue and Roosevelt's concern with it. While attacking Bullitt's proposal, he therefore informed the president that Britain's approach of holding "the leg for Stalin to skin the deer . . . will be dangerous business for us at the end of the war. Stalin won't have much of an opinion of people who have done that and we will not be able to share much of the postwar world with him."[73]

While Stimson pressed such points on Roosevelt, the COS discovered that the Americans were more united, organized, and determined than they had been at Casablanca. The OPD and the revamped joint committees bolstered the JCS with daily position papers and summaries stressing the validity of the American program and warning that London's approach would be of little military value, was politically inspired, and would sap resources needed for a 1944 cross-Channel assault.[74]

Such warnings were supported by Brooke's comment at the May 14 CCS meeting that major operations in France would not be possible until 1945 or 1946,[75] and by his private statement to Marshall that an early cross-Channel attack would not end the war "the way we hope to finish it!"[76] The American Army chief responded by warning the COS that the Mediterranean would be a "vacuum" that would destroy the possibility of ROUNDUP "for virtually all of 1944," and that this prolongation of the European war would in turn prolong the war against Japan, a situation "which the people of the U.S. would not tolerate." Joined by the rest of the JCS, he threatened to turn American strength toward the Pacific if the British clung to their position.[77]

While such threats convinced Brooke that the Americans desired to totally shut down the Mediterranean and left him "thoroughly depressed,"[78] JCS planning papers and meetings show that they were basically tactical ploys meant to weaken British opposition to a 1944 cross-Channel assault. The Americans were in actuality willing to continue in the Mediterranean, provided operations in that theater were so limited as to help rather than hinder a modified ROUNDUP and enabled them to advance further in the Pacific.[79] The COS, however, saw this theater in the same light as the Americans saw the Mediterranean—as a politically inspired diversion from the Germany-first concept—and insisted that major action along the southern periphery of Europe was more important in order to help Russia and insure a successful cross-Channel attack.[80]

In effect, each side was demanding "a loophole permitting it to carry on its own favorite sideshow while talking of the major effort against Germany."[81] Each side interpreted this fact to mean that his ally had no intention of defeating Germany. The result was what one participant called an "unmistakable atmosphere of tension" and what others more bluntly labeled an atmosphere of "mutual suspicion" that led to a complete deadlock.[82] As a result, on May 19, Marshall suggested an "off the record" CCS discussion, and the British readily agreed. All planners and assistants left the room, and the JCS and COS had a "heart to heart" talk, followed by more of the same in the ensuing days.[83]

After those talks, the CCS were able to report a compromise whereby the Americans conceded what they already knew, that a full ROUNDUP in 1944 was logistically impossible. and the British in turn agreed to a new assault of twenty-nine divisions, appropriately designated ROUNDHAMMER, with a target date of May 1, 1944. COSSAC was ordered to plan for this assault as well as for an emergency reentry onto the continent in the event of German collapse before the target date. The JCS further agreed to Mediterranean operations in exploitation of HUSKY "as are best calculated to eliminate Italy from the war and to contain the maximum number of German forces," but with a specifically limited force and provisions to withdraw seven divisions by November 1 for ROUNDHAMMER. Moreover, rather than list any specific Mediterranean operations, the CCS ordered Eisenhower to submit recommendations directly to them. In the Pacific, the COS agreed to an extension of the war against Japan, while the JCS acquiesced in curtailing the Burma operation. Plans were also made to meet again during the summer to review the entire situation.[84]

Churchill, intent upon a commitment to invade Italy proper, was opposed to this compromise. Correctly fearing that the Americans might insist on a minor attack against Sardinia instead, he attacked the CCS accord vehemently on May 24 and pleaded for an invasion of Italy and perhaps the Balkans.[85] Brooke was appalled at this breaking of a hard-won agreement and correctly perceived that Churchill's "tragic" stance would again arouse American suspicions.[86] Leahy noted in his diary that day that the prime minister's attitude fitted in perfectly with the "permanent" British policy "of controlling the Mediterranean Sea regardless of what may be the result of the war."[87]

Roosevelt responded by acting upon his May 17 conclusion that he might have to "read the Riot Act to the other side . . . and be stiff." Feeling that Churchill was acting like a "spoiled boy," Roosevelt told him pointblank to "shut up" and, with Hopkins' assistance, succeeded in forcing him to accept the CCS compromise. In return Churchill obtained presidential approval for Marshall to join him in Algiers for a strategy conference with the Mediterranean commanders which he hoped would decide upon an invasion of Italy. The army chief objected to being "traded around like a piece of baggage" but agreed to go.[88]

With the exception of Churchill, all parties expressed satisfaction with the TRIDENT compromise. Feeling that he had talked the Americans out of completely closing down the Mediterranean theater, Brooke considered the conference "a triumph" in which he got almost exactly what he wanted.[89] Since the JCS had used this threat as a bargaining tactic, however, they felt that the Mediterranean limitations coupled with what King called "the most important decision"—the fixing of a definite date for a 1944 cross-Channel attack—constituted an American victory.[90] Such a victory did not mean that American suspicion of the British had ceased. As Stimson stated, London could still take advantage of the TRIDENT decisions by dragging out "comparatively minor efforts" in the Mediterranean "until we lose the chance for the big one."[91]

Both sides also expressed concern about Russia at the conference. Hull spoke with Churchill about talking Stalin "out of his shell" in order to determine his postwar aims,[92] but was none too hopeful about those aims. By May 11, Hull had expressed agreement with Stimson's earlier judgment that the best hope for the postwar world was a "close association between the English speaking countries."[93] Churchill was no more optimistic, telling a group of American officials on May 22 that it was important to reconstitute a strong France in the postwar world since "the prospect of having no strong country on the map between England and Russia was not attractive."[94] Militarily, the newly emerging policy toward the Soviets was reflected in the decision to plan for an emergency reentry onto the continent in the event of German collapse and in the lower priority given the Russian aid program, a decision General John E. Hull of the OPD called "a continuation of the recently adopted hard-headed diplomatic relations with the Soviet Union."[95]

It was too early, however, to throw away the possibility of postwar Soviet cooperation with the West, especially since Russia was still needed to defeat Germany. The problem that arose as the conference ended was how to tell Stalin that the second front would not be launched until 1944 when Churchill had spoken to him of 1943 only two months earlier.[96]

Roosevelt and Churchill struggled over drafts and redrafts of the proposed message to Stalin but could not come up with an acceptable statement. In desperation, Churchill decided to attempt an acceptable letter on his way to Algiers. Marshall, who was on the prime minister's plane, tried his hand and came up with a draft satisfactory to both Allied leaders. But even the brilliant Marshall could not cover up the fact that the invasion would not be launched until 1944. The telegram sent to Stalin on June 2 could only state that it was "now feasible" to resume the United Kingdom buildup so that an invasion could be launched in the spring of 1944.[97] Ironically, this message prophesying the final second front at Normandy would bring the Grand Alliance to its supreme political crisis over the issue.

CHAPTER SEVEN

THE SUMMER CRISES

MAY TO AUGUST 1943

The TRIDENT Conference had further impressed upon the planners the fact that it was, in the words of the JWPC, impossible "to divorce political considerations from strategic planning."[1] During the next three months, crucial military and political events revolving around the second-front issue reinforced this lesson and led the planners and their chiefs toward further clarification of their position.

THE ITALIAN LURE

From May 29 to June 3, Churchill pressed Marshall at Algiers to agree to an invasion of Italy, including the capture of Rome, as the only "worthy objective" capable of drawing German forces from the East and creating favorable conditions for ROUNDHAMMER. He "very passionately" desired such an offensive and even offered to cut British rations again to provide the necessary shipping. The British Parliament and people were becoming "impatient" with Allied inactivity, Churchill explained, and he was "willing to take almost desperate steps to prevent such a calamity."[2]

From his bitter 1942 experience with TORCH, Marshall well understood such a point. Yet he remained unmoved, partially because of the inopportune but revealing statements of Churchill's subordinates. On May 29, Eisenhower informed the conference of Brooke's private comments to him that "the Russian Army was the only land force that would yield decisive results" and that "any Anglo-American force that could be put upon the continent was merely a drop in the bucket." The Mediterranean commander interpreted these statements, both then and later, as complete opposition to a cross-Channel assault. Two days later, Eden further raised American suspicions by stating that elimination of Italy would aid British efforts to bring Turkey into the war and that Ankara "would become much more friendly when our troops reached the Balkan area."[3]

Churchill immediately attempted to counter these statements. Although there was "no chance" of matching Russian strength in Europe, he stated on May 29, it was still necessary to assemble in Great Britain the largest force possible in order to launch in May 1944 "a considerable operation which was likely to be accompanied by very heavy fighting and casualties." On May 31, he interrupted Eden "to observe emphatically that he was not advocating sending an army into the Balkans now or in the near future." But the damage had already been done, and Marshall continued to insist that final decision await the results of HUSKY and the looming battles on the Eastern front. On June 3, the prime minister was forced to agree.[4]

Nevertheless, Churchill left the conference convinced he had converted Marshall to his Mediterranean position. He apparently reached this conclusion on the basis of Marshall's refusal to engage in a prolonged and hopeless debate on the merits of such a strategy as well as his insistence on awaiting Eisenhower's recommendations. Since Eisenhower had stated that he would recommend invasion if HUSKY proved an easy operation, Churchill deduced that both Americans felt as he did and would "almost certainly" pick the mainland over a lesser assault on Sardinia.[5]

Such conclusions had little to do with reality. Marshall was now willing to invade Italy if Eisenhower so recommended, but he saw such an operation as a limited one to be carried out within the TRIDENT allocations and as a way of terminating the Mediterranean campaign in preparation for ROUNDHAMMER. This conception differed drastically form Churchill. The chief of staff returned to Washington convinced he had preserved all the American gains made at TRIDENT, a judgment with which Leahy concurred.[6]

While Churchill bathed in the glow of his nonexistent victory, American fears of his goals in the Mediterranean were heightened by a dispute over future civil affairs in Sicily, increased American interest in Arabian oil, and attempts by General de Gaulle, considered by many in Washington to be a British puppet, to gain control of French forces in North Africa. By June 1, Stimson had concluded that the British were "straining every nerve to lay a foundation throughout the Mediterranean area for their own empire after the war is over." Joined by Hull, he decided to make sure Roosevelt understood "the depth and far reaching character of the issue."[7]

A few weeks later, Stimson visited England and warned Churchill and Eden of "the political danger" involved in any further delay of the cross-Channel assault. The American people, he stated on the evening of July 12, viewed the Italian armed forces as "a joke" and had agreed to defeat Germany before Japan "only by an intellectual effort." Mediterranean action that would delay ROUNDHAMMER would therefore be "a serious blow to the prestige of the President's war policy," he warned, and to "the interests of the United States." When Churchill countered "that any such blow could be cured by victories," Stimson remarked that victories would not help if the people were disinterested and saw no strategic importance in them. Three days later, on July 15, COSSAC planners strengthened his position by warning that ROUNDHAMMER could only be launched if Mediterranean delays ceased.[8]

By mid-July, those delays were threatening to increase sharply. In response to a request from Eisenhower for more forces, the JCS agreed to divert a BOLERO convoy to HUSKY. The quick success of that operation led Marshall, upon advice from G-2, to propose on July 16 an assault in the Naples area as the best and quickest way to knock Italy out of the war and thus close down the Mediterranean campaign. Eisenhower and the COS concurred,[9] but Churchill interpreted Marshall's stance as agreement to an extensive Mediterranean campaign that included giving "succour to the Balkan patriots."[10]

An alarmed Stimson telephoned Marshall on July 19 and was reassured that Churchill's interpretation was incorrect. Three days later, the secretary attempted to disabuse Churchill of the notion that Marshall favored an extensive Mediterranean campaign, but the prime minister responded by attacking ROUNDHAMMER and drawing images of a "Channel full of corpses." This response infuriated Stimson and, according to him, "for a few minutes we had it hammer and tongs." In answer to Stimson's charges of bad faith, Churchill swore fidelity to ROUNDHAMMER, stated that he only wished to advance to Rome unless Italian collapse opened the entire peninsula, and insisted that he had no intention of sending troops into the Balkans.[11]

If Stimson remained suspicious, it was with good reason, for only three days earlier Churchill had told the COS the exact opposite. Feeling a May ROUNDHAMMER to be beyond Western strength, he insisted on July 19 that the correct strategy for 1944 consisted of JUPITER preparations and a "maximum post-'HUSKY,' certainly to the Po, with option to attack westwards in the South of France or north-eastward towards Vienna, and meanwhile to procure the expulsion of the enemy from the Balkans and Greece."[12] When the COS pointed out that Italian landings would require resources set aside for ROUNDHAMMER and the Burma campaign, and now due by the TRIDENT accords to leave the Mediterranean, Churchill insisted on delaying their departure. "It is true, I suppose," he told his chiefs, "that the Americans think we have led them up the garden path in the Mediterranean—but what a beautiful path it has proved to be. They have picked peaches here, nectarines there. How grateful they should be!"[13]

The JCS were neither grateful nor interested in Churchill's Mediterranean fruit, for by late July there was only one American division in Britain and Churchill seemed determined to make sure no more arrived in time to launch a 1944 assault. To make matters worse, the Army had by this time adopted its ninety-division program, a sharp cut from the 215 divisions envisioned in 1941, which left no room for dispersion of forces and demanded long-range strategic planning for proper manpower mobilization and material procurement. On July 20, Army Service Forces Chief General Brehon Somervell warned Marshall of "serious inroads" in ROUNDHAMMER troop allotments, which were making the operation's status "indefinite" and leading to "prevalent" fears "that it may go the way of our previous experience." Unless definite and precise strategic plans were made by January, he concluded, Army Service Forces would be in serious trouble.[14]

Twenty-four hours later, the COS requested even further inroads by calling for delay in transferring the seven divisions from the Mediterranean to Britain until the Italian situation cleared. The JCS promptly refused and pointed out that such a delay would postpone cross-Channel and Far Eastern operations and lead to the complete overthrow of the TRIDENT agreements. Countering that the invasion of Italy was totally in line with the TRIDENT decisions and would insure a successful ROUNDHAMMER, the COS informed the Americans on July 24 that they had unilaterally issued a "stand fast" order to British forces in the Mediterranean scheduled for transfer and asked the JCS to reconsider and do likewise.[15] A day later Mussolini fell from power. With the entire Italian Empire hovering on the brink of collapse, Churchill immediately began a lengthy correspondence with Roosevelt on the importance of an extended Mediterranean campaign at the expense of ROUNDHAMMER.[16]

With their views of British aims, strategy, and promises supported by these events, American planners spoke out during the summer, again maintaining that London's political goals necessitated a long war of attrition to bleed Germany and Russia white as well as Mediterranean action to gain control of areas of imperial interest. The American people, they warned, would not countenance such a lackadaisical approach to victory and would respond by demanding decisive action against Japan.[17] The OPD recommended that Marshall should warn Roosevelt against making any statement that the British could twist to their own advantage, as they had the Army chief's advocacy of the Naples attack, and should win presidential commitment to the now-revised and renamed cross-Channel attack (OVERLORD).[18]

On July 25, Marshall explained to Roosevelt that London's strategy was based "on the speculation that a political and economic collapse, without a military invasion, can be brought about in the occupied territories, especially in the Balkans." If this assumption was proven incorrect, he cautioned, the British approach would lead to a long European war which the American people would not tolerate, insisting instead "that our efforts in the Pacific should be increased." According to Marshall, the president expressed "general agreement" with these ideas which he had dismissed three months earlier.[19]

News of Mussolini's fall turned Roosevelt back to the Mediterranean. On July 26, he suggested to Churchill that the Allies move against all Italian-held areas "in the north and . . . the whole Balkan peninsula," a proposition to which the prime minister immediately agreed.[20] On the same date, Leahy told the JCS that the president felt "it may be necessary to change our entire conception of the war in Europe." Roosevelt insisted, however, that Burma operations not be delayed and that the United States "should continue to consider plans for at least a limited cross-Channel operation." With the resources available, such a "limited" operation could only mean RANKIN in the event of severe German weakening or collapse. Leahy therefore informed his colleagues that, in view of the Italian situation, "we may not mount OVERLORD" and should consider an alternative invasion of Europe from the south.[21]

Many planners agreed that Mussolini's fall opened opportunities in the Mediterranean that justified postponement or cancellation of OVERLORD. Only the Red Army, they argued further, could play the key role in any decisive defeat of Germany.[22] Their logic was strengthened in early August by COSSAC's insistence that a successful OVERLORD depended upon fulfilling a set of preconditions involving German defensive capabilities,[23] preconditions some planners claimed the West could not meet without drawing heavily from the Far East.

Speaking for these planners, on August 4 Rear Admiral Charles W. Cooke of the JPS recommended reducing OVERLORD to "an opportunistic operation" since diverting forces "from more certain operations in the Mediterranean and Pacific to a contingent operation" was unsound and gave the initiative to the Germans.[24] On August 6, King repeated these ideas by suggesting in a JCS meeting that the West abandon OVERLORD and use its resources elsewhere because the British would probably attempt to use COSSAC's limiting factors to kill the cross-Channel assault.[25] Although the Army and AAF objected vehemently, it was obvious by now that the JCS and their planners were badly split over the proper strategic concept for 1944. Nor was anyone clear on exactly where the president stood.

During the first week in August, the JCS called for all planning and position papers and made preparations to attempt to form a united front among themselves and with Roosevelt. As in the past, any American position would have to be based at least in part on the Russian situation, and by early August that situation had reached crisis proportions.

DIPLOMATIC CRISIS WITH RUSSIA

The tense atmosphere within the Grand Alliance had cleared somewhat during May when Stalin acknowledged Western aid, dissolved the Comintern, cordially received Davies, and approved the idea of a summer summit meeting with Roosevelt.[26] But when Davies returned to Washington, he warned the president that failure to "deliver" on the second front during the summer could easily destroy this new atmosphere and have "far reaching effects" on Soviet actions both during and after the war.[27]

At the same time Davies sent this warning, the Germans were preparing their last great Eastern offensive near Kursk, while Marshall and Churchill were simultaneously preparing the message telling Moscow that there would be no second front in 1943. The embattled Stalin angrily replied by informing Roosevelt on June 11 that this decision ran counter to the

Casablanca accords, created "exceptional difficulties" for the USSR, and
left the Red Army "to do the job alone, almost single-handed." The Soviet government, he concluded, could not agree to the TRIDENT plans,
which had been made without Russian participation or discussion and were
capable of "gravely" affecting "the subsequent course of the war."[28]

Churchill, who in June had so feared Stalin's response that he had seriously considered going to Moscow again,[29] informed the Soviet leader on
June 19, with Roosevelt's concurrence, that disaster in France would not
help Moscow while the Mediterranean campaign would offer the best and
only possible aid.[30] At the same time, he informed his ambassador in Moscow that he was

> getting rather tired of these repeated scoldings considering that
> they have never been actuated by anything but cold-blooded
> self-interest and total disdain of our lives and fortunes. At the
> proper time you might give Stalin a friendly hint of the dangers
> of offending the two Western Powers whose war-making strength
> is growing with every month that passes and who may play a
> helpful part in the Russian future. Even my own long-suffering
> patience is not inexhaustible.[31]

Apparently, such a hint was not delivered, for on June 24 Stalin sent
Churchill a long and virulent reply that made his earlier response to Roosevelt seem mild in comparison. Citing promises over the past year regarding
a 1943 second front, repeating his anger over not being consulted, and
terming Western losses "insignificant" in comparison to those of Russia,
Stalin stated that his government "cannot become reconciled to this dis-
regard of vital Soviet interests." The main point, he added, was not Russian "disappointment" over the lack of a second front, "but the preserva-
tion of its confidence . . . which is being subjected to severe stress."[32]

Churchill now found his "long-suffering patience" exhausted. Infuriated
at this message, he at first refused to respond, but on June 26 lashed back
by informing Stalin, without consulting Roosevelt beforehand, that his
reproaches "leave me unmoved."[33] A few days later, he forwarded the recent exchange of insults to Roosevelt along with word that he would cease
objecting to the Big Two meeting Roosevelt had been attempting to arrange with Stalin.[34] When Stalin made no response to the June 26 blast,
the prime minister concluded that he had reached the end of the "Churchill-
Stalin correspondence."[35]

By early July, that correspondence seemed to be the least important casualty of this latest second-front crisis. Moscow recalled its ambassadors from London and Washington, began a virulent public campaign for a second front, attacked Allied policy in North Africa, and angrily complained when the West refused to allow a Soviet representative to visit the area. In the European sphere, the Soviets again repeated their claim to the Baltic States and strengthened their ties with de Gaulle and the Czechs.[36] Equally menacing was the lack of action on the Eastern front in June, which Churchill admitted was "not necessarily due to our Mediterranean activities" and which raised "anxious questions" of a separate peace in his mind.[37]

Those questions became even more anxious when in July Stalin sent no congratulatory message on the invasion of Sicily and indefinitely postponed the meeting with Roosevelt, while his government complained about the lack of consultation over the Italian situation and publicly credited Mussolini's fall to Soviet military action in the East. That action had by the end of the month demolished the German offensive at Kursk, broken Hitler's Center Army, and endangered the entire German position on the Eastern front. At the same time, the Soviets announced the formation of a "Free Germany" Committee, composed of captured German officers and soldiers as well as communists, which soon issued a manifesto calling upon the German people to overthrow the Nazi government. To many, Hitler's empire seemed to be on the verge of collapse, and Soviet moves implied not just an attempt at a separate peace, but also a possible effort to overthrow Hitler and replace him with a Moscow-controlled puppet government. Such a coup would give the Soviets control of Europe and negate their need for postwar Western aid. In late July, a worried Hull and Berle asked their representatives to forward all known information on the Free Germany Committee and similar Soviet moves toward other European countries.[38]

Within the armed forces, fears of a separate peace took on increasing gravity. Such a peace, the planners noted in early August, would mean indefinite postponement of OVERLORD and thus increased time for Japan to consolidate and expand her gains and war potential. In such a situation, the United States would have to forget quick victory in Europe and turn its major effort towards the Pacific.[39] These conclusions once again underscored the greater logic of a cross-Channel assault rather than further Mediterranean action. Postponement of the operation had led to the crisis in the first place, while launching it in 1944 would, hopefully, restore Allied harmony and maintain the Russian participation mandatory for a successful assault.

Equally important, only a cross-Channel assault could prevent Soviet domination of Europe and the peace conference by getting American troops onto the continent the minute Germany showed signs of collapse. American leaders had made this point during the spring of 1943,[40] and the military and political events of the summer lent increased urgency to their warnings. On August 4, Arnold received a report from AAF Intelligence which bluntly stated in this regard that the United States must be prepared to invade the continent before December 1943. Germany was "on her last legs" and an Axis collapse without such preparation would leave only Russia in a position to "move in with force and quell the anarchy which is certain to explode throughout Europe" and thus to "dictate future political arrangements and territorial assignments on the 'future' of world peace." In such a situation, it would be "too late . . . to attempt to beat Russian forces to the occupation of more than a fringe of France, Belgium and Holland," and the United States would "merely sit on the sidelines while Russia dictates the European politics."[41]

Such a report was, of course, highly political, but from the military's point of view, these political factors infringed upon the conduct of the war and could no longer be avoided. The joint committees had on numerous occasions commented on the link between national goals and military strategy, and the second-front controversy had for two years emphasized the inseparability of the two issues. As early as July 25, that controversy had led two members of the JWPC to state that, while the armed forces should not dictate national policy, they "must advise in its preparation, have cognizance of its implications, and be prepared strategically and operationally to carry it out" if its implementation was to be assured.[42]

In this regard, the planners had noted in late July the necessity for discussing postwar assistance to Russia, the arming of liberated countries, and occupation forces needed for Europe. They had further stated that the number, nature, and duration of those forces "will depend to a large extent on the political situation" existing at the time of the Axis surrender.[43] With a German collapse possible in 1943 and the "political situation" far from promising, military discussion of the issue seemed all the more mandatory. Furthermore, as an OSS correspondent had commented in mid-June,

Soviet domination of Europe would probably lead to another world war,[44] thus giving the military a direct reason for discussing the relationship of its moves to the political situation.

The planners realized their need for expert guidance from departments more directly concerned with political issues. Accordingly, in early August they asked for and received information on the Free Germany Committee and manifesto from both the State Department and the OSS.[45] While these reports were being prepared, the JCS were concluding their debate on proper strategy and discussing the issue with the president.

THE AMERICAN DECISION

The planners' reports on the dangers and consequences of a separate peace in the East had pointed out a very weak link in any argument for extended Mediterranean action at the expense of OVERLORD. Such a peripheral campaign depended for success upon continued Russian resistance, which might not be forthcoming if a second front was not launched. Furthermore, even if the Russians did continue to fight, the lack of cross-Channel operations could easily leave them in control of Europe.

On August 6, General Ray W. Barker of the COSSAC staff informed the JCS of additional flaws in the Mediterranean approach. In response to King's claim that the British would use COSSAC's preconditions to kill OVERLORD, Barker observed that German strength across the Channel was presently far below the limitation set by the planners. Special planning considerations, he further maintained, could assure a successful OVER-LORD even if the Germans surpassed that limitation. Russia, however, "must still be in the picture and largely absorbing German strength." While a Mediterranean assault to further disperse the Germans would help the invasion, a threat in the Mediterranean "would have the same effect."[46]

These comments succeeded in convincing the JCS of the feasibility and necessity of OVERLORD. King showed his conversion when discussion shifted to a JSSC report. Insisting, despite statements by Embick and Marshall to the contrary, that one paragraph in the report had implied reducing OVERLORD to a RANKIN in order to continue Mediterranean operations, the CNO questioned the report's assumptions, stated that he did not want to see it in British hands, and pressed for revision.[47] Further reinforcement for OVERLORD came on the following day, August 7, when a member of Eisenhower's staff informed the JPS that his chief felt he could advance as far as the Po valley in Italy without violating the TRIDENT allocations.[48]

On the same day, the JCS approved as a guide for themselves at the coming conference with the British the revised JSSC report. This document now recommended that Mediterranean operations be "strictly subordinated" to the cross-Channel assault "and invoke no means that are needed for OVERLORD or for approved undertakings in the Pacific." Italian operations could continue to the Pisa-Ancona line, but only with allotted resources, and further advances should be examined in light of the situation existing at the time. Plans for an advance into the Balkans, "a British concept since we entered North Africa," should be rejected as militarily "eccentric." Politically, such plans "would not receive popular support in this country and there are probable implications with the Soviets, which should be avoided." Violation of these guidelines, the JSSC warned, would mean "indefinite prolongation of [the] war in Europe and a corresponding postponement of decisive measures against Japan." The JCS would therefore have to consider transferring resources to the Pacific if the British refused to agree with the American concept.[49]

Wedemeyer backed up these arguments at the August 7 JCS meeting by pointing out that transfer of the seven Mediterranean divisions as envisioned in the TRIDENT accords would mean "less pressure" for "extensive operations in that theater." Cooke objected that the Italian campaign was a "going operation" and would probably require further reinforcement, but the JCS supported Wedemeyer and ordered the JPS to revise its estimates.[50] By August 9, Cooke had completely acceded to the cross-Channel approach.

At this time, Marshall presented his colleagues with an OPD paper he rated "formidable." The rest of the JCS apparently agreed, for a copy was sent to Roosevelt and every American delegated to attend the coming conference. Stating that the Allies had now reached the "crossroads" in European strategy, the OPD warned that the Mediterranean approach would "imperil the final victory" through its lack of decisive objectives, creation of small diversions which led to "disproportionate disruptions and delays in preparations for the decisive effort," failure to relieve the Eastern front, and predication on the "very doubtful" assumption that the Germans and Russians would "continue to weaken and destroy each other while the U.S. and Great Britain succeed in crumbling the internal support of the German war machine" by various limited operations. Such an approach invited a "protracted European war" and might lead to Soviet "unilateral action culminating in peace short of complete victory." Germany could only be defeated, the OPD concluded, by using the maximum power of all three allies through OVERLORD and a subsequent two-front war in France and the East.[51]

The overwhelming bulk of the papers and arguments presented to the JCS had made clear that a 1944 cross-Channel assault was not only practical but mandatory to achieve a host of American military and political objectives. Between August 7 and 10, the JCS therefore approved a series of papers calling for OVERLORD as the basic 1944 effort, with subordination of the Italian campaign to that operation.[52] Stalemate in Europe was now possible, they warned the COS on August 9, and the Allies must accordingly abandon the earlier "opportunistic" strategy forced upon them by weakness in favor of a cross-Channel assault which, if given "*wholehearted* and *immediate support*," could "bring about the early and decisive defeat of the Axis."[53]

OVERLORD should therefore be given "overriding priority" in the allocation of supplies, the Americans insisted, with the TRIDENT decisions holding and the seven Mediterranean divisions going to the United Kingdom. With previously allocated resources, Eisenhower could continue his Mediterranean campaign to Rome with the objective of knocking Italy out of the war. His forces should then be used for an attack on southern France in conjunction with OVERLORD, while the Balkans received only supplies for guerrilla forces and strategic bombing raids. A basic assumption of all these plans, the JCS pointed out, was continued Russian participation, and the "unlikely event" of a separate peace would call for a careful strategic reexamination and probably reconcentration of American forces in the Pacific.[54]

With agreement reached on proper strategy, the JCS and their planners turned to the question of tactics at the coming conference, once again approaching the issue with a battlefield frame of mind. As early as May 25, the JWPC had suggested "war gaming" American and British proposals in advance so that the JCS could be prepared to answer any British points, as well as including within the American delegation representatives from political agencies.[55] Such representation was needed, Wedemeyer had informed Marshall on June 8, to give the JCS "information and advice as to how their military decisions will affect our foreign and national effort which is so well exemplified in the British organization."[56]

On August 4, the JWPC further suggested that the JCS "seize the initiative" at the conference by submitting their papers early and preparing backup studies.[57] By August 9, the JSSC had presented a complete battle plan calling for full agreement on positions in advance, avoidance of discussion on issues for which the JCS were unprepared, caution in accepting British proposals until the planning committees had thoroughly examined them, special assignments to individual JCS members, and a secret warning signal if any American chief felt that an issue needed further private discussion.[58]

The obvious first step in any such plan was, of course, full agreement on positions in advance. While the JCS had achieved such unity among themselves by August 9, they still did not know whether the president would support them, and without his agreement their united front was rather worthless. Despite the July 25 assurances to Marshall, Mussolini's downfall had revived Roosevelt's interest in the Balkans. The JSSC had warned its superiors that the British would probably "endeavor to capitalize on that interest if possible."[59] At that very moment, Churchill was notifying Roosevelt that Italy had "turned Red overnight," that there was now nothing between the king and "rampant Bolshevism," and that the Germans were preparing to take Rome. If the Allies could not attack the Balkans immediately to forestall this latter move, Churchill concluded, then "the sooner we land in Italy the better."[60]

A recently returned Stimson moved on August 4 to counteract Churchill's influence by submitting to the president a full report on his trip. He pointed out that the British conception of an Italian campaign differed sharply from the American one and was part of an approach not to aid OVERLORD, but to be "a substitute for it" by invading Europe from the south. Churchill was "constantly and vigorously" searching "for an easy way of ending the war without a trans-Channel assault" and would agree to OVERLORD only "if pressed by us." The United States, Stimson concluded, must therefore "be constantly on the lookout against Mediterranean diversions." He requested an interview with Roosevelt to discuss the issue further.[61]

An impressed Roosevelt agreed to meet Stimson.[62] On August 9, Roosevelt informed Marshall that he favored OVERLORD over the Italian campaign and opposed Balkan operations because of shipping problems and the relationship of action in Eastern Europe "to the political situation." Nevertheless, he still wanted to conquer Sicily, Sardinia, and Italy up to Rome before crossing the Channel. He suggested replacing the seven Mediterranean divisions scheduled for transfer with seven fresh ones from the United States in order to accomplish these goals. Marshall replied that this transfer would

weaken OVERLORD, but he promised to review the situation and report
back on the next day.[63]

While the JCS discussed the issue on August 10, Stimson arrived for
his conference with Roosevelt. Stimson immediately handed Roosevelt a
new letter of conclusions that he had written that morning and felt were
"among the most serious that I have had to make since I have been in this
Department." OVERLORD, the secretary insisted, would never be launch
if placed under a British commander, for Churchill as well as Brooke dis-
liked the concept and "The Shadows of Passchendale and Dunkerque still
hang too heavily over the imagination of these leaders of his government.
Though they have rendered lip service to the operation, their hearts are nc
in it."[64]

Rather, London felt that Germany could be beaten by a "series of at-
tritions" in the Mediterranean, and that "the only fighting which needs to
be done will be done by Russia." Such an attitude, Stimson warned, was
"terribly dangerous" in light of probable postwar problems, for the West
was "pledged" to open a second front and such "pinprick warfare" would
not "fool Stalin into the belief that we have kept that pledge." The time I
therefore come for Roosevelt to decide that the United States must assum
responsibility for and leadership of OVERLORD by placing Marshall in
charge of the operation.[65]

After reading the letter, Roosevelt informed Stimson that he had come
to the same conclusions. The secretary rated their subsequent discussion
"one of the most satisfactory conferences I have ever had with the Presid
and by Roosevelt's invitation remained for the ensuing session with the
JCS. During that session, Roosevelt stated his outright opposition to
Balkan operations. The British, he said, wanted these operations in order
to forestall Soviet influence, but he felt that Russia only desired to establish "kinship with other Slavic people" in the area. Furthermore, he agree
with his advisers that it was "unwise to plan military strategy on a gambl
as to political results," and he strongly backed OVERLORD. When King
gested dropping the assault if the British insisted on postponing or abandoning it, Roosevelt responded that, if necessary, the United States woul
mount the operation alone. In any event, he desired more American than
British troops in the invasion so that he could insist on an American com
mander.[66]

In the Italian theater, Roosevelt again expressed his desire to replace t
seven divisions scheduled for transfer with fresh American forces. Repea

the judgments they had made in the earlier private session, the JCS responded that shipping for such divisions would hurt Pacific operations and that Eisenhower felt he did not need the extra troops. Giving them to him "would simply invite having these extra divisions used for an invasion in the Balkans," Marshall warned, which would in turn "make Mediterranean operations so extensive as to have a disastrous effect" on OVERLORD. Furthermore, Arnold and Stimson pointed out, air bases north of the Po were unnecessary for the bombing of Germany; those in the Rome area would be just as good. Roosevelt acquiesced under this combined pressure and logic; Eisenhower would continue to Rome with forces already allotted to him.[67]

Stimson was overjoyed. The president, he wrote in his diary, had been "more clear and definite" at this meeting "than I have ever seen him since we have been in this war and he took the policy that the American staff had been fighting for fully." The JCS were also "astonished and delighted at his definitiveness," for he had backed them completely on European strategy for the first time since early 1942.[68] Interestingly enough, he had in the process agreed with virtually every JCS judgment he had attacked in May 1943.

CHAPTER EIGHT

____SHOWDOWN AT QUEBEC____

AUGUST 1943

With unity achieved, the JCS felt ready to meet the British in Quebec. By the time that conference ended, military and political events had combined with the solid American stance to produce a clearcut victory and a series of intensive statements on the ability of the cross-Channel approach to achieve American goals in the war.

OVERLORD VERSUS ITALY

When the QUADRANT Conference opened on August 14, the JCS fou many of their fears unrealized. As Brooke was able to point out on Augus there was "great similarity" between the British and American positions. London now agreed that the Italian campaign be subordinated to OVERLORD, that operations in the eastern Mediterranean be limited to supply guerrilla forces and launching commando raids, and that some forces from Italy be used for an invasion of southern France in conjunction with the cross-Channel assault. Despite earlier plans and Churchill's continuing interest in taking the Aegean islands and landing a few divisions to "activate the Balkan guerrillas, the COS had concluded that present difficulties prevented any Turkish entrance into the war or operations in the eastern Mediterranean.[1]

Nevertheless, fundamental differences between the American and British programs still existed. The JCS insisted that OVERLORD could be launche

only if BOLERO were given "overriding priority" in the allocation of supplies. The COS, concentrating on the assault rather than the buildup, countered that the attack could only succeed if COSSAC's preconditions regarding German strength across the Channel were met. Achieving those preconditions would require an Italian campaign perhaps as far as the Milan-Turin
area in order to disperse German strength, Brooke stated on August 15.
Since such a campaign might require the seven divisions scheduled for transfer to the United Kingdom, "overriding priority" for OVERLORD would
be "too binding." Decision on movement of the divisions should be postponed, with fresh American forces eventually replacing them in the Mediterranean so that the cross-Channel assault could have battle-tested forces
while the Italian campaign continued.[2]

With BOLERO still far behind schedule and the fact clear that trans-
porting seven fresh divisions would hurt proposed Pacific action as well as
the cross-Channel buildup, the Americans insisted that Eisenhower stay within the TRIDENT allocations while OVERLORD received his seven divisions
and "overriding priority." They also questioned British loyalty to the cross-
Channel assault and denied the validity of Brooke's position on the relationship between the Italian campaign and OVERLORD. COSSAC's preconditions, King maintained, could also be met by the bomber offensive and by
action on the Eastern front and in Sicily. Furthermore, Marshall observed,
failure to meet those preconditions would not doom the assault, but simply
necessitate "more extensive use . . . of available means to reduce the enemy's
ability to concentrate his forces."[3]

An extensive Italian campaign, on the other hand, would continually
require BOLERO resources and would in reality, according to Marshall,
mean a new strategy involving only an "opportunist landing" in France
which would be "cheaper in lives" than OVERLORD but "speculative."
Refusal to agree to "overriding priority," he warned, "doomed" the operation, "weakened our chances of an early victory and rendered necessary
a reexamination of our basic strategy with a possible readjustment towards
the Pacific."[4] Such refusal, Marshall further informed Sir John Dill later
on August 15, would also result in his resignation.[5]

As at TRIDENT, the CCS were forced into "off the record" conversations during which extremely harsh words were exchanged. Brooke correctly pointed out the basic problem on August 16: "we were not trusting each
other."[6] At the JCS meeting earlier that day, in fact, Marshall and King had
agreed that London had never been serious in regard to the TRIDENT trans-

fer of seven divisions and had acquiesced in the proposition only to gain American acceptance of the entire conference document.[7] Nor were the British any less suspicious, seeing the Americans as more interested in mair taining landing craft for Pacific offensives than in assuring OVERLORD by transferring them to Europe for further Mediterranean action and/or an increase in the size of the initial assault across the Channel.[8]

To further complicate matters, word arrived of successful completion of the Sicilian campaign and Eisenhower's subsequent decision to attack Salerno on September 9, as well as serious Italian peace overtures to the Allies if they could invade so as to prevent the Germans from taking over the country.[9] Convinced that these events vindicated their previous strateg and justified holding the seven divisions, the COS continued to refuse to agree to "overriding priority" while the Americans just as adamantly insist upon such a clause. The arguments and recriminations reached such intensity that when an experiment with pistols was conducted during one of th closed sessions, the guards outside concluded that the military leaders had finally begun to shoot one another.[10]

By August 17, tempers had cooled and a compromise had begun to emerge. As communicated to Roosevelt and Churchill on August 19, that compromise listed OVERLORD as the "primary" operation for 1944 with a target date of May 1, while approving an Italian campaign at least up to Rome. Resources were to be distributed with the "main object of insuring the success of OVERLORD," and Mediterranean operations would be car ried out within the TRIDENT allocations unless this decision was later "v ied" by the CCS.[11]

Since the JCS had agreed to an Italian offensive and had given up on th "overriding priority" clause, Brooke viewed this compromise as an acceptance of British proposals and "quite fair" in its outcome. Some historian have recently concurred with this judgment.[12] In reality, the victory belonged to the Americans, for despite the lack of an "overriding priority" clause, the seven divisions would be transferred on November 1 unless the JCS changed their minds before that date, and London's "stand fast" order in the Mediterranean was immediately revoked.[13] Furthermore, the COS had retreated from their call for an Italian advance to the Po to a she er line north of Rome which the Americans had been willing to agree to i the TRIDENT transfer held.

This victory was largely a result of the fact that the American united front was for the first time stronger than London's. Churchill had visited

Roosevelt at Hyde Park between August 12 and 14 and had found the president solidly behind his military chiefs. Churchill, on the other hand, had split with the COS by insisting upon the recapture of the northern tip of Sumatra as well as the Aegean islands and had proved willing to acquiesce in American demands to keep these projects alive. While at Hyde Park, he approved an American commander for OVERLORD, apparently in return for a British commander for the new Southeast Asia command. On August 17, he agreed to stop the Italian campaign at the Pisa-Ancona line rather than at the Po or the Alps, since the former position would enable the West to launch "minor descents" across the Adriatic without hurting OVER-LORD.[14]

Churchill thus approved the preliminary compromise on August 19. He stated that while he had opposed the 1942 and 1943 cross-Channel operations, he favored OVERLORD and wanted it "definitely understood" that he was not committed to an Italian campaign beyond the Pisa-Ancona line. He still had some minor reservations about the CCS accord, disliking the idea of an invasion of southern France and insisting a few days later upon a clause mentioning the possibility of JUPITER in case OVERLORD could not be mounted.[15]

These reservations were fairly meaningless at the time, for no one except Churchill ever took JUPITER seriously and disagreement over the attack on southern France would not flare up for another five months. In effect, the Americans had won every strategic point for Europe except the "over-riding priority" clause and had accepted the content of those two words instead of the form: commitment to OVERLORD in 1944 with an American commander, a limited and subordinated Italian campaign, an end to the "stand fast" order, and restatement of the TRIDENT allocations with a veto over any future changes. In the Pacific they did just as well, winning approval for offensives designed to defeat Japan within twelve months of German surrender. In return, Churchill received only British leadership in the new Southeast Asia theater, further examination and study of the Sumatra project which no one else favored, and the unstated possibility of using some Mediterranean landing craft in the Aegean and Adriatic after the capture of Rome if such moves would not interfere with OVERLORD.[16]

QUADRANT, however, was more than just a military conference. With Hull, Eden, Stimson, and Hopkins joining the CCS and the two Allied leaders, the Quebec meetings dealt with world politics as well as strategic plans, and the line between the two was by no means firmly drawn. As the public communique at the end of the conference stated, agreements had been reached not only in the military sphere, but also "upon the political issues underlying and arising out of the military operations."[17] These "underlying issues" included, of course, postwar planning and the future of Germany. In both areas, the subject of Russia and her future course of action, during and after the war, dominated all thoughts.

OVERLORD, RANKIN, AND THE RUSSIANS

By the time the Quebec Conference opened, the tense diplomatic situation within the Alliance had eased somewhat. In response to an August 7 message from the British Foreign Office, Stalin had resumed his correspondence with Churchill by expressing interest in a "Big Three" summit meeting and in a preliminary conference of Allied foreign ministers.[18] Churchill could therefore report to his king on August 11 that he and the "Great Bear" were on "speaking, or at least growling, terms again."[19] Balancing this correspondence were the activities of the Free Germany Committee, incessant public demands for a second front, and continued rumors of both a rupture within the Grand Alliance and a forthcoming separate peace.[20] In an interview with the British and American ambassadors on the evening of August 11, Stalin expressed his dissatisfaction with the military and political aspects of the Italian campaign and stated that "with Italy out of the way, *now*, you should be able to open a Second Front."[21]

In effect, future military and political cooperation from Moscow still hinged on the cross-Channel operation, a fact well recognized by the conferees at Quebec. Leahy warned the JCS on August 15 that abandonment of OVERLORD "might create a bad political situation and that the United States would be accused, particularly in Russia, of failure to open a second front."[22] On August 19, Eden and Hopkins agreed that without a firm commitment to launch this operation and without a position on Russian frontiers and the future of Germany, the proposed foreign ministers' meeting "was almost certain to do more harm than good."[23]

The Free Germany Committee had raised serious doubts, however, as to whether future Soviet cooperation would be forthcoming even if OVERLORD was launched. By the time the conference opened, the JCS had begun to receive the requested OSS and State Department reports on the committee and future Soviet policy. On August 6, the OSS Planning Group had warned the War Department and the JCS that the committee's manifesto indicated a Russian desire to provoke "at least a limited revolution in Germany before any peace negotiations," and that it could serve as a possible cover for a separate peace with a German militarist regime or the beginnings of a "far-reaching program of eventual invasion and Bolshevization." Success in these efforts, it maintained, might result in a communistic Germany or a breakdown of German resistance which would enable the Red Army to arrange the peace and German government "to its liking." Even if such fears were unfounded, the manifesto still gave Russia a great advantage over her allies in negotiations with Berlin. Its implications were thus "not only far-reaching . . . but disturbing from the ideological and political viewpoint."[24]

Appendices to this report linked Free Germany's manifesto to Soviet diplomatic moves in other countries, called the dissolution of the Comintern merely "a clearing of the decks for intensifying nationalistic policy" which had begun in late 1942, and cautioned that the Soviets seemed bent on an imperialistic policy in Europe. If Germany was on the verge of collapse, the manifesto would make her susceptible to Soviet manipulation. "In such an event, the U.S. and Great Britain might find themselves unable to effectively intervene politically" in Germany or Eastern Europe.[25]

Conceivably, the Planning Group admitted, the Free Germany movement might be nothing more than wartime propaganda, but such a conclusion seemed unwarranted in the face of deteriorating Allied relations. To the contrary, Soviet policy towards postwar political developments as reflected in the manifesto was "dangerous." If the United Nations did not soon establish a unified policy towards Germany, the United States should review its unconditional surrender policy in order to "be prepared at the psychological time to present Germany conditions which will offset the Russians' proposals in the armistice and the peace." In this regard, the group pointed out, "our political position will be greatly enhanced as our military forces arrive on the continent of Europe."[26]

On August 10, Wedemeyer forwarded this memorandum to Marshall, noting that it was "of sufficient interest to merit your attention," and warning his chief that the Germans might be willing to accept communism as the only alternative to "the terrible implications of the unconditional surrender terms of the Allies."[27] A day later, the State Department reinforced the OSS conclusions in a response to a G-2 request for information on Soviet foreign policy. Signed by Political Adviser James C. Dunn but probably

the work of at least four high-level officials of the department, this respons
analyzed Soviet foreign policy attitudes in the same terms George F. Kenn;
would later use in his "Containment" article. The department maintained
that these attitudes were dominated by the "basic feature" of Bolshevik
doctrine—the inevitable hostility between capitalist and communist worlds
and by Stalin's "absolute dictatorship" which enabled the Soviets to revers
foreign policy overnight if necessary. During the present war, these factors
had led the Soviets to keep their distance in the Alliance. Their recent military victories and political actions, especially the creation of the Free Ger-
may Committee, showed an even more independent line which might resul
in a negotiated peace with Germany.[28]

On August 14, General Hull forwarded this memorandum to Handy an(
noted that the OPD chief, Wedemeyer, and another subordinate should rea
what he termed an "excellent paper," probably representing "some of the
best thought of State Department personnel." Handy was so impressed tha
he sent the memorandum and Hull's comments to Marshall at Quebec with
the recommendation that the chief of staff read them "before [the] Russian discussion."[29]

What Handy meant by the "Russian discussion" is unclear. In all likelihood he was referring to an August 20 CCS agenda item entitled "Military
Considerations in Relation to Russia." During the discussion of that issue,
Marshall cited the establishment of the Free Germany Committee and recent Soviet blasts in regard to a second front as signs that "Russia was turn
ing an increasingly hostile eye on the capitalistic world, of whom they wer
becoming increasingly contemptuous." Picking up on a theme the Joint
Intelligence Committee (JIC) had discussed in a July 19 report,[30] Marshall
stated that such a situation might necessitate the redeployment of Western
forces; "for example, in the event of an overwhelming Russian success,
would the Germans be likely to facilitate our entry into the country to
repel the Russians?"[31]

Brooke appeared to share Marshall's fears, responding that "he had in
the past often considered the danger of the Russians seizing the opportunity of the war to further their ideals of international communism." But
citing Czech leader Edouard Benes' insistence that the Russians would require peace after the war to rebuild, the CIGS concluded that the Soviets
"would be anxious to assist us in maintaining the peace of Europe" if they
received concessions in Eastern Europe.[32]

Whether Marshall would have favored taking the possible "opportunity
with the Germans against the Russians cannot be determined, for the con-

versation ended soon after Brooke's comments. The issue, however, remained
open, and within a month of QUADRANT British planners were discussing
necessary peacetime forces in terms of Russia as the only possible enemy
and what side Germany would take in such a conflict. Although they re-
cieved a "stern rebuke" from their political superiors for delving into such
issues,[33] Churchill too was worried about future Soviet actions. As early
as July 5, he had informed Harriman that Stalin's second-front demands
were aimed at keeping the West out of the Balkans.[34] A month later,
Churchill had justified an invasion of Italy partially in terms of stopping
communism in that country,[35] and during the Quebec Conference he expressed similar thoughts in regard to Greece.

Earlier British attempts to unify all Greek partisan forces with the Lon-
don-backed king had met with failure, and by August the guerrillas were
insisting upon Cabinet positions and a plebiscite before the king returned.
The king refused to agree to these demands and was supported by both
Churchill and Roosevelt at QUADRANT.[36] On August 19, a worried prime
minister informed Eden that British forces could reinstate the king if they
took part in the liberation of Greece, but that if the guerrillas pushed the
Germans out by themselves, "we shall have a good deal less to say in the
matter." A day later, Jan Smuts of South Africa warned Churchill of the
possibility of "wholesome Communism" in the Balkans as well as the "Bol-
shevisation of a broken and ruined Europe."[37] According to Secretary Hull,
the prime minister grafted these fears onto his dislike of the cross-Channel
concept to push for an alternative invasion via the Balkans, stating that
OVERLORD would involve frightful casualties and

> that a victory under such conditions would be barren for Britain;
> she would never recover from it and would be so weakened that
> the Soviet Union would inevitably dominate the European con-
> tinent. He said that the southern European coastline was long
> and badly defended and offered huge tactical advantages. . . . He
> also felt that an Anglo-American entry into the Balkans and south-
> ern Europe would prevent a Soviet rush into that area which would
> permanently establish the authority of the Soviet Union there, to
> the detriment of Britain and incidentally of the United States.[38]

While no record exists of such a statement by Churchill at Quebec, it is
conceivable that he verbalized these thoughts in one of the conference's
numerous unrecorded conversations. Furthermore, even if he did not bring

up the idea of a Balkan invasion to block Soviet expansion at this time, certain Americans did. Bullitt had been pressing for just such a strategy since early 1943, and according to State Department official Loy W. Henderson, he and OSS Chief Colonel William Donovan discussed the idea with Bullitt at the latter's house in July. In response to a request from Donovan, Henderson put his thoughts into a memorandum that was read and discussed in G-2.[39] Bullitt sent a draft of a similar memorandum to Hull on August 6 and forwarded the final copy to Roosevelt four days later. Stressing the importance of an East European invasion, Bullitt justified such an operation by pointing out that war was "an attempt to achieve political objectives by fighting; and political objectives must be kept in mind in planning operations."[40]

American military planners were in full agreement with this paraphrase of and addition to Clausewitz but had concluded from it that they should oppose a Balkan invasion. While the area was of great importance to Britain, American interests centered on the Pacific and Western Europe and necessitated quick victory over Germany via the mutually dependent cross-Channel attack and continued Russian participation, in order to be able to turn as rapidly as possible against Japan. Moscow had also made clear that it would join in the Far Eastern war only after Hitler's defeat and if the West aided in that defeat through a second front. Furthermore, a Balkan invasion would do nothing to forestall the Red Army in France and Germany, while the mountainous terrain of southeastern Europe would make it impossible to land enough troops there to defeat the Germans *or* block the Russians.[41] Ironically, the only place where enough troops could be landed to defeat Hitler and prevent Russian domination of all Europe was across the Channel.

The planners thus rejected the Balkan invasion not because it was "politically inspired," but because it was logistically unfeasible as well as harmful to American interests. Their recognition of these facts emerged clearly in two QUADRANT documents. A high-level military estimate which Hopkins brought to Quebec stated point-blank that Russia occupied the "dominant" and "decisive" position in the defeat of Germany and would continue to occupy such a position in relation to the rest of Europe in the postwar world. With Germany crushed, no power would be able to oppose her, and even Britain's Mediterranean position could not be maintained unless "otherwise supported."

The United States, however, could not afford to support London at the cost of Soviet enmity. In addition to the European war, Washington had to consider the war in the Pacific, which was *"the most important factor"* in its relations with Russia. An "unfriendly" or "negative" Soviet attitude in the Far East, the estimate warned, would "immeasurably" increase American difficulties to the point where "operations might become abortive." Since Russia was the decisive factor in both wars and would dominate Europe at the end of the hostilities, it was "essential" for Washington to "develop and maintain the most friendly relations with her."[42]

Those relations obviously required establishment of the consistently demanded second front, but even completion of this operation would not lead to harmony if Moscow had already decided to pursue an expansionist and unilateral postwar policy. Such a possibility, the Research and Analysis Branch of the OSS explained in an August 22 memorandum to the JCS, made cross-Channel operations all the more mandatory in order to prevent Soviet domination of the continent. "The future of Europe," it warned, "will be affected profoundly, *and perhaps decisively*, by the strength and the geographic disposition of the armed forces at the cessation of hostilities."

Strategy, the memorandum maintained, was "literally inseparable from policy" and determined "to a very considerable extent" the war aims that nations could achieve. This fact was "particularly true in the present war" because of the "serious lack of unanimity among the prospective European victors." Both Russia and the United States defined their security in terms of preventing a hostile power or group of powers from dominating Europe, but for the Soviets such a definition could easily lead to "a considerable westward extension of the Soviet revolutionary system" and the establishment "of new Soviet governments under the domination of Moscow." If extended to Germany, this system "would assure Russia the domination of Europe," and in that eventuality, "we have lost the war."

Unfortunately, the United States simply did not have the power to prevent such domination. It could and should rebuild Europe and establish close alliances with the reconstituted governments to increase its power, but such moves could not in and of themselves stop the Soviets. Nor could Washington let an undefeated Germany concentrate her forces against Russia, for such a policy, besides being intolerable to the American public, might result in German domination of the continent. The only two alternatives open to the United States were compromise with Russia combined with attempts to build common interests, or pursuit of an independent strategy in hopes of defeating Germany quickly and achieving a good postwar bargaining position.

Either of these alternatives, the memorandum stressed, required immediate concentration of powerful forces across the Channel. If compromise
was possible, the Soviets would demand this second front as a prerequisite
to further discussion. If it were not possible, then only the presence of such
forces in Europe could "make a policy of hostilities costly and unattractive"
to the Soviets. Furthermore, from "an American point of view," concentration in Western Europe was

> *the one move* that is best calculated to give the Western Allies, in
> advance, an effective bargaining position for a compromise settle-
> ment with Russia, and a base for participating in such an agreed
> occupation of Germany by the United States, Britain, and Rus-
> sia, as will secure the bargain.[43]

A Balkan landing, on the other hand, would only increase present friction between the Allies while being incapable of maintaining itself against
a future attack. It would thus "do little to improve our bargaining position
vis-a-vis Russia, but would divert allied forces from Western Europe where
they could materially help" that position.

The Research and Analysis Branch of OSS favored an attempt at compromise over an independent policy. It believed that the Soviets preferred
such an approach too, as shown by their continued insistence, despite recent and overwhelming victories, on the one operation that could insure
the West a voice in the future of Europe. But cooperation was only possible
the memorandum maintained, if the Allies compromised *before* American
troops landed in Europe and came into conflict with Soviet forces. It sketch
out such a compromise in terms of a protocol covering all outstanding wartime and possible postwar areas of disagreement. In the "last analysis," con
centration in Western Europe was a cornerstone for either approach:

> The policy of compromise will produce results of great value, if
> it proves workable. If it breaks down, the open rivalry that then
> develops will be no sharper than it would have been if no com-
> promise had been attempted, and the large Anglo-American force
> on the continent will be in the best possible position to deal with
> the situation.
>
> One indispensible element in any policy of compromise with
> the Soviet Union is, apparently, a firm agreement as to the launch-
> ing of a major Allied operation in Western Europe. If compromise

fails, America and Britain will then have no choice but to pursue
their own aims independently. For this independent strategy and
policy vis-a-vis Germany and Russia, a major allied action in Western Europe again seems indispensable.[44]

This extraordinary document was brought to the attention of the JCS
while the American chiefs were discussing COSSAC's RANKIN plans for
emergency reentry onto the continent in the event of severe German weakening or collapse before OVERLORD could be launched. In effect, the OSS
report had boldly highlighted the political need for such plans and the cross-
Channel invasion, as well as the weaknesses of any Balkan alternative. COS-
SAC had also recognized the political importance of RANKIN, recommending the use of a rather large force of twenty-four to twenty-six divisions in
case of total German collapse and noting that "for both political and military reasons speed of entry will be of the first importance." On August 23,
both the JCS and the CCS approved the RANKIN plans "in principle" and
directed that they be kept under "continuous review" in regard to the forces
required for success.[45]
    In a plenary session that afternoon, Roosevelt showed that he was think-
ing along similar lines when he pointedly asked "if a study was being made
regarding an emergency entrance of the Continent and indicated that he
desired . . . to get to Berlin as soon as did the Russians."[46] Such a desire was
reinforced on the following day when he received a telegram from Stalin
complaining bitterly over the lack of Soviet inclusion in surrender discussions with the Italians. The USSR, he complained, had been "a passive third
observer" to agreements reached by Britain and the United States, and it
was "impossible to tolerate such [a] situation any longer."[47]
    On the evening of August 24, an angry president informed Harriman that
he and Churchill were "both mad" at Stalin for this latest blast.[48] Attempts
by subordinates to calm the two Western leaders met with little success.
Churchill warned that evening of "bloody consequences in the future" and
"grave troubles" with this "unnatural man."[49] On the following day, he
reported home that the "black spot at the present time is the increasing
bearishness of Soviet Russia," and that Roosevelt had been "very much
offended" at the tone of Stalin's recent messages, to the extent of refusing
to see the new Soviet charge d'affairs.[50]
    As QUADRANT ended, future cooperation with Russia seemed far from
assured. In such a situation, the second front, be it OVERLORD or RAN-
KIN, appeared more necessary than ever.

CHAPTER NINE

OVERLORD IN TROUBLE

SEPTEMBER TO NOVEMBER 1943

American suspicions of Churchill did not end with the QUADRANT victory, for as Hopkins told Lord Moran, even though the prime minister "came clean" and "threw in his hand" at Quebec, "I don't believe he is really converted."[1] Such fears were soon proven completely valid, for Churchill had not really given up on his eastern Mediterrenean projects and by October he had once again succeeded in placing the cross-Channel attack in doubt. This time, however, he received support from the most unlikely of sources.

CHURCHILL AND THE AEGEAN

Churchill had agreed to the QUADRANT decisions largely because of his belief that the Allies now had enough power simultaneously to cross the Channel and to accomplish his goals in the eastern Mediterranean. He enunciated this belief to Roosevelt and the JCS immediately after Eisenhower announced Italy's surrender and landed at Salerno on September 9. While there was no question of "whittling down" OVERLORD, Churchill insisted, enough forces would still be available both to open the Dalmatian ports and to give supplies to "all forces that will obey our orders." Furthermore, after meeting the main German forces in Italy, the West could establish a defensive line and transfer some troops eastward to "emphasize a movement North and North-Eastward from the Dalmatian ports" and take over the Italian-held islands in the Aegean.[2]

Army planners opposed such ideas as "dangerous" diversions.[3] Since
Churchill had vowed not to disturb OVERLORD, however, the JCS on September 10 approved the occupation of the Dodecanese Islands and the opening of the Dalmatian ports provided these operations did not use resources
needed for the cross-Channel assault or Italy.[4] Churchill meanwhile had
not even waited for formal approval of his plan, writing on September 9
to General Sir Henry Maitland Wilson, commander of Allied forces in the
Middle East, that "this is the time to play high. Improvise and dare."[5]

Wilson did just that in an attempt to wrest the Dodecanese from the
demoralized Italians before the Germans could move in. By mid-September, he had succeeded in taking the small Aegean islands of Cos, Leros, and
Samos. He failed, however, in his attempt to beat the Germans to the big
prize, the island of Rhodes, and Hitler soon counterattacked against Cos,
the only British-held island with an airfield. Unless Rhodes could be taken,
the entire British position in the Aegean would be hopeless. In late September, Churchill and Wilson both pressed Eisenhower for reinforcements to
take the island (ACCOLADE).[6] The Mediterranean commander was able
to send some aid, but when the Germans took Cos in early October, he requested guidance from the CCS. Eisenhower informed them of his personal opposition to ACCOLADE on the grounds that the Italian campaign required all supplies available, while Aegean operations in the present situation "will probably assume the aspect of a major bitter battle."[7]

The OPD agreed with Eisenhower completely, pointing out to Marshall
and the JCS that while ACCOLADE might force the Germans to withdraw
from Greece, it was no longer the easy operation originally envisaged and
there was thus "no excuse for it." In fact, it was at this stage "the perfect
set-up for the creation of a vacuum" capable of drawing forces that could
be put to better use in England or Italy. It would be a "wasteful dispersion
of forces" that could have "but one ultimate objective—the Balkan mainland."[8] The JSSC reached similar conclusions, calling the Rhodes attack
a worthless diversion that would mean "a continuing drain on our resources"
and lead to further operations against Crete and Greece.[9] Roosevelt and
the JCS agreed and on October 5 insisted that Wilson only be provided with
equipment that Eisenhower could spare from the Italian campaign.[10]

On October 7, however, Churchill pressed Eisenhower and Roosevelt
for supplies to mount ACCOLADE, informing the president that Italy and
the Balkans were part of the same theater and that the assault would require
only one "first class division" and landing craft which could be returned
in time so as not to affect OVERLORD. Sending an army into the Balkans,

he insisted, had never been his aim. He only wished to send supplies to the area and conduct commando raids to "activate" the guerrillas and further disperse the Germans. Rhodes was the key to this entire operation, and its importance now warranted such a diversion of resources.[11]

Once again, Churchill was not being honest, and the American planners were quite correct in assessing his political motives for such an attack. In th aftermath of Rome's surrender, the Greek guerrillas had disarmed the Italian troops in their country and now seemed capable of pushing the Germans out and establishing their own government. Churchill's August 19 desire to prevent this outcome by landing British forces with the king had by mid-September been bolstered by Smuts' warnings of "wholesale Communism" in the Balkan area.[12] On September 12, however, Brooke advised that any such plan would require at least two divisions and would thus prejudice the Italian campaign. Despite this warning, Eden and his associates insisted on the importance of the landing, regardless of its military effect. On September 29, Churchill backed the Foreign Office but cut the two-division figure to 5,000 highly mobile troops, a force cabable of restoring the king without unduly hindering either the Italian campaign or OVERLORD.[13]

Such a small force could not by itself force the Germans out of Greece, but taking Rhodes and the rest of the Aegean islands would badly compromise Hitler's strategic position and bring Turkey into the war. Hence, Hitler would be forced to withdraw and the mobile British force would be able to restore the king. Realizing their exposed position, however, the Germans were rapidly moving into the Aegean. In addition, the communist-controlle Greek guerrillas attacked the smaller Republican partisans on October 8.[14] Clearly Churchill had to move fast and take Rhodes immediately.

Opposed to the entire scheme, Brooke attempted after the fall of Cos to talk Churchill out of ACCOLADE, but the prime minister was adamant. A "heated argument" between the two men solved nothing. On October 8, the CIGS wrote despairingly in his diary,

> I can now control him no more. He has worked himself into
> a frenzy of excitement about the Rhodes attack, has magnified
> its importance so that he can no longer see anything else and
> has set his heart on capturing this one island even at the expense
> of endangering his relations with the President and the Americans and the future of the Italian campaign. He refused to listen to any arguments or to see any dangers.[15]

Brooke had accurately anticipated Washington's reaction to Churchill's plea. While Admiral Leahy concluded that the British were "prepared to sacrifice success elsewhere in order to assure their full control of the Mediterranean,"[16] the JCS prepared a reply that Roosevelt approved and sent on October 8 stating that ACCOLADE would jeopardize the Italian campaign and that "no diversion should prejudice OVERLORD."[17] An undeterred Churchill responded with two more telegrams to Roosevelt pleading for the one division as well as a meeting with Eisenhower, Marshall, and the COS.[18] Again using a JCS draft, Roosevelt informed Churchill on October 9 that such a conference would in effect be a CCS meeting which he could not attend, and that ACCOLADE would mean a long campaign beyond Rhodes, drawing heavily from resources needed for OVERLORD as well as the Italian and Burma campaigns. The choice, the president stated, was now Rome *or* the Balkans, and the Rome objective was the more important of the two.[19]

Churchill later stated that this message "quenched my last hopes," but the evidence again says otherwise. On October 9, he told Wilson to "press most strongly" for ACCOLADE at the Mediterranean commanders conference scheduled for that day. At the same time, he pleaded with Roosevelt to allow free discussion of the issue by Eisenhower, warning that cancellation of the Rhodes attack meant the loss of Leros and " complete abandonment by us of any foothold in the Aegean, which will become a frozen area, with most unfortunate political and psychological reactions in that part of the world instead of great advantages."[20]

Roosevelt agreed to let Eisenhower make up his own mind, but by this time Hitler's decision to reinforce and hold Italy had become obvious. With the choice definitely Rome *or* Rhodes, the Mediterranean commanders unanimously chose Rome.[21]

It would seem that Hitler's decision would have destroyed all chances of mounting ACCOLADE, but it actually kept Churchill's plans alive. Both Eisenhower and the COS now began to fear that transfer of the seven divisions and landing craft to OVERLORD could easily lead to defeat or stalemate in Italy, and in mid-October they requested retention in the Mediterranean.[22] Such retention, Churchill realized, could mean eventual use in the Aegean, though this move would involve more than the minor delay in holding OVERLORD forces which Eisenhower had envisaged and could not be accomplished until the Italian theater stabilized.

Churchill solved these problems by an interesting reversal of strategic plans. He had originally perceived ACCOLADE as an operation to be undertaken without prejudice to OVERLORD and as a necessary prerequisite to Turkish entry into the war. Now, however, he began to push for both a delay in the cross-Channel assault and Turkish entry as prerequisites to the Rhodes attack. On October 19, he directed the COS to prepare a paper on the current Mediterranean situation with special reference to the partisan movement in the Balkans, and on the next day he asked Roosevelt for a full conference in November before any meeting with Stalin in order to review all 1944 plans.[23] Brooke wrote in his diary on the evening of October 19 that the prime minister wanted "to swing the strategy back to the Mediterranean at the expense of the Channel. I am in many ways entirely with him, but God knows where this may lead us as regards clashes with the Americans."[24]

Churchill as well as the CIGS knew that those clashes would be explosive and that by themselves the British could never convince Washington to delay OVERLORD. The prime minister therefore began to look for support from other quarters and found it in the most unlikely place—Moscow.

THE MOSCOW CONFERENCE

The QUADRANT reaffirmation of the 1944 cross-Channel assault led to a sharp improvement in relations between Russia and her Western allies. Molotov agreed to Italian surrender terms, which did not include a Soviet veto on future Allied actions, and he also empowered Eisenhower to sign for the Russians. For his part Stalin congratulated the West on the Salerno landings, expressed a willingness to go to Iran for a tripartite summit meeting, and agreed to a preliminary foreign ministers' conference in Moscow.[25] The Soviets also informed Washington on September 16 that they had rejected German overtures, made through the Japanese, for a separate peace.

Nevertheless, numerous issues still divided the Allies in September,[27] and a full conference of foreign ministers appeared necessary to determine how much the Russians truly desired postwar cooperation. The aging Hull agreed to take the first airplane flight of his career so that he could personally attend the Moscow Conference.

The Soviets soon made clear that the second front remained the prerequisite for future cooperation by insisting that the first item on the conference agenda be "measures for shortening the war against Germany" and by defining such measures in terms of a cross-Channel attack.[28] Not wishing to have the meeting turn into a military conference, Hull foresaw "trouble" on this Soviet demand but realized that the West would "have to reassure Stalin completely on this point before we could induce him to come in with us on the political decisions."[29] An OSS report used even blunter language, stating that the "atmosphere of suspicion can only be removed by military action. Without it, the chances of the Allies winning the peace are very slim."[30] General John R. Deane, head of the new American military mission to Moscow, and General Ismay of the COS therefore accompanied the diplomats to Moscow to explain the OVERLORD plans.[31]

After being elected permanent presiding officer, Molotov began the conference on October 19 by asking if the June 1943 promises regarding a second front still held. He also suggested that the Allies launch moves to bring Turkey into the war immediately and obtain air bases from Sweden. Hull and Eden quickly cabled home for instructions on these two points, while Ismay and Deane informed the conference on October 20 that the TRIDENT promise still held, provided certain military preconditions were fulfilled. Ismay was "fairly confident" they would be, and he joined Deane in stressing the combined bomber offensive in this regard. Molotov appeared dissatisfied and again asked if the TRIDENT promise had been reaffirmed at Quebec. Eden said yes, subject to the conditions explained, and he was backed by Deane and Hull. On the following day, the Soviet minister stated he was satisfied.[32] With the issues of Turkey and Sweden postponed pending instructions from Washington and London, the conferees then moved on to political matters.

Hull's method of discovering if the Soviets were willing to cooperate in the postwar world revolved around their reaction to his cherished Four Power Pact, the State Department's Declaration on Germany, and the idea of a summit meeting in the near future between the three Allied heads of state. If the Russians signed the Four Power Pact, they would be agreeing to the unconditional surrender of Germany and future cooperation within the framework of a new League of Nations. The Declaration on Germany also contained an unconditional surrender clause, as well as a tripartite occupation plan. If Stalin agreed to these two documents and a meeting with Roosevelt and Churchill, he was obviously not going to sign a separate peace or attempt to communize Europe.

The Russians, not yet at war with Japan, balked at the inclusion of China as one of the signatories to the Four Power Pact. Hull was adamant on this point, however, and resorted to the Army's old Pacific threat, warning Molotov that leaving China out would have "the most terrific repercussions, both political and military, in the Pacific area, and that this might call for all sorts of readjustments by my Government for the purpose of keeping properly stabilized the political and military situation in the Pacific."[33]

Molotov apparently understood the implication, for the Soviets accepted
the pact with Chinese signature and thereby publicly endorsed the unconditional surrender principle for the first time. Moreover, Stalin seemed en-
thusiastic over the Declaration on Germany, showed interest in a summit
meeting, and told Hull he would enter the war against Japan after Germany's defeat. His subordinates, meanwhile, denied separate peace rumors
and stated their opposition to postwar spheres of influence.[34]

An overjoyed Hull concluded that the Soviets were perfectly willing to
cooperate, provided a second front was established in 1944. He now dis-
counted the threats of a separate peace and a Sovietized Europe that had
been fanned by the Free Germany manifesto. Not bothered by the fact that
many important political issues, especially in Eastern Europe, had been virtually ignored at the conference in order to maintain the atmosphere of
goodwill, he returned to Washington convinced that he had laid the basis
for a new Wilsonian world order. As he told Congress: "There will no longer
be need for spheres of influence, for alliances, for balance of power, or any
other of the special arrangements through which, in the unhappy past, the
nations strove to safeguard their security or to promote their interests."[35]

Nor was such optimism limited to the secretary of state. Deane informed
Roosevelt and the JCS on October 30 that he had "been tremendously
impressed with the possibilities for cooperation engendered during this conference,"[36] and two days later the JWPC canceled an October 9 request for
a JIC appreciation of separate peace possibilities on the Eastern front.[37]
Roosevelt, perhaps influenced by his recent break with Bullitt over the re-
moval of Sumner Welles from the State Department,[38] also appeared to
share Hull's optimism. Even the hard-headed Eden later recalled that Moscow had been "the high tide, if not of good, at least of tolerable, relations
between us."[39]

Churchill too was pleased at the outcome of the conference, though for
reasons quite different from those of Washington. By the beginning of November, the prime minister appeared to have accomplished one of his greatest politico-military coups by getting Stalin to support further delay in the
cross-Channel assault in order to gain immediate aid in the eastern Mediterranean.

On October 20, Churchill had wired his worries regarding European
strategy to Eden, as well as his belief that the seven divisions should remain
in the Mediterranean. Still convinced of the "great importance" of taking
Rhodes and refusing to accept American arguments on the ability of air power
to "flatten everything out in the battle zone or its approaches," he objected

to the "lawyer's bargain" for a May OVERLORD. He concluded that, "in
the absence of a German collapse," no Channel crossing should be attempted
"with less than forty divisions available by the sixtieth day, and then only
if the Italian front were in strong action with the enemy." Citing Molotov's
expressed interest in getting Turkey into the war, Churchill directed his foreign secretary to find out how the Russians "really" felt about Anglo-American action in the Balkans.[40]

Eden's response that the Soviets were "completely and blindly" set on
OVERLORD[41] only led Churchill to damn Stalin and his obsession with
"this bloody second front" and to state that he could "be obstinate too."[42]
During the lsat week in October, Churchill complained to Marshall about
the opening withdrawals being made from the Mediterranean for OVER-
LORD and reiterated to Roosevelt his desire for a military conference to
review the QUADRANT decisions before any summit meeting with Stalin.
Present plans for 1944, he warned the president, "seem open to very grave
defects," for the split in forces between the United Kingdom and Italy invited successful German counterattacks and the Italian theater could not
be allowed to "degenerate into a deadlock." Rome and its airfields had to
be won "at all costs," and the Mediterranean should therefore receive needed supplies "no matter what effect is produced on subsequent operations."[43]

At the same time, Churchill instructed Eden not to discourage any Russian desire to bring Turkey into the war. On October 26, he forwarded to
Eden General Harold Alexander's pessimistic estimate of the Italian situation, with instructions to show it to Stalin and inform the Soviet leader that
the West would not let the Italian campaign end in disaster for the sake of
a May OVERLORD. The assurances already given on the cross-Channel assault would have to be modified, with a possible delay in launching the attack
until July.[44] Intensely worried over Alexander's estimate, the COS warned
the JCS on the same date that they would demand postponement of OVER-
LORD if reverse or stalemate ensued in Italy. The Cabinet concurred on
October 27, with Churchill stating that he was willing to resign over the
issue.[45]

Italy was not Britain's sole concern in the Mediterranean. On October
29, the COS informed Churchill that Leros could neither be defended nor
evacuated and that its only hope was outside assistance from Turkish airfields. Following their advice, Churchill immediately forwarded this report
to Eden with instructions to tell the Russians.[46]

The impact of these messages on Eden was soon apparent. When the Soviets on October 28 inquired into the rigidity of OVERLORD's precondi-

tions and again asked if the Quebec pledge still held, the foreign secretary once more responded in the affirmative but added that his statement was "not a binding legal contract."[47] That evening, he presented Alexander's estimate to Stalin and admitted in response to a direct query that OVER-LORD might be delayed for a few months. The Soviet leader calmly accept this news, and Eden wired home that the entire talk "went off surprisingly well."[48]

With the possible postponement of OVERLORD explained, Eden went to work on the Turkish issue. Originally he had been cool to the idea of forcing Ankara into the war at this stage. Hence, he had at first agreed with the American position, expressed by Hull on October 28, that inquiries be limited to the lease of air bases since probable Turkish demands for supplies needed for OVERLORD and Italy made her entrance presently inadvisable.[49] Eden soon changed his mind under the impact of the COS report on Leros and a warning from his own Foreign Office that Turkish entry wa the best, if not the only, way to prevent Russian domination of the Balkan by allowing British troops to arrive in the area before the Soviets.[50]

Reversing his earlier antipathy to meeting the Turks, Eden now agreed to a conference in Cairo to be held immediately after the Moscow talks, and he asked Hull for permission to change the proposed agreement on Turkey with the Soviets. Interpreting such remarks to signify only minor changes, Hull agreed. On October 31, Eden and Ismay informed Molotov that they planned to speak with the Turks immediately after the conferenc and ask for the use of airfields to protect Leros.[51]

In actuality, Eden perceived this request as the first stage in gaining Turkish entry into the war, a fact he had not explained to Hull. Ironically, Molotov found the British approach too gradual and still favored demandin immediate Turkish entry. A compromise was reached by November 1, afte the conference had ended, whereby Molotov agreed to Eden's plan in retur for later British support in demanding full Turkish belligerency. With the Soviets adamant, Roosevelt and the JCS agreed to this compromise on November 4, providing no British or American resources which the field commanders thought necessary for OVERLORD or Italy be committed to the eastern Mediterranean.[52] At Cairo, Eden found that the Turks would not cooperate under such conditions. Ankara declared that it would not even grant the use of air bases without an Anglo-American commitment to send an army into the Balkans. Eden was thus forced to return home with his mission a failure.[53] Leros fell to the Germans on November 16.

This defeat did not end British pressure for action in the Mediterranean, for the battle in Italy continued to bog down. Furthermore, Eden and the Middle East Defense Command had agreed in Cairo that London must break relations with Greek leftists, while British representatives in Yugoslavia reported that Tito's partisans were a much larger force than originally thought and were likely to be a decisive factor in that country when the war ended.[54]

Even with Leros lost, Churchill and the COS continued therefore to demand a conference to revise the QUADRANT decisions. They also pressed for a unification of commands so as to put Italy and the eastern Mediterranean in the same theater and under a British commander.[55] Washington got a taste of what would follow such a move when London simultaneously asked for delays in the transfer of Mediterranean landing craft over and beyond those already requested and received by Eisenhower and told Alexander to plan his campaign on the basis of CCS acceptance of the request.[56]

The Americans were incensed. Many of the planners felt that the Italian campaign had already achieved its stated objectives and that there was no need to continue up the peninsula.[57] Moreover, the six- to eight-week delay in launching OVERLORD which the British were now suggesting could easily destroy any possibility of mounting the operation in 1944. COSSAC had already pointed out that weather conditions prevented launching the operation after July.[58] On November 5, General Sir Frederick Morgan, head of COSSAC, further warned the CCS that the delay in the transfer of landing craft which the British were advocating "would reflect seriously on OVERLORD preparations."[59]

Fully informed by Deane and the State Department of the events in Moscow, the American planners were further infuriated by British moves at the conference. Especially galling had been the sending of Alexander's estimate to Stalin, with its implications of delay in OVERLORD, rather than Eisenhower's more optimistic report.[60] The JCS quickly responded by informing Deane of their disagreement with some of Alexander's statements and their belief that the Italian situation would not cause delay in crossing the Channel.[61] Stimson labeled the British move "dirty baseball" and concluded that Churchill "wanted to stick a knife in the back of OVERLORD." Feeling "more bitterly" about the issue "than I ever have before" and worried about the effect of these moves on Roosevelt, Stimson went to see the president on October 29. He received Roosevelt's reassurance that he "would not think of touching the Balkans" unless the Russians stated their desire for such a move.[62]

By this time such a statement was not very reassuring. In September, the idea of the Soviets demanding a Balkan invasion in preference to a second front would have seemed ridiculous, and at Moscow they had insisted on reassurances in regard to OVERLORD. At the Moscow meeting, however, the Soviets had also demanded Turkish entrance into the war and immediate measures to relieve their front, and they had not objected to possible delay in launching OVERLORD in order to accomplish these goals and keep the battle going in Italy.

American observers in Moscow could not agree on the significance of these contradictory moves and statements. Harriman reported in early November that, although the conference had been a great success and had "delighted" the Soviets, "our whole permanent relations depend in a large measure on their satisfaction in the future with our military operations. It is impossible to over-emphasize the importance they place strategically on the initiation of the so-called 'second front' next spring."[63] At the same time, however, Deane reported that the Soviets were more interested in immediate military action in Italy and the Balkans, even at the expense of delaying OVERLORD, and that Stalin had indicated the Italian theater might be developed as a second front. Even Harriman was forced to admit Moscow would have a difficult choice to make if informed that it could have either a spring OVERLORD or immediate help elsewhere.[64] Unfortunately, that was exactly what the choice now boiled down to.

A worried Stimson attempted to reassure Roosevelt by telling him that the Russians were under pressure from Churchill.[65] While this was to an extent true, Stalin was not the kind of man to break under the prime minister's assaults. The reasons for his acceptance of British plans have remained a mystery. With Soviet forces continuing their great 1943 offensive and appearing capable in November of totally smashing the German armies on the southern portion of the Eastern front, he may have concluded that immediate Western aid in the Mediterranean could end the war that year, thereby obviating the necessity for launching a second front in 1944.[66] Whatever his motivations, the Americans were forced to conclude in November that Stalin might indeed back Churchill's plans at the expense of OVERLORD. Washington could not resist such combined pressure, especially after the optimism engendered by the Moscow Conference. International cooperation and the possibility of quick victory definitely took precedence over favored strategy. Thus, the future of the cross-Channel assault was once more up in the air. Ironically, the final decision on this operation now rested in Soviet hands.

CHAPTER TEN

FINAL ARGUMENTS AND DECISION

NOVEMBER TO DECEMBER 1943

With the cross-Channel assault again uncertain, the Americans prepared for the now necessary series of strategic discussions with their allies. Once again, political considerations dominated military planning, for the final decision on future operations would now have to be made totally within the context of Allied diplomatic relations.

PLANS AND DECEPTIONS

In early November, the planners recommended rigid adherence to the QUADRANT accords, with Balkan activities and efforts to bring Turkey into the war remaining severely limited in scope so that OVERLORD could be launched on time. Neither the American public nor the Soviets, they warned, would tolerate delay or cancellation of the operation which was "essential, not only to prevent the creation of a strategic stalemate in Europe, but also to preserve and strengthen the favorable future relations of the United Nations heralded by the results of the Moscow Conference."[1] According to one planner, Stalin would interpret cancellation as part of a British scheme to bleed the Russians dry and would respond by demanding not only a Balkan invasion, but possibly domination of Eastern Europe as well and by considering himself a "free agent" in the postwar world.[2]

If London insisted on revision of the QUADRANT allocations and a subsequent delay in OVERLORD, the United States should threaten to turn to the Pacific, for as the OPD emphasized, *"further indecision, eva-*

sion and undermining of agreements cannot be borne. . . . the time has arrived to 'fish or cut bait.' "[3] To bind the British further, insure the launching of OVERLORD on time, and prevent a repetition of Churchill's autumn moves in the Aegean, the planners also suggested unifying the European and Mediterranean theaters under an American commander who would have the power and will to decisively pursue the proper strategic approach Stimson made clear his preference for Marshall for this position.[4]

The planners knew, however, that they could not refuse a Soviet demand for further Mediterranean action. Final decision on European strategy would therefore have to await a tripartite conference in which the Russians should be informed that they could have such action or OVERLORD in 1944, but not both, and that the Mediterranean approach would take much time and be rather ineffective in relieving German pressure. Furthermore, as King pointed out to his JCS colleagues in late October, this conference would have to precede any CCS discussions in order to avoid increased Russian suspicion of Western collusion and "political and propaganda repercussions" which "would be extremely dangerous to the allied cause."[5]

Roosevelt agreed wholeheartedly but found himself unable to act on the planners' suggestions. While Churchill continued to insist on CCS discussions before any meeting with Stalin, the Soviet leader refused to travel farther than Tehran for the proposed summit conference. Fearing that he could not fulfill his constitutional duties at such a distance from Washington, Roosevelt vetoed the Iranian capital. The ensuing deadlock kept the summit meeting hypothetical through early November and forced him to agree to Churchill's proposed Anglo-American conference in Cairo (SEXTANT). Still hoping to avoid Soviet suspicion, Roosevelt suggested that this meeting include a Russian military representative and be followed by a conference with either Stalin or Molotov and Chiang Kai-shek.[6]

Churchill was willing to meet Molotov and Chiang after Cairo but objected vehemently to any Russian sitting in on CCS discussions, since the Russian would have no power and "would simply bay for an earlier second front and block all other discussions." European strategy for 1944, the prime minister insisted, should remain an Anglo-American affair.[7] Stalin's unexpected stance at the Moscow Conference led him to shift position a few days later and back a meeting with the Russian and Chinese representatives in Cairo, as well as the proposed summit meeting. Nevertheless, Churchill was still unwilling to let the Soviets play a role in determining Anglo-American strategy, insisting that the CCS meet in Malta *before* joining their allies in Cairo. In effect, the Soviets would receive already agreed upon CCS decisions.[8]

Such a plan was exactly what Roosevelt wished to avoid, and between November 8 and 10 he torpedoed Churchill's idea. Roosevelt informed Stalin that he could go to Tehran after all and set November 26 as the tentative opening date for the conference. Simultaneously, the president requested the Soviet leader to send Molotov to Cairo on November 22, asked Chiang to arrive on the same date, vetoed the idea of preliminary CCS discussions in Malta, and called for SEXTANT to begin on November 22. Although he had informed Churchill that the CCS would have "many meetings" before the Russians or Chinese arrived, Roosevelt had arranged the conference so that no such meetings could take place by having everyone arrive on the same date, thereby insuring its preliminary nature.[9]

Unfortunately, Roosevelt had overstacked the deck. On November 12, an angry Churchill struck back by informing Stalin that Chiang had also been invited to Cairo, a fact Roosevelt had conveniently left out of his November 8 message to the Soviet leader. Since Russia was not at war with Japan, Stalin responded by informing the president that Molotov could not attend the conference.[10] Nevertheless, Roosevelt's deception had worked to an extent, for with Chiang arriving on November 22, SEXTANT would be dominated by Far Eastern affairs while European decisions would await the summit meeting to follow immediately in Tehran.

En route to Cairo on board the U.S.S. *Iowa*, Roosevelt met with the JCS on November 15 and 19. He showed himself to be in full accord with their views on OVERLORD, the eastern Mediterranean, and an American supreme commander for the entire European-Mediterranean theater, and he even went so far as to state his preference for Marshall for this position.[11] But Roosevelt also stated that the Soviets might well demand immediate aid in the form of a Balkan invasion and that their position on the issue would be decisive. In reply, Marshall reiterated the military's view of the situation. Balkan operations would prolong the war "materially," he said, and would "reduce United States potentialities by two-thirds." Commitments and preparations for OVERLORD now extended "as far west as the Rocky Mountains," and any British insistence on a Balkan alternative could be met by an American threat to "pull out and go into the Pacific with all our forces." The Soviets should be informed of the serious implications of any demand for a Balkan attack and of the fact that OVERLORD would provide them with more effective aid.[12]

Roosevelt and the JCS also discussed the RANKIN plans that COSSAC had now completed and forwarded to Washington, along with a proposed military occupation division of Germany. The division plan allocated the eastern portion of the *Reich* and continent to the Russians, northwestern Germany and Europe to the British, and southwestern Germany and France to the United States. This allocation had been based on the probable positions of the Allied armies at the time of German surrender, for by the OVERLORD plan, American forces were concentrating in southwestern England and would form the southern flank of the cross-Channel invasion. Despite the logistical rationale, American planners had immediately noted the immense political implications of COSSAC's division. They had concluded that General Morgan "apparently coordinated thoroughly his plans with British post-war political and economic policies." Similar American coordination, they felt, was necessary before RANKIN could be approved or disapproved. They and the JCS had therefore decided to defer action until guidance could be obtained from the State Department and the president.[13]

Roosevelt gave that guidance during the *Iowa* talks by blasting the proposed division, stating that COSSAC's plan had been motivated by "British political considerations," and insisting that the United States be allocated the northwestern rather than the southwestern zone so as to have as little to do with France and Italy as possible. London, he stated, wished to restore France to great power status, a move he felt impossible for at least twenty-five years. The British were welcome to try, but he wanted no part of the ensuing political chaos. Furthermore, southwest Europe was an area in which London "would undercut us in every move we make." A northwest occupation zone would free him from any dependence on Britain or France for lines of communication, as well as from any responsibility for France.[14]

Such a zone would also enable the Americans to control at least part of Berlin, for despite the improved relations with the Soviets, the president still desired to occupy the city as soon as possible for postwar political purposes. The *Iowa* discussions strengthened this desire. If France could not be a great power for at least twenty-five years and Stalin did demand a Balkan assault over OVERLORD, then only the RANKIN forces would stand between Russia and the Atlantic. Roosevelt thus told the JCS that the American zone in the northwest should include Berlin, that there "would definitely be a race" for the city, and that Washington might have to place divisions there "as soon as possible." Hopkins further suggested dropping an airborne division into Berlin "two hours after the collapse of Germany," while the president mapped out a massive American occupation zone in northwest Germany stretching as far east as Berlin and encompassing about half the country.[15]

The extra American territory came, of course, from the now diminished Soviet and British zones in the east and southwest. Considering the fact that this division was based on a German collapse and a subsequent "railroad" invasion rather than OVERLORD, Roosevelt's political desires were incredibly greater than his present military capabilities. How he expected to convince London and Moscow to agree to such a partition he did not explain, except to state that Stalin "might 'okay' it." Nor did he bother with the fact that his plan would involve a logistically nightmarish crossover of British and American forces. Marshall and King pointed the problem out to him, but with Roosevelt agreeing to virtually every JCS point they did not stress the issue. To the contrary, King concluded that the crossover "did not present insuperable difficulties."[16] With logistics taking a back seat to unity, the Americans were now prepared to meet their allies.

The opening sessions of SEXTANT proceeded almost exactly as Roosevelt had planned. Far Eastern affairs and personnel, as well as reports from field commanders, dominated both formal and informal talks. The Allies did not even discuss European strategy until November 24. At the plenary session on that date, Roosevelt stated that Cairo should be a "preliminary survey" of European operations, with final decisions depending "on the way things went at the conference shortly to be held with Premier Stalin." The Soviet leader, he felt, "would be almost certain" to demand both Mediterranean action and OVERLORD. Roosevelt himself thought Aegean operations would go "nowhere," but he admitted that Turkish entrance into the war "would put quite a different complexion on the matter."[17]

Seeing his opening, Churchill responded on November 24 by arguing that OVERLORD, though still the primary operation, should not be a "tyrant" ruling out further Mediterranean action. After sketching every possible operation in that sea, he asked for a further delay in transferring landing craft and suggested bringing more into the Mediterranean from the Southeast Asia Command in order to launch ACCOLADE. Turkish entrance, he maintained, would enable the Allies to make the German position in the Aegean untenable at a cost of only a few divisions and landing craft, and the effect of operations in the area on the Balkan countries would be "profound." The West should therefore plan to capture Rome in January and

Rhodes in February, open the Aegean if Turkey entered the war, and unify the Mediterranean command. All preparations for OVERLORD should go ahead "full steam," but within this framework.[18]

On November 25, the COS presented the JCS with a paper reiterating these points and stating it was now "absolutely essential" to delay OVERLORD so as to insure its ultimate success. They also announced their firm opposition to the American concept of a supreme Allied commander for all of Europe, largely, as Churchill stated, because of the "divergencies of view" between the two staffs and governments over future operations. The differences were "political as much as military" and would result in making the commander either powerless or too powerful.[19]

While the CCS did discuss European strategy in closed session on November 25, they reached no decisions, and the formal session on that date was again dominated by Far Eastern affairs. Not until November 26, the last day of the conference, did they openly discuss Europe, and by that time tempers on all sides had reached, and in some cases passed, the boiling point. In line with Churchill's suggestion, the COS had pressed for the transfer of landing craft from Asia to the Aegean, a move they perceived as insuring ACCOLADE and OVERLORD but one that the Americans saw as another attempt to place British political interests in the Aegean ahead of winning both wars. The early CCS sessions on Southeast Asia were thus explosive, and King at one point, according to a participant, "almost climbed over the table at Brooke."[20]

The informal sessions were no less heated. Frustrated in his attempts to see Roosevelt privately to convince him of the validity of the British viewpoint, Churchill vented his rhetoric on Marshall. On the evening of November 23, he kept Marshall up until 2:00 A.M. with pleas for a delay in OVERLORD and a transfer of landing craft from Southeast Asia. After the November 24 plenary session, he continued his arguments for Rhodes by telling Army chief that "his Majesty's Government can't have its troops standing idle. Muskets must flame." The harassed Marshall shot back that "not one American soldier is going to die on [that] goddamned beach,"[21] but his firmness and bluntness were matched by a growing sense of despair regarding the probable Russian position at Tehran.

On November 20, General Hull of the OPD had informed the planners en route to Cairo that State Department officials who had attended the Foreign Ministers' Conference felt the Soviets would find "any action" resulting in delay or abandonment of OVERLORD "unacceptable," and the such action "might result in undoing the results of the Moscow Conference." OVERLORD, according to one high-ranking department official, remained the "basic thing" for the Soviets. Anything else they had asked for at Moscow was in addition to this operation "and in no way a substitute for it," a conclusion Harriman seconded on the following evening.[22]

On November 23, however, the War Department informed the planners in Cairo that the Germans had recently transferred six to twelve divisions to the East and had launched an attack in the Kiev region on a sixty-mile front. Berlin claimed a forty-mile advance, while Moscow reported that the situation was serious.[23] At the same time, Deane reasserted before the JCS his view that the Soviets would demand immediate relief over "operations scheduled for the future," that their emphasis at Moscow on OVERLORD had been only "for the purpose of testing Anglo-American sincerity," and that they viewed the operation "more in the nature of desirable insurance than as an immediate necessity." Assistant Secretary of War John J. McCloy seconded this assessment, while Winant informed the JCS that Churchill had reached the same conclusions. Even Harriman admitted that Moscow was under "tremendous pressure" to end the war quickly and was likely to demand immediate action to relieve the Eastern front.[24]

To make matters worse, Eisenhower now insisted he must retain some landing craft "indefinitely," expressed his desire to advance to the Po in Italy, and stated that such an offensive or ACCOLADE would delay OVERLORD not six to eight, but eight to twelve, weeks and so put the target date somewhere between July and August 1.[25] On November 26, the Joint Logistics Committee admitted that OVERLORD could be launched this late, but only if landing craft were shifted from Southeast Asia and amphibious operations in that theater were canceled. Otherwise, ACCOLADE would cripple OVERLORD and have repercussions on Pacific operations. The JPS was even more pessimistic, reporting on the same day that the Rhodes attack would cut into both OVERLORD and the Italian campaign and thus "weaken and indefinitely postpone" the cross-Channel assault.[26]

With Chiang Kai-shek demanding an Allied offensive, Roosevelt refused to sanction any cancellation in Southeast Asia. To the contrary, after checking on landing craft production schedules, he promised the Chinese leader on November 25 an amphibious operation in the Bay of Bengal (BUCCANEER), thereby forcing a choice between ACCOLADE and OVERLORD on schedule.[27] But with the JCS convinced that the Soviets "were certain to press for some immediate action" and the president determined to support Stalin's demands, cancellation of the Rhodes assault was out of the question. Leahy concluded at the November 26 JCS meeting that, unless delay in OVERLORD until July 15 could be accepted, "the problem appeared insoluble." Equally depressing, King warned his colleagues that delay beyond July 15 would definitely destroy any 1944 assault.[28]

Completely trapped by political factors beyond their control, the JCS reversed themselves on November 26 by accepting British Mediterranean proposals "as a basis for discussion" with the Soviets, provided these oper ations "in no way" interfered with BUCCANEER. When Brooke noted that this meant a definite postponement of OVERLORD, Marshall replied that he "quite understood" this point, but that for "political reasons" BUCCANEER "could not be interfered with."[29]

To the stunned and bitter COS, the Americans were now doing in the Far East exactly what they had accused the British of doing in the Mediterranean—prolonging the war for the sake of political goals. Brooke thus pressed for the postponement of BUCCANEER in order to end the European war at an earlier date, while Portal warned that Stalin might ask for OVERLORD *and* operations in the eastern Mediterranean. The JCS refus to budge. They had already decided to inform Stalin of the impossibility of such a program, and Leahy emphasized that only Churchill and Roosevelt could decide to abandon BUCCANEER.[30]

This was too much for Brooke. Going "off the record," he and Marsha proceeded to have "the father and mother of a row" which, according to Arnold, almost ended in a brawl.[31] When the smoke had cleared, the COS had agreed with the adamant JCS, although the JCS obviously had no gre love for the position they had so fiercely defended. The CCS therefore ap proved unification of command in the Mediterranean and "tentatively ac cepted" British proposals for operations in that theater, provided it was understood that such operations would "necessitate" delay in OVERLO and that the JCS could not accept abandonment of BUCCANEER without further discussion by Roosevelt and Churchill.[32]

As the Cairo Conference ended, European strategy had reached its ultimate crossroads. Roosevelt's promise to Chiang meant a definite choice between the Mediterranean and OVERLORD, and the Americans insiste that this choice be left to Stalin. According to his son Elliot, the preside was optimistic that the Soviet leader would favor OVERLORD,[33] but Lord Moran found Hopkins and Marshall worried by the end of the conference that Roosevelt was "wobbling" in his support of the cross-Chanr assault.[34] Furthermore, the JCS and their planners were convinced Stali would choose the Mediterranean. Winant had informed them that Churchill shared this belief, and according to Handy's later recollections, the Americans were "glum" and the British "elated" as SEXTANT ended.[35] Such elation was not shared by Brooke, who concluded in his diary that Stalin would insist upon OVERLORD at the earliest possible date.[36] With everybody second-guessing the Soviet leader, only three facts remained clear: a definite choice now had to be made between the Mediterranean and OVERLORD; Stalin would make this choice; and military factors had had little, if anything, to do with either the creation of the choice or the throwing of it into his lap.

DECISION AT TEHRAN

On the morning of November 28, the JCS met with their planners in Tehran and then discussed with Roosevelt the appropriate American response to probable Soviet demands for immediate Mediterranean action. Reiterating the fact that a definite choice between OVERLORD and such action now had to be made, Leahy warned Roosevelt that the latter alternative would mean only an eventual RANKIN across the Channel. Marshall modified this somber conclusion by explaining that a delayed OVERLORD *could* be combined with ACCOLADE and an Italian advance to the Pisa-Rimini line. Conquering Rhodes, however, would do nothing more than open a new supply route through the Dardanelles six to eight months hence and thus in no way fulfill Stalin's demand for immediate help. Moscow would probably demand even more action in the Mediterranean, and that action would in turn destroy OVERLORD.

As an alternative to ACCOLADE, the planners and their chiefs suggested allowing Eisenhower to advance to the Po and then to push eastward toward Austria and/or westward into southern France, while launching "limited" operations to open the Adriatic ports and send more supplies to Tito. Unlike the Rhodes assault, such movements could immediately engage numerous German divisions and thus fulfill Stalin's demand. Interestingly, they would also accomplish the original purpose of the Italian campaign—stretching German forces so as to insure a successful OVERLORD. Clearly implied was the possibility of combining such action in Italy with a delayed cross-Channel assault, for the planners and JCS had rated OVERLORD doomed *only* if a Po advance were undertaken *in conjunction* with ACCOLADE.[37]

Roosevelt seemed favorably impressed with this alternative, but the meeting ended inconclusively, as it had to until Soviet demands were clarified. As Marshall had clearly pointed out during the meeting, the "real issue" was what the Russians had in mind by "immediate help." They "definitely want something, and we should find out what it is."[38]

The meeting that afternoon to determine Soviet desires began in circumstances boding ill for the Americans. Arriving in Tehran with a bad cold which would eventually culminate in pneumonia, Churchill had originally postponed this meeting. Though he soon changed his mind and rescheduled it, Marshall and Arnold had in the meantime gone sightseeing. Hopkins was thus the only strong cross-Channel proponent near the president during this crucial discussion.

After preliminary remarks that included a blunt "let us get down to business" by Stalin, Roosevelt began the session by giving a lengthy discourse on the Pacific war. Shifting to Europe, he then stated that all plans and preparations for the last year and a half had revolved around the problem of relieving Russia and that OVERLORD was now planned in this regard for the spring of 1944. The pressing question at the moment was what to do in the Mediterranean to aid the Soviets. Possibilities included action in Italy, the Adriatic, the Aegean, and Turkey, but any "large expedition" would cancel OVERLORD while "certain contemplated operations" might postpone the assault one to three months. Stalin would have to decide if such efforts would be worth the postponement, though Roosevelt added his belief that OVERLORD could offer the Soviets more relief and should not be delayed by any "secondary operations."[39]

Stalin's response shocked the assembly. He welcomed Allied successes against Japan and stated that Russia would enter the Far Eastern war as soon as Germany was defeated. Hence, the Americans had immediately achieved one of their major goals. After reviewing recent developments on the Eastern front, Stalin then attacked further Mediterranean operations on the basis that they could not crack Germany. The Italian campaign would help the shipping situation, but the Alps constituted "an almost insuperable barrier" against an attack on Germany proper. Turkish entrance into the war would be "helpful" in opening the Balkans, and operations in the area would be "useful" but not decisive since the Balkans were too far from the heart of Germany. A cross-Channel assault, though difficult, was from the Soviet viewpoint "still the best" way to get at the heart.

Churchill responded by asking what the Allies were to do between the planned conquest of Rome in January and the summer of 1944. Although further Mediterranean operations might involve a two-month delay in OVER-LORD, they could lead to an Italian advance to the Pisa-Rimini line and a subsequent move into southern France or across the Adriatic while Tito was assisted and Turkey brought into the war. Turkish belligerency would in turn open the Aegean and the Dardanelles, and thus another supply route to Russia, as well as make possible an attack on Rhodes and other Aegean islands and possibly start a "landslide" in the German satellite states. Did the Soviets, Churchill asked, think such operations were worth a two- to three-month delay in OVERLORD?

Roosevelt now interjected his thoughts in regard to an operation at the head of the Adriatic to make a junction with Tito and then link up with the Russians in Rumania. He stated that such an operation, "together with a movement into Southern France," was being considered, although plans had not yet been worked out in detail. A worried Hopkins scribbled to King, "Who's promoting that Adriatic business that the President continually re-turns to?" King answered that as far as he knew it was Roosevelt's own idea.[40] Both men apparently had short memories, for in reality it was Eisen-hower's idea, backed by the JCS and expressed to the president that morn-ing as a way of fulfilling Stalin's demands for immediate action without mounting ACCOLADE or destroying OVERLORD. Furthermore, Roose-velt was doing exactly what he and the JCS had decided to do on board the *Iowa*—explain all the possible alternatives and let Stalin make his own de-cision.[41]

Churchill, however, had been invited to neither the *Iowa* meetings nor the morning conference with the JCS. Continuing to see an Italian-Adriatic operation as a way of keeping supplies in the Mediterranean so that they could be used in the Aegean, he backed the idea of moving east or west from Italy, but after the capture of Rome rather than the Po river line, thereby keeping alive his plan to invade Rhodes in February.

Before responding, Stalin asked Churchill if the Italian campaign would affect the OVERLORD divisions, if there was a plan to invade southern France, and whether the West would allocate forces to the eastern Medi-terranean if Turkey entered the war. Churchill replied that Italy would not affect the OVERLORD divisions, that a skeleton plan existed to invade southern France as a diversion to help the cross-Channel assault, and that aid was available for Turkey and the capture of the Aegean islands. Stalin then stated that the proposed Mediterranean operations appeared to have no direct connection to each other and would result in an unwise disper-sion of forces. He therefore thought it "better to take OVERLORD as the

basis for all 1944 operations," and since he was "convinced" Turkey woul
not enter the war, to use troops available after the capture of Rome for a
supporting operation in southern France.

Churchill was not prepared to give up so easily. Again he asked what
the Allies were to do for the next six months, and he reminded Stalin of
the woe Soviet propaganda had caused by stating that he and Roosevelt
were "most anxious" to continue fighting so as not to be "exposed to the
criticism that they were letting the Soviet Union bear the brunt of the wa
Stalin replied that the West should go on the defensive in Italy, attack
southern France two months before OVERLORD as a diversion to ensure
its success, and capture Rome "at a later date." Churchill objected vehemently. Failure to capture Rome in January would be a "crushing" blow.
Parliament would conclude he was not aiding the Soviets, and it would "r
longer be possible for him to represent his government."

Roosevelt had remained silent during this exchange. Now knowing wh
Stalin stood, he interjected that "nothing should be done to delay the car
rying out of OVERLORD which might be necessary if any operations in
the eastern Mediterranean were undertaken." Instead of such operations,
the staffs should immediately make a study of southern France so that ar
assault in that area could be launched "one or two months before the firs
of May and then conduct OVERLORD on the original date."

Such comments not only backed Stalin fully, but went even further in
demanding OVERLORD on time by revealing to the Soviets for the first
time its exact target date. An angry Churchill struck back at the revelatio
and the growing Russo-American front by stating that he could not leave
British forces idle in the eastern Mediterranean "merely for the purpose
of avoiding any insignificant delay in OVERLORD." Admitting that his
plans were "meaningless" if Turkey decided to remain neutral, the prime
minister still insisted on "some flexibility" in the cross-Channel target da
and suggested that the staffs look into the matter. Stalin agreed to the pr
posal, but both he and Roosevelt made clear their belief that Turkey wou
insist on staying neutral. Churchill felt the Turks would be "crazy" to ma
tain such a position, but Stalin replied that some people "apparently preferred to remain crazy." On that note the session ended.

This meeting had, in effect, determined future Allied strategy in Euro
As planned, Roosevelt had presented Stalin with all the alternatives. The
Soviet leader had chosen OVERLORD on schedule with supporting actic
in southern France, and the president had then backed him completely a
further solidified the decision by linking it to the TRIDENT target date

of May 1. Stalin's reinforcement consisted of his promise to enter the war against Japan as soon as Germany was defeated, a promise Roosevelt interpreted as a means of getting Washington to turn its undivided attention to OVERLORD.[42]

The Americans were overjoyed, but confused, for they had won all their basic points on the first day of the conference while Stalin's demands for immediate action had virtually disappeared. What they failed to realize was that the German counteroffensive, rather than reinforcing the demand for immediate help, may have actually destroyed it by ending hopes for total victory in 1943. No Western attack in the Balkans could retrieve those hopes. With the war definitely continuing into 1944, OVERLORD was once again the best supporting action.[43] Furthermore, the German counterattack meant that British and American troops might arrive in the Balkans ahead of the Red Army if Stalin backed such operations. From both military and political viewpoints, his desire for Western action in the eastern Mediterranean no longer made sense; the short flirtation had ended.

Churchill, however, still hoped Turkish entrance into the war could realize his Mediterranean plans. He also adamantly refused to sacrifice the capture of Rome for OVERLORD. Both he and the COS pushed their position again on November 29. At the meeting that morning between the CCS and Marshal Kliment Voroshilov, the Soviet military representative, Brooke reiterated Churchill's themes of the day before but once again met combined Russo-American opposition. Marshall stated that OVERLORD would be "inevitably delayed" by operations in the eastern Mediterranean, while Voroshilov bluntly asked if the CIGS viewed OVERLORD's importance as did the American army chief. Furthermore, did both men think the cross-Channel assault could be carried out, or did they feel it could be replaced by another operation if Turkey entered the war?

Brooke replied that the British had always considered OVERLORD "an essential part of this war," but that its preconditions necessitated further Mediterranean action and retention of landing craft in the Italian theater which would delay the assault. The alternative was not OVERLORD on time but total cancellation, for without the landing craft Italian operations would come to a "standstill" and the preconditions could not be met. Voroshilov refused to accept such pessimism. Again asking if Brooke considered OVERLORD to be as important as Marshall did, he stated that Stalin and the Soviet staff attached "great importance" to the cross-Channel attack and that action in the Mediterranean could only be regarded as "auxiliary." The West's "firm will and desire," coupled with strength, could solve all

problems and insure the success of an operation he claimed "would go
down in history as one of our greatest victories." Diversionary operations
were necessary, but they should be planned to assist, rather than hurt,
OVERLORD, and they should therefore consist of an invasion of southern
France. Stalin, he pointed out, did not insist on this diversion, but he did
insist on "the execution of OVERLORD on the date already planned."[44]

Stalin made this fact abundantly clear that afternoon by insisting on
the immediate appointment of a supreme commander for OVERLORD
and stating that the operation would come to nothing unless this was done
Churchill again pleaded for a delay in order to bring Turkey into the war
and start his chain reaction in the Balkans. He tried to reassure Stalin by
claiming that he had no intention of landing an army in Yugoslavia and "n
ambitious interests" in the area. But the Soviet leader remained firm. Turk
ish entrance, Yugoslav partisan activities, and even the occupation of Rom
were "not really important operations" from the Soviet viewpoint. OVER
LORD, Stalin insisted, "was the most important and nothing should be do
to distract attention from that operation." The Big Three should therefore
set a definite date for the assault, which should not be postponed, so that
the Soviets could launch an offensive in the East to coincide with it. Landings in southern France should also be undertaken, two months beforehan
if possible, with or after the assault if not, and a supreme commander ap-
pointed as soon as possible.[45]

Roosevelt again backed Stalin completely. Operations in the eastern
Mediterranean, the president maintained, did not warrant a delay in OVEF
LORD. The Allies should therefore work out plans to contain German for
in the area but "on such a scale as not to divert means from doing OVER-
LORD on the agreed time," a scale, he argued, that meant only command
raids and supplies to the guerrillas. "You are right"–"You are right," Stali
responded. With this support, Roosevelt then suggested adhering to the or
iginal May 1 target date; in no case, he insisted, should the operation be
launched after May 20.

Refusing to agree, Churchill returned to his theme of the day before by
stating that six months of inaction "would lay the British open to reproac
from the Soviets for having the Soviets bear nearly all the burden of land
fighting." Stalin replied that he was not asking the British to do "nothing.
Churchill abruptly shifted to a military argument by insisting that OVER-
LORD's preconditions could not be met unless the Germans were pressed
from all sides, and he then launched into a full defense of action in the ea
ern Mediterranean. Stalin tried to break in by sarcastically asking what th

British would do if there were thirteen rather than the maximum twelve
German divisions across the Channel. The prime minister threw the question aside, continued his verbal barrage, and suggested giving the entire landing craft question to a technical committee. When the Soviet leader hinted
his displeasure at the suggestion by asking how many more days the conference would continue, Churchill replied that he was willing to stay "for-
ever, if necessary."

With his sarcasm failing to make any impression on Churchill, Stalin
bluntly stated that committee work was not necessary, but that decisions
on a commander and date for OVERLORD as well as a supporting operation in southern France were. These matters could and should be resolved
quickly, for he would have to leave no later than December 2. Churchill
continued to press for committee work, however, and the president, apparently tiring of endless debate, appeared willing to agree. An annoyed Stalin
again stated his opposition to such a proposal and then asked Churchill "an
indiscreet question, namely, do the British really believe in OVERLORD
or are they only saying so to reassure the Russians?"

Such bluntness finally stopped Churchill, who according to one participant was "irked, to put it mildly," by the insulting inference. He "glowered,
chomped on his cigar,"[46] and replied that if the preconditions set down
at Moscow were met, "it was the duty of the British Government to hurl
every scrap of strength across the Channel." With the tension mounting,
Roosevelt suggested recessing for "a very good dinner." After more arguments on the role of committee work, his two colleagues agreed.

The cuisine may have been excellent that evening, but the prime minister was in no condition to enjoy it. While his physical condition continued to deteriorate, Stalin taunted him throughout the evening on his attitude toward OVERLORD, sarcastically stating at one point his inability
to

> understand you at all; in 1919 you were so keen to fight and now
> you don't seem to be at all. What happened? Is it advancing age?
> How many divisions do you have in contact with the enemy? What
> is happening to all those two million men you have in India?[47]

Nor were such taunts limited either to the issue of OVERLORD or to
the single voice of Stalin. The Soviet leader also accused Churchill of being
"soft" on the Germans. Roosevelt, apparently enjoying the display and
anxious to befriend Stalin, joined in the needling. When Stalin humorously

suggested shooting 50,000 German officers and Churchill objected vehemently, the president offered a "compromise" figure of 49,000. Taking the suggestions seriously, an infuriated Churchill denounced the whole idea and stalked out of the room. Stalin and Molotov had to chase after him and reassure him it was all a joke before he agreed to return to the table.[48]

Reality that evening seemed just as threatening as the jokes. Consistently supported by Roosevelt, Stalin insisted upon a harsh peace for Germany. When the prime minister asked what the Soviets desired territorially after the war, Stalin ominously replied that there was "no need to speak at the present time about any Soviet desires, but when the time comes, we will speak."[49] By evening's end, Brooke felt like "entering a lunatic asylum or a nursing-home,"[50] while Churchill warned Lord Moran that after Hitler had been defeated "there might be a more bloody war."[51]

The British could not resist the combined Soviet-American front. As Churchill stated later, he was forced to realize at Tehran what a small nation Britain was: "There I sat with the great Russian bear on one side of me, with paws outstretched, and on the other side the great American buffalo, and between the two sat the poor little English donkey who was the only one . . . who knew the right way home."[52] After the dinner, Hopkins apparently visited Churchill and convinced him of the hopelessness of his position and the wisdom of yielding with grace.[53] On the following day, which was the prime minister's sixty-ninth birthday, he formally surrendered on OVERLORD.

Before that surrender, however, the British made one more attempt to save their strategy. Although delay of OVERLORD for Mediterranean operations was now out of the question, the possibility of launching those operations by canceling BUCCANEER and shifting its landing craft still existed. The Americans would, of course, refuse to agree to such a shift, but if they and the Russians could be convinced of its necessity to insure OVERLORD and the attack on southern France (ANVIL) as well as ACCOLADE, it might alter Washington's stance.

While Churchill went to see Stalin, Brooke argued at the November 30 CCS meeting for cancellation of BUCCANEER and a one-month delay in OVERLORD so as to allow Eisenhower to take Rome in January, Rhodes in February, and southern France before the cross-Channel assault. The JCS, however, refused even to discuss cancellation of BUCCANEER and insisted that OVERLORD could be launched on May 1, even if Eisenhower retained landing craft until January 15 for the Rome assault. ANVIL, they further maintained, could be launched within present Mediterranean allocations by mounting the operation simultaneously with, rather than ahead of, the cross-Channel assault. Taking a page out of the Russian book, Leahy bluntly asked Brooke "whether he believed that the conditions laid down for OVERLORD would ever arise unless the Germans had collapsed beforehand." The CIGS replied in the affirmative, "provided the enemy were engaged on other fronts as well," a precondition which he maintained necessitated a one-month delay in OVERLORD and cancellation of BUCCANEER. Crossing the Channel on May 1 would mean no more than a RANKIN. The Russians, he added in the understatement of the conference, "would not understand the RANKIN operation if it were put to them."[54]

The JCS continued to hold firm. The COS therefore agreed to a compromise whereby Eisenhower would retain landing craft until January 15 to advance to the Pisa-Rimini line, while OVERLORD would be launched "during May" with a simultaneous ANVIL on as large a scale as permitted by the landing craft situation. Agreement on Aegean operations, the compromise held, was not possible until the CCS received "further instructions" from Roosevelt and Churchill—in other words, until the two men decided the future of BUCCANEER.[55]

Churchill had no better luck in his attempt to win Stalin's support for canceling the Southeast Asia operation. Arguing that Russia's promise to enter the war against Japan negated the need to give the Far East many landing craft and that the real choice was not OVERLORD versus the Mediterranean but OVERLORD versus BUCCANEER, the prime minister informed the Soviet leader on November 30 that cancellation of BUCCANEER would insure both Mediterranean action and an early date for the cross-Channel assault. Stalin refused to get involved in this Anglo-American dispute, which Washington insisted had no direct relationship to OVERLORD. He limited his reply to an ominous warning: if the cross-Channel attack did not materialize in May, the Red Army would conclude that no assault would take place in 1944. This conclusion would lead to "disappointment" in the Army which "could only create bad feeling. If there was no big change in the European war in 1944, it would be very difficult for the Russians to carry on. They were war-weary. He feared that a feeling of isolation might develop in the Red Army."[56]

That settled the issue, and a defeated Churchill approved the CCS agreements with Roosevelt later that morning. At lunch, Stalin expressed "great satisfaction" and promised a Russian offensive to coincide with the landings. The president in turn promised to name a commander in three to four days. These agreements were restated at the afternoon plenary session and signed on the following evening. The long debate was over. Churchill still hoped to continue action in the eastern Mediterranean by convincing Roosevelt to cancel BUCCANEER, but he now realized that Stalin would not aid him and that OVERLORD could not enter this strategic debate.[57]

The feeling of elation surrounding these agreements was obvious at Churchill's November 30 birthday dinner party. Finally surrendering with grace, the prime minister joined Roosevelt and Stalin in a series of effusive toasts in striking contrast to the insults of the previous evening. According to the minutes:

> It was clear that those present had a sense of realization that historic understanding had been reached and this conception was brought out in the statements and speeches. Back of all was the feeling that basic friendships had been established which there was every reason to believe would endure.[58]

So impressive were these statements, speeches, and feelings that they called forth one incredible display of discipline. As Stalin rose to make a toast, his waiter froze in his tracks, thereby losing his balance and inadvertently spilling an elaborate ice cream desert. The confection narrowly missed Stalin but landed directly on his interpreter, who kept on translating as if nothing had happened. The British later rewarded such conduct "under fire" by making the interpreter a commander of the Order of the British Empire.[59]

The comments of the Big Three that evening were only slightly less amusing. Churchill, the great anti-Bolshevik, toasted the "proletarian masses" of Russia and "Stalin the Great," and he even admitted that the political complexion of Britain was becoming "pinker." Stalin pointed out that this was a sign of good health, and Roosevelt picked up the metaphor to produce a vision of all political colors blending into a future rainbow while maintaining their individuality. Stalin praised American production and referred to the president and prime minister as his "fighting friends," but then added "if it is possible for me to consider Mr. Churchill my friend." According to one story, the prime minister muttered, "Yes, you may call me 'Winston' if you like—I always call you 'Joe' when you aren't there," and then raised his voice to speak on translating the great decisions reached into action. In the meantime, he warned, the Germans must be mystified and misled as to Allied intentions. Apparently intent upon getting in the last crack, Stalin thereupon remarked audibly, "That's all right, so long as one of your mysteries is not the Second Front."[60]

Such asides could not detract from the overall atmosphere of elation and goodwill, and no one was more pleased than the president. From his point of view, this dinner was the culmination of all his efforts in the fields of strategy and diplomacy. As he had planned in early 1942, the second front had become not only the primary Anglo-American operation in Europe, but also the basis of understanding and collaboration with the Soviet Union. Furthermore, agreement to launch that operation had been achieved only because of Stalin's strong stand, and the Americans were impressed as well as elated. Marshall wired Stimson that the agreements reached had been "unexpectedly favorable,"[61] while McCloy informed the secretary of Stalin's key role in the victory. The conference minutes, he stated, gave the impression "that Marshal Stimson was talking and not Marshal Stalin."[62]

Some Americans were a bit less sanguine. Bohlen, for one, realized that the time for military agreements replacing political ones had long since passed, if in fact it had ever existed. Two months earlier, he had stated that the "basic question" in regard to cooperation with the USSR was not a second front, but "whether we have prepared to abandon certain traditional American principles in regard to territorial adjustments on a power politics basis in the hope of obtaining real cooperation from the Soviet Government in the post-war world."[63]

Roosevelt had tried to avoid this question in 1942 with a second front, and he might have succeeded had the operation been launched at that time. By 1944, however, the cross-Channel assault would no longer save Russia but would simply quicken the defeat of Germany and relieve some of the pressure on the Eastern front. In no sense would the Soviets again view the operation as a substitute for political and territorial agreements. Furthermore, the ensuing delay in reaching final agreement on the assault had increased Russian suspicions.

Yet, Roosevelt persisted in acting as if Tehran was taking place in the spring of 1942. He avoided any hard political discussions at the conference, and with the exception of Polish boundaries, all political issues were swept under the Persian rugs. He did not even bother to bring up the crucial issue of postwar reconstruction aid, informing Harriman on December 1 that he was "sorry I did not get the time to talk with the Russians about the whole question."[64] This attitude meant that the agreements reached were only the military preliminaries to the real issues.

Few of the Americans at Tehran were willing to face this unpleasant fact in their hour of triumph. Some, however, did recognize the contradictions and weaknesses inherent in a victory based on second-front diplomacy When Bohlen on December 2 warned Hopkins and Leahy of probable Soviet territorial aims in Europe, the admiral turned to the presidential adviser with a "sardonic smile" and replied, "Well, Harry, all I can say is, nice friend we have now."[65]

CHAPTER ELEVEN

AFTERMATH, SUMMARY AND CONCLUSIONS

DECEMBER 1943 TO AUGUST 1944

The second-front issue properly ends not with the Normandy invasion but with the Tehran agreements, for by those accords, OVERLORD became politically sacrosanct. Barring a major Allied catastrophe or a German collapse, nothing would be allowed to interfere with the timing of the cross-Channel assault. Nevertheless, the second-front controversy had become inextricably linked to a host of military and political issues which continued far into 1944.

Roosevelt, Churchill, and the CCS continued to meet in Cairo after Tehran in order to clear up loose ends of Allied strategy. Fearing the loss of Marshall from Washington and worried about the domestic political controversy already brewing over his possible shift to OVERLORD command,[1] Roosevelt decided at Cairo to appoint Eisenhower to command the cross-Channel assault. General Wilson took over the new, unified Mediterranean command, and General Alexander was placed in charge of the Italian theater.

Meanwhile, Churchill pressed for cancellation of BUCCANEER and further Mediterranean action on the grounds that the Southeast Asia operation would delay OVERLORD and ANVIL and that Stalin's promise to enter the Pacific war negated its importance. Privately, however, he told Lord Moran that Alexander "may be our last hope. We've got to do something about these bloody Russians," who he warned the CCS on December 7, "breed like flies."[2] Mountbatten's simultaneous insistence on additional landing craft to launch BUCCANEER persuaded Roosevelt to agree to its cancellation and transfer of its landing craft to the Mediterranean, where Churchill hoped to use them in the Aegean before they would be needed for ANVIL.

Such a plan depended upon prior Turkish entry into the war and conquest of Rome in January. Neither prerequisite materialized. At Cairo Churchill "pleaded, cajoled, and almost threatened" the Turks, according to Leahy, but to no avail.[3] In addition, the Italian campaign remained deadlocked, and Churchill soon decided on the need for an amphibious assault behind the German lines in order to break the stalemate. But such an assault would further delay return of landing craft to OVERLORD and totally destroy the possibility of mounting ACCOLADE. Moreover, the attack plan was dated and dangerous, and had already been rejected by the Mediterranean commanders.

Undaunted by these facts and intent upon getting to Rome and the Balkans, Churchill pleaded with Roosevelt for a three-week delay in the transfer of landing craft in order to launch an amphibious assault behind the German lines at Anzio (SHINGLE), stating that it would not postpone OVERLORD and that he was willing to cancel ACCOLADE. As an alternative to the Rhodes assault, he now hoped to advance up the Italian leg and then move into Yugoslavia and Austria. Since he did not communicate this part of his plan to Washington, the Americans agreed to the landing craft transfer delay and SHINGLE on the condition that ACCOLADE was out of the question and nothing would allow postponement of OVERLORD or ANVIL.

While Churchill had thus solved the first two problems involved in the Anzio attack, he could not come up with a successful solution to the third one. By sheer force of personality, he had been able to convince the Mediterranean commanders, against their better judgment, to launch SHINGLE in January, but his powers of persuasion did not affect the Germans, who came dangerously close to pushing the beachhead back into the sea. Desperate Allied defense efforts succeeded, but at the cost of making Anzio the fourth largest port in the world and thus causing postponements everywhere else.[4]

Ironically, this massive effort did absolutely nothing to break the Italian stalemate. The COS therefore decided that further offensives in Italy were necessary. To prevent delay in OVERLORD, they recommended cancellation of ANVIL and use of its resources as well as those in the Pacific for an assault on Rome. Washington objected to cancellation of a south ern France assault which it saw as a crucial aid to OVERLORD, a promise to the Russians, and a way of preventing any Western descent into the Balkans. The JCS therefore refused to allocate Pacific forces for an attack on Rome unless a delayed ANVIL remained on the timetable.

Brooke considered this position militarily stupid and politically immoral, referring to it as "blackmail" which London would never forgive.[5] But he realized that America's demand was based on her growing preponderance within the Alliance which he could no longer fight. Churchill, however, refused to give up. With his military options rapidly disappearing, the Russian menace increasing, and his pride wounded over the Anzio failure and America's growing preponderance, he remained determined to gain both a British victory in Italy and a subsequent move into the Balkans. He thus began a massive campaign to replace ANVIL with a move through the Ljubljana gap. But Washington refused to budge, and by July Churchill at last had to accept defeat, though this time without the grace exhibited at Tehran. He renamed the attack on southern France DRAGOON, perhaps to reflect his own feelings on being roped into the operation, and fought it up until the very day it was launched in mid-August 1944.[6]

As early as the spring, Churchill had faced the possibility of defeat on ANVIL and had begun to pursue his goals on a political as well as a military level. Unwilling to acquiesce "in the Cummunisation of the Balkans and perhaps of Italy," he decided to settle the issue directly with the Soviets in May by offering them the "lead" in Rumania for the duration of the war in return for a British "lead" in Greece. The Russians agreed, and in October the prime minister made his second trip to Moscow to formalize the arrangement and broaden it to include the entire Balkan area. Two months later, he used the accord to land British troops in Greece and restore the king at bayonet-point; Stalin refused to intervene when severe fighting ensued.[7]

Such Soviet quiescence seemed to be a logical continuation of the improved atmosphere within the Grand Alliance which had followed the Tehran agreements on OVERLORD. The invasion itself produced a flood of congratulatory telegrams from the Russians, with Stalin describing the operation as "an unheard of achievement, the magnitude of which had never been undertaken in the history of warfare."[8] Churchill later wrote that at this juncture in the war "harmony was complete."[9]

Unfortunately, this was far from the case. Stalin's private musings were in sharp contrast to his congratulatory messages and showed that the two-

year delay in crossing the Channel had only increased his suspicions of the
West. On the evening of June 5, he expressed his displeasure and mistrust
to Yugoslav leader Milovan Djilas:

> Perhaps you think just because we are the allies of the English
> that we have forgotten who they are and who Churchill is. They
> find nothing sweeter than to trick their allies. During the First
> World War they constantly tricked the Russians and the French.
> And Churchill? Churchill is the kind who, if you don't watch
> him, will slip a kopeck out of your pocket. Yes, a kopeck out
> of your pocket! By God, a kopeck out of your pocket! And
> Roosevelt? Roosevelt is not like that. He dips in his hand only
> for bigger coins. But Churchill? Churchill—even for a kopeck.

When Stalin received a telegram from Churchill later in the evening announc-
ing that OVERLORD would begin on the following morning, he sneered
that a landing would take place "if there is no fog. Until now there was
always something that interfered. I suspect tomorrow it will be something
else. Maybe they'll meet up with some Germans! What if they meet up with
some Germans! Maybe there won't be a landing then, but just promises as
usual."[10]
    While such feelings were not revealed to the West, Stalin's actions during
the first half of 1944, especially in Eastern Europe, demonstrated both his
mistrust and goals. The Polish issue, rather than OVERLORD, dominated
Big Three correspondence, and Stalin's adamancy and sharp words soon
turned Western elation over Tehran into apprehension. As early as January
17, Cadogan was referring to the Russians as "swine" and "the most stink-
ing creepy set of Jews I've ever come across."[11] Within a few months of
this statement, Harriman and members of the State Department had become "increasingly concerned" over Soviet moves and soon concluded that
Lend-Lease aid should be used to bring the Soviets back into line.[12] Deane
felt the time had come to reverse "our soft attitude toward Russia."[13]
Even Hull concluded in April that "the tide of Moscow and Teheran" had
ebbed; it was time, he stated, for a "very plain-spoken approach" to Stalin.
    The change in atmosphere in 1944 even affected retrospective analyses
of Russian aims in demanding a second front. In October 1943, Edward
Stettinius of the State Department had brought to Hull's attention a col-
umn in which Walter Lippmann pointed out that Soviet insistence on the

cross-Channel assault showed that Moscow was not interested in dominating Europe, for "you do not invite in an army of a million men if you do not wish to cooperate with the Governments which sent in the army."[15] But by September 1944, George F. Kennan in the Moscow Embassy was writing that Soviet insistence on a second front had been nothing more than a demand for the military prerequisite to Russian expansion after the war. With the invasion accomplished, he said, Stalin was now showing his true colors.[16]

Stimson and Marshall carefully took note of the growing Russian truculence as a sign that a separate peace or inaction on the Eastern front was once more a possibility. Stimson thus continued to press for overwhelming American force in Europe,[17] while Marshall told Roosevelt on March 31 that Lend-Lease was the American "trump card in dealing with [the] U.S.S.R. and its control is possibly the most effective means we have to keep the Soviets on the offensive in connection with the second front."[18]

Other military planners carried their analyses into the purely political realm. In an interesting reversal of position, some OPD members concluded in April that the United States should take an interest in Balkan affairs and oppose Russian moves in the area, for "acknowledgement of the Soviets' hegemony over the Balkans can easily result in a lowering of United States prestige with the U.S.S.R. and an inability to back British interests in the area, even though it might be to our advantage to do so."[19] At the same time, a member of the British Foreign Office informed his superiors that Americans, "particularly in military circles, were saying that their army would be useful in time to fight the Russians."[20]

In line with such thinking, many of the planners joined State Department officials before the invasion was launched in questioning the "no strings" aid policy of the United States toward the Soviets and in pleading with Roosevelt, on both political and military grounds, for modification of the unconditional surrender policy.[21] But the pleas fell on deaf ears. Continuing to believe in the "spirit of Tehran" and the idea that Stalin was "getatable," Roosevelt refused to alter his previous decisions. Moreover, in a strange irony, the mistrust of British motives that the military had helped instill in him now reached its peak and prevented the president from taking any action to block Soviet moves. Rather than modify unconditional surrender or establish a tougher Lend-Lease policy, Roosevelt expended most of his efforts in an attempt to get the northwestern occupation zone of Germany, despite the almost-unanimous opinion of his advisers that the issue was rather meaningless. This obsession not only dominated his time and thoughts, but also paralyzed the European Advisory Commission in London and prevented any effective decisions from being reached until September 1944, when Roosevelt finally accepted the southwestern zone.[22]

In the face of direct presidential orders, the planners could not and would not push their foreign policy ideas, but this did not mean that they ceased to interest themselves in foreign policy. On the contrary, the second-front controversy had highlighted for them in bold relief the inseparability of political and military affairs, and they continued to prepare papers on political subjects. By September 1944, the military had delved into the postwar issues of Soviet-American relations, the "proper" role of the European Advisory Commission in postwar planning, territorial trusteeships and settlements, aircraft markets, and the inhibiting effect of spheres of influence on American manufacturers in Europe. In early 1945, one OPD member stated what had by then become the obvious: "The time has come when, whether we like it or not, the War Department must face the fact that it has a real interest in political matters of varying categories."[23]

* * *

The second-front issue was basically a political controversy within the Grand Alliance based on differing national conceptions of the proper way to defeat the Axis. These conceptions were in turn products of the histories, interests, and immediate positions of each member of the Alliance. London, Moscow, and Washington all perceived the war from their own vantage point and generalized their particular positions into concepts of the only "proper" way to win. Each viewpoint was thus as incorrect for an ally as it was correct for the nation propounding it. The result was a politico-military conflict that became the basic theme of Allied diplomacy through 1943.

Army planners in Washington developed the second-front concept as a way of winning the war on American, rather than British, terms. They defined those terms through a host of politico-military factors that represented a generalization of Army into national as well as national into Allied interests. While their position seemed to rest on the military need to achieve concentration and aid Russia in order to gain a quick and decisive victory, these needs were highly political.

Britain's peripheral approach through the Mediterranean, designed to minimize casualties and place troops in areas of imperial interest, would take longer to defeat Germany than a massive cross-Channel assault. The American Navy and public, insistent upon revenge against Japan, would not countenance such a dilatory approach and would demand further action in the Pacific, perhaps to the extent of overthrowing the Germany-first strategy. Such a move would not only imperil final victory, but would also replace Army influence in the White House with that of the Navy. From the War Department's viewpoint, the Mediterranean approach had already succeeded in replacing its influence with that of Churchill, thus creating this series of problems in the first place. Furthermore, continued dispersion of forces in either the Mediterranean or Pacific would destroy both Army power in Washington and American power within the Grand Alliance.

The necessity to aid Russia through a second front was based not only on the military situation, but also on the fact that Moscow had made the operation a political prerequisite for continued participation in the war. That participation was in turn mandatory in order to successfully launch the cross-Channel attack and maintain the Germany-first approach. Moreover, Russia's aid would be needed in the Pacific, and Stalin would eventually supply such aid only if he were given equivalent help against Germany.

While agreeing to the Army plan, Roosevelt perceived it as providing an immediate as well as a decisive front in Europe. Besides keeping Russia in the war, such immediate action would enable him to counter the Pacific thrust in American thought and mollify the offensive demands of the American public, thus silencing his critics and protecting his own political position. It would also allow him to take the lead in Allied diplomacy and define the alliance on American terms by offering Stalin a second front in return for an end to Russian demands for recognition of the 1939-1940 conquests in Eastern Europe.

Such an approach to foreign and domestic problems suffered from numerous deficiencies. The Army had developed the 1942 assault as an emergency operation in case disaster threatened on the Eastern front and as a method of forcing concentration for the massive 1943 assault. The 1942 operation was thus too small to fulfill Russian needs and too risky to guarantee the victory Roosevelt needed for domestic purposes. Furthermore, it depended upon British troops, and London was totally unwilling to risk another Dunkirk.

Most of these facts were known to all three partners. Yet, each ignored them in hopes of achieving specific aims. London agreed to the 1942 plan in order to prevent an American shift to the Pacific, but from the beginning had absolutely no intention of launching the operation. Despite strong hint of the true British position, Roosevelt promised the Russians a 1942 second front on a scale that was logistically impossible in return for a nonterritoria treaty. The Soviets demanded such a promise from him, although they kne London would have to supply the forces and would not agree to such a sacrifice. Churchill then played on Roosevelt's need for a 1942 victory in Europe so that the British could replace the cross-Channel attack with an invasion of North Africa. This switch in turn virtually destroyed the possibility of any second front until 1944.

In the short run, this series of deceptions produced benefits for all three countries. Roosevelt gained his nonterritorial treaty and 1942 action in Europe for domestic political purposes; London kept American forces in Europe and operations centered in the Mediterranean; and the Soviets received a "promise" they could show their war-weary people and perhaps use as a bargaining point in later Allied negotiations. In the long run, the deceptions proved disastrous, however. The political necessity for 1942 action, coupled with the British refusal to cross the Channel that year, led to a two-year delay in the second front and a slowing down of Western aid to Russia. Together with the nonterritorial treaty, this meant that Stalin had been denied everything he had demanded from his allies at the most critical juncture of the war. His suspicions of the West were increased by this "second-front diplomacy," rather than decreased as the Americans had hoped, and his reaction precipitated a diplomatic crisis within the Grand Alliance. The wounds engendered by this conflict never fully disappeared.

The episode also split the American military services, hardened the plan ners' beliefs regarding British motives and their inherent danger to American interests, and forced the military to further recognize the inseparability of political and strategic issues. As a result, in late 1942 and 1943 the planners began to delve deeply into the political aspects of strategy-making in order to convince the president of the validity of their views and to defeat the British in combined staff discussions. Those discussions increasingl resembled battles rather than conferences between allies.

The planners had long recognized the inseparability of political and military issues, but they had always felt that the political leadership of the country should play the key role in defining the relationship between the two. Roosevelt refused to give such a definition beyond unconditional surrender, and he appeared to be under British influence to a dangerous extent. As a result, the planners insisted on a greater role for themselves in defining the political and military aspects of national goals. By mid-1943, they had evolved a statement of these goals as well as those of Britain and Russia, the relationship of strategy to national aims, and the necessity of a second front to accomplish American desires. In the process, they called upon the State Department and the OSS for political advice and achieved a degree of unofficial liaison with these two services. At the same time, the military improved its own coordination through the JCS and joint committees, planned combined staff conversations on a political basis, and increased its influence with the White House.

The planners' basic conclusion was that London's Mediterranean strategy was a reflection of British political interests and ran counter to American interests as defined during the 1942 debate. In 1943, however, new political interests were added to these old ones. Most important was the fear now expressed, often in terms quite similar to Kennan's 1947 "Containment" theory, over the combination of Russian victories and diplomatic truculence resulting from the postponement of the second front. This combination seemed to threaten either a separate peace or Soviet domination of the peace conference and postwar Europe.

According to the planners, the only way to avoid this menace without negating either unconditional surrender or the goals expressed in 1942 was to establish a second front. The Soviets had demanded such an operation in return for continued cooperation both during and after the war. Furthermore, only a second front could enable the West to land enough troops in Europe to give it an effective bargaining position at the peace conference and block any Soviet attempts to dominate Europe without alienating Moscow before the war ended. An approach via the Balkans would immediately alienate the Russians and was logistically incapable of defeating either them or the Germans. In short, the planners perceived the second front as an "umbrella" policy, capable of fulfilling all American goals and handling any future possibility with the Soviets. British Mediterranean strategy was rejected not because it was political, but because it was logistically unfeasible and attempted to fulfill British goals at the expense of those of the United States.

Roosevelt's military advisers stressed these points in their conversations with him, and by mid-1943 the president was in complete accord with them. During that entire year, his degree of support for the cross-Channel assault increased as the Red armies moved westward and Soviet-American relations deteriorated. Stalin had already told him that any future cooperation hinged on this operation. His advisers reinforced this point as well as the fact that only a second front could block Soviet domination of the peace conference and Europe.

The results of this united American front were the TRIDENT and QUAD RANT decisions on Operations OVERLORD and RANKIN, the successors to the original ROUNDUP and SLEDGEHAMMER projects in 1942. RANKIN, however, was a good deal more political than its predecessor. It had little military value, and it was basically designed to get Western forces onto the continent rapidly if Germany collapsed before OVERLORD could be launched. Not the least of the reasons for such a plan was the desire to prevent Russian domination of the peace conference and Europe.

RANKIN was, of course, never communicated to the Soviets. OVERLORD was, and it led to a great improvement in relations between the USSR and the West, culminating in the Moscow Foreign Ministers' Conference and the promise of a future Big Three meeting. The Soviets again made clear, however, that future cooperation depended upon a successful OVERLORD.

London now attempted to postpone the cross-Channel assault once more so that further operations could be launched in the Mediterranean. In an ironic twist, the Soviets backed this proposal. The worried Americans decided to explain their position to Moscow. They realized, however, that cooperation was the key goal and, if the Soviets insisted, OVERLORD would have to be delayed or canceled.

The final decision on the second front at Tehran was thus arranged not as a military decision, but as a political one to be made totally within the context of Allied diplomatic relations. Ironically, Stalin would determine future Anglo-American strategy. But before the conference opened Roosevelt moved to protect American interests, in case the Soviets sided with the British, by insisting on Far Eastern action to aid China and on a RANKIN plan to get American forces into Berlin. Stalin, however, backed the American position fully at Tehran, and the British were overruled. Roosevelt, still thinking in terms of 1942, saw this agreement as the foundation for all future cooperation. He never did realize the changes in the situation caused by the two-year delay, nor did he understand that a 1944 second front could not be the all-encompassing politico-military operation he had hoped the 1942 assault would be. Hard political compromises were now necessary. Unfortunately, they were not forthcoming.

The findings developed in this study contradict many popular assumptions regarding the second front and American advocacy of that operation. From its very inception, the cross-Channel controversy was heavily involved in political issues and was a basic factor in the origins of the Cold War. Furthermore, both President Roosevelt and his military planners were well aware of the political factors involved and acted accordingly. In retrospect, the American plan appears more realistic on both military and political levels than Britain's approach.

While historians have recognized the crucial importance of the second-front controversy in the coming of the Cold War, most of them still maintain that the planners, and perhaps the president, were naive regarding the political aspects of this operation. Such conclusions appear to stem from two basic facts: the nature of the documents involved and the questions historians have asked relating to politics and strategy.

World War II records are so enormous that no individual historian can read all of them. Consequently, each historian writing on this period has concentrated on a specific set of documents. Studies based on such examinations have been extremely valuable, and this work has relied heavily upon many of them. Such concentration, however, can easily lead to a distorted view of the entire picture. Certain Army records, for example, show that logistical problems were the basic factors in delaying and modifying the cross-Channel assault. But such a conclusion ignores the fact that many of these logistical problems were caused by earlier political decisions. TORCH is a prime example.

Furthermore, the documents themselves do not tell the entire story. Roosevelt's statements (or lack thereof), if taken literally, would lead one to the conclusion that the president was a political and strategic moron. Yet, his political wisdom is famous, and as an ex-Navy man, he was well aware of Mahanite principles regarding the link between strategy and politics. One of the problems here stems from the fact that Roosevelt's goals, by his very position as the chief of state, were broader than and often different from those of his advisers. Although these advisers theoretically realized this fact, they as well as later historians reached the erroneous conclusion that Roosevelt was either ignorant of strategic and political realities or naively under the influence of Churchill.

Neither judgment is correct. Roosevelt was usually very consistent, and his few inconsistencies were the result more of the contradictory nature of his many goals than of any ignorance of the realities of the situation. Roosevelt may have been indulging in wishful thinking, for example, in his belief that the Soviets would accept TORCH as an effective second fron But since a true second front was impossible for 1942 and his political goal demanded some offensive action, he was forced to hope that the North African assault could accomplish everything the defunct cross-Channel attack would have achieved.

Another key problem regarding Roosevelt and the documentation available is his notorious insistence upon secrecy. Throughout his White House career, Roosevelt refused to divulge his innermost thoughts to the men around him. By his standards, only the president should weigh all the facto involved in a decision, and no one, future historians included, should know how he reached such a decision. Nor was Roosevelt above the temptation of distorting the record for the sake of his future reputation, as is clearly shown by his desire to expunge the 1942 record of all references to the Pacific alternative. Even more revealing of his secretiveness was his 1943 com ment to Cordell Hull that the notes of conversations between Wilson, Lloy George, and Clemenceau should never have been written.[24] Had the president been able to have his way, there probably would have been no official record of the Tehran Conference.

Such secretiveness is in no way ignorance. Roosevelt's refusal to inform his advisers of his political goals beyond unconditional surrender may have been a grave error which led the military into political discussions, but that is not equivalent to a total ignorance of or refusal to deal with political goa His actions and statements during the war clearly show that those goals we constantly on his mind.

The situation is similar in regard to the planners on both sides of the Atlantic. Because of their beliefs and training, these men seldom set down their political thoughts in official documents. Historians reading these documents have thus concluded that the American planners ignored political factors. Furthermore, since British strategic papers show no strong politica desire either to enter the eastern Mediterranean or to cancel OVERLORD, Washington's stated beliefs in this regard appear to be figments of paranoid imaginations rather than reflections of the facts. Again, one must realize that the official documents do not tell the entire story. In their memoirs and unofficial correspondence, the planners expressed their concern with political factors, and this concern sometimes did spill onto official papers.

Some unguarded British comments even suggest that the American suspicions were correct.[25]

Furthermore, even the political leadership often discussed political matters on purely military grounds because of the standards of the times. According to Eisenhower, Churchill once argued for a change in strategy on military grounds for seven straight hours, although both men knew the rationale for such a change was political. Since military men were not supposed to consider these issues, and since the Americans had carefully kept such issues out of their official statements, Churchill apparently concluded that he would be on safer ground if he stuck to military arguments with Eisenhower. The American commander quickly realized this, informed Churchill of his knowledge as to the real situation, and suggested he discuss the issue with Roosevelt on political grounds if he desired a change in strategic plans.[26]

The second key problem centers on the questions historians have asked regarding the relationship between strategy and politics. Most have searched for a "right" versus a "wrong" approach to strategy and have often based their conclusions on statements of "military" versus "political" factors. Both dichotomies are artificial. The key question here is not right or wrong, but right or wrong for *whom*; the missing factor is the *merging* of the political and military aspects of an issue into a truly grand strategic design. Churchill's primary motive for pushing Aegean operations in the fall of 1943 was not his fear of communism in the area. However, this was definitely *one* of the factors in his mind, and he merged it with his other desires—the indirect approach to victory, low casualties, a purely British victory, proving his World War I ideas correct, and placing British troops in areas of great imperial interest—into a grand strategic design. As he himself stated later, "It is not possible in a major war to divide military from political affairs. At the summit they are one."[27] The American planners wholeheartedly agreed with such a judgment and planned accordingly. Ironically, future historians, and not the characters themselves, created this artificial split.

In later years, American planners spoke out sharply against the growing belief in their political naivete during the war. General Marshall in particular pointed out that, with the exception of the landing craft shortage, nothing "came to out minds more frequently than the political factors."[28] Dean Acheson, who worked under Marshall in the State Department during the postwar era, often discussed this point with the general and later concluded that when Marshall thought about military problems, "non-military factors played a controlling part." In fact, Marshall's explanation and knowledge of the complex political and military factors involved in the second-front controversy convinced Acheson of the brilliance of the man considered by many to have been America's greatest soldier.[29] One might also add that such knowledge enabled Marshall to become secretary of state. He, along with his advisers and JCS colleagues, learned a valuable lesson during the war in the inseparability of political and military factors.[30] Hence, within the second-front controversy may lie one of the origins of military influence in the formulation of post-World War II foreigh policy.

If one disagrees with that foreign policy, then one may conclude that Roosevelt's greatest failing as a war leader was his unwillingness to share his political thoughts with his advisers. Yet from a larger vantage point, his very ability to perceive the link between strategy and politics, and to act accordingly, proved his greatest failing. This ability, shared by the other two heads of state and the different advisers, meant that no one within the Grand Alliance was capable of viewing the war, politically or militarily, frc an *Allied* rather than a national perspective. Such a broad outlook was beyond the power of men trained in terms of national interest and facing the supreme threat to the very existence of their countries. While this situatio may appear natural, or even inevitable, it set definite limits to the cooperation possible within the alliance both during and after the war. Common danger may bring nations together, but the desire to survive as a national entity means that the cooperation stops far short of its desired goals.

In World War II, those goals included future international cooperation. Men hoped that the second front and the alliance as a whole would bring the anti-Axis nations together and further the idea of internationalism in the process of defeating the enemy. The merging of strategy and politics did the exact opposite by reinforcing national desires and suspicions, and thus future rivalries. No one during the war wanted this to happen, but no one proved capable of breaking through established national thought patterns to prevent it. No national leader has to this very day.

APPENDIX ONE

ABBREVIATIONS

AAF	Army Air Forces
ABC	American-British Conversations
ACofS	Assistant Chief of Staff, U.S. Army
AGWAR	Adjutant General, War Department
AMSME	American Military Mission, Middle East
App.	Appendix
CAD	Civil Affairs Division, U.S. Army General Staff
CCS	Combined Chiefs of Staff
CF	Conference File
CIGS	Chief of the Imperial General Staff
CM-IN	Incoming Message to War Department
CM-OUT	Outgoing Message from War Department
CNO	Chief of Naval Operations, U.S. Navy
CofS	Chief of Staff, U.S. Army
Col.	Colonel
Comm.	Committee
Conf.	Conference
Corres.	Correspondence
COS	British Chiefs of Staff
COSSAC	Chief of Staff, Supreme Allied Commander (designate) and staff
CPS	Combined Planning Staff
Dept.	Department

Disp.	Dispatch
Diss.	Dissertation
Div.	Division
DS	Department of State Records, National Archives
ETO	European Theater of Operations, U.S. Army
EW	European War
Exec.	Executive
FDRL	Franklin D. Roosevelt Library, Hyde Park, N.Y.
F.R.	U.S. Department of State *Foreign Relations* series
G-2	Intelligence Division, U.S. Army General Staff
JCS	Joint Chiefs of Staff
JIC	Joint Intelligence Committee
JPC	Joint Planning Committee
JPS	Joint Planning Staff
JPWC	Joint Psychological Warfare Committee
JSSC	Joint Strategic Survey Committee
JUSSC	Joint U.S. Strategic Committee
JWPC	Joint War Plans Committee
Ltr.	Letter
LOC	Library of Congress
Memo	Memorandum
Min.	Minutes
MM	Modern Military Records, National Archives
MRF	Map Room File
Mtg.	Meeting
N.	Note
NH	Naval History Division, Department of the Navy
OCMH	Office of the Chief of Military History, Department of the Army
OF	Official File
OPD	Operations Division, U.S. Army General Staff
OSS	Office of Strategic Services
PPF	President's Personal File
Pres.	President
PSF	President's Secretary's File
Pt.	Part
RG	Record Group, National Archives
Rpt.	Report

S & P	Strategy and Policy Group, OPD
Sec.	Section
SF	Subject File
SN	Secretary of the Navy
SOF	Special Official File
Sp.	Special
SS	Strategy Section, S & P, OPD
Supp.	Supplementary
SW	Secretary of War
Tel.	Telegram
Unpub.	Unpublished
WDCSA	War Department Chief of Staff Army
WPD	War Plans Division, U.S. Army General Staff

CODE NAMES

ACCOLADE	Plan for 1943-1944 capture of Rhodes.
ANVIL	Plan for invasion of southern France in conjunction with a 1944 cross-Channel assault.
ARCADIA	Anglo-American conference in Washington, December 1941 to January 1942.
BOLERO	Plan for a 1942-1943 buildup of forces in United Kingdom in preparation for a cross-Channel assault.
BUCCANEER	Plan for 1944 amphibious assault in Bay of Bengal.
CRUSADER	Plan for 1941 British offensive in Libya.
DRAGOON	Plan for invasion of southern France to follow 1944 cross-Channel assault.
EUREKA	Anglo-American-Soviet conference in Tehran, November 1943.
GYMNAST	Plan for 1941-1942 invasion of North Africa.
HADRIAN	Plan for August 1943 cross-Channel assault.
HUSKY	Plan for 1943 invasion of Sicily.
JUPITER	Plan for 1942-1944 invasion of Norway.
MAGNET	Plan for 1941-1942 replacement of British troops in Ireland by American troops.
OVERLORD	Revised plan for 1944 cross-Channel assault.
QUADRANT	Anglo-American conference at Quebec, August 1943.

RANKIN	Plan for reentry onto continent in late 1943 or early 1944 in case of German weakening or collapse before OVERLORD.
ROUNDHAMMER	Plan for 1944 cross-Channel assault.
ROUNDUP	Plan for 1943 cross-Channel assault.
SEXTANT	Anglo-American and Anglo-American/Chinese conferences at Cairo, November to December 1943.
SHINGLE	Plan for 1944 assault at Anzio, Italy.
SLEDGEHAMMER	Plan for 1942 emergency cross-Channel assault.
SYMBOL	Anglo-American conference at Casablanca, January 1943.
TORCH	Revised plan for 1942 invasion of North Africa.
TRIDENT	Anglo-American conference at Washington, May 1943.
VELVET	Plan for 1942 for sending an Anglo-American Air Force to the Caucasus.
WHIPCORD	Plan for 1941-1942 invasion of Sicily.

NOTES

PREFACE NOTES

1. See Hanson W. Baldwin, *Great Mistakes of the War* (1948); Chester Wilmot, *The Struggle for Europe* (1952).

EPIGRAPH

1. Winston S. Churchill, *The Second World War,* vol. 3, *The Grand Alliance* (1950), p. 28.
2. Albert C. Wedemeyer, *Wedemeyer Reports!* (1958), p. 81.
3. Forrest C. Pogue, *George C. Marshall,* vol. 3, *Organizer of Victory* (1973), p. 315.
4. Dean Acheson, *Sketches From Life of Men I Have Known* (1959), pp. 163-64.

CHAPTER 1: PRELUDE TO CONTROVERSY

1. Michael Howard, *The Mediterranean Strategy in the Second World War* (1968), pp. 1-18, and "The Mediterranean in British Strategy in the Second World War," in *Studies in War and Peace* (1972), pp. 122-26.
2. Trumbull Higgins, *Winston Churchill and the Second Front* (1957), pp. 29-58, and *Soft Underbelly* (1968), pp. 1-22.
3. Howard, *The Mediterranean Strategy,* pp. 1-18.

4. Stetson Conn and Byron Fairchild, *The Framework of Hemispheric Defense* (1960), pp. 65-67, 83-84, 113-15; Robert Sherwood, *Roosevelt and Hopkins* (1950), pp. 11, 296-98; Richard W. Steele, *The First Offensive, 1942* (1973), pp. 6-15.

5. Conn and Fairchild, *Hemispheric Defense,* pp. 119-25.

6. Maurice Matloff and Edwin M. Snell, *Strategic Planning for Coalition Warfare, 1941-1942* (1953), pp. 29-30.

7. Ray S. Cline, *Washington Command Post* (1951), p. 44.

8. Fred Greene, "The Military View of American National Policy, 190 1940," *American Historical Review* 66 (Jan. 1961): 354-77.

9. Memo, CNO to SN, Nov. 12, 1940, MM, RG 165, WPD 4175-15.

10. Matloff and Snell, *Strategic Planning, 1941-1942,* pp. 15-17, 21.

11. Ibid., pp. 13-14; Forrest C. Pogue, *George C. Marshall,* vol. 2, *Ordeal and Hope* (1966), pp. 76-78; Theodore A. Wilson, *The First Summit* (1969), pp. 132-35.

12. Memo, CNO to SN, Nov 12, 1940, MM, WPD 4175-15.

13. Memo, WPD to ACofS, WPD, "Staff Conversations with British," Jan. 1941, MM, RG 165, OPD Exec. 4, Item 11; see also memo, Col. J. W. Anderson, Acting ACofS, "National Policy of the United States," Nov. 13 1940, MM, WPD 4175-15.

14. This was part of a larger accord (ABC-1) to concentrate on defeating Germany first if both powers found themselves at war with Berlin and To see 79th Cong., 1st sess., *Hearings Before the Joint Committee on the Investigation of the Pearl Harbor Attack* (1946), Pt. 15, Exhibit 49, pp. 1-1550.

15. See memos cited in n. 13.

16. OPD Diary, June 19, 1941, MM, OPD Exec. 10, Item 11, Tab A; Steele, *The First Offensive,* pp. 16-18.

17. Sherwood, *Roosevelt and Hopkins,* pp. 314-15; Winston S. Churchi *The Second World War,* vol. 3, *The Grand Alliance* (1950), pp. 424-25; Si John Kennedy, *The Business of War* (1957), p. 153. Full min. of July 24 mtg. in Tracy Kittredge, "U.S.-British Naval Cooperation, 1940-1945" (unpub. and unfinished manuscript), Sec. V., Pt. A, pp. 518-25, and App. pp. 349-56, in NH.

18. Sherwood, *Roosevelt and Hopkins,* pp. 315-18.

19. Wilson, *The First Summit,* pp. 125-54.

20. Ibid.

21. All memos in MM, WPD 4402-64; see also Albert C. Wedemeyer, *Wedemeyer Reports!* (1958), pp. 442-45.

22. Reprinted in Kittredge, "U.S.-British Naval Cooperation," Sec. V, Pt. B, App. A.

23. Roosevelt to Stimson and Knox, July 9, 1941, Franklin D. Roosevelt Papers, PSF, Box 40, Stimson Folder, and Box 28, Knox Folder, FDRL.

24. Sherwood, *Roosevelt and Hopkins,* pp. 410-11. Marshall objected to inclusion of such statements since they were "purely political and therefore somewhat out of place in this paper," but they appeared in the final estimate; see memo, Marshall to Stark, "United States Over-All Production Requirements," Sept. 10, 1941, MM, WPD 4494-10.

25. Sherwood, *Roosevelt and Hopkins,* pp. 410-18.

26. Ibid., p. 418; memo, Marshall to Stark, enclosing memo from Gerow to CofS, "United States Over-All Production Requirements," Sept. 10, 1941, MM, WPD 4494-10. See also Mark S. Watson, *Chief of Staff* (1950), p. 362.

27. WPD "Estimate of Army Requirements," Sept. 1941, MM, WPD 4494-21; memo, Marshall to Pres., "Ground Forces," Sept. 22, 1941, in *Pearl Harbor Hearings,* Pt. 15, Exhibit 60, pp. 1636-39; Watson, *Chief of Staff,* pp. 354-57; Matloff and Snell, *Strategic Planning, 1941-42,* pp. 59-61.

28. Henry L. Stimson Diary, Sept. 25 and 26, Oct. 6 and 7, 1941, Stimson Papers, New Haven, Conn.

29. Ibid., Oct. 6-9, 1941.

30. Sir Hastings Ismay, *The Memoirs of General Lord Ismay* (1960), p. 226.

31. Sherwood, *Roosevelt and Hopkins,* p. 417. See also William L. Langer and S. Everett Gleason, *The Undeclared War, 1940-1941* (1953), p. 563; Wilson, *The First Summit,* pp. 140, 146-47.

32. WPD "Strategic Estimate," Oct. 1941, MM, OPD Exec. 4, Item 9, Book I; see also Stimson Diary, Oct. 30, 1941.

33. Memo by Lt.-Col. Edwin E. Schwien, "An Essential Strategic Diversion in Europe," Aug. 1941, MM, WPD 4402-77.

34. Unpub. app. to Cline's *Washington Command Post,* pp. 1409-10, OCMH, OPD Misc. 314.7.

35. Churchill, *The Grand Alliance,* pp. 369-73, 380-83.

36. David Dilks, ed., *The Diaries of Sir Alexander Cadogan, 1938-1945* (1972), p. 389; Anthony Eden, *The Memoirs of Anthony Eden, Earl of Avon: The Reckoning* (1965), pp. 313-14; Ivan Maisky, *Memoirs of a Soviet Ambassador* (1967), p. 157; *F. R., 1942,* vol. 3 (1961), pp. 472-73; tel., Steinhardt to Hull, June 30, 1941, DS, RG 59, 740.0011 EW 1939/12644.

37. *F. R., 1941,* vol. 1 (1958), p. 182; Langer and Gleason, *The Undeclared War,* pp. 553-55; Maisky, *Memoirs,* pp. 173-74; Edward J. Rozek, *Allied Wartime Diplomacy* (1958), pp. 54-57.

38. Arthur U. Pope, *Maxim Litvinoff* (1943), pp. 461-62; Maisky,

Memoirs, pp. 161-63; Don E. McIlvenna, "Prelude to D-Day" (Ph.D. diss., 1966), p. 12.

39. Churchill, *The Grand Alliance,* pp. 380-84.

40. Sir Llewellyn Woodward, *British Foreign Policy in the Second World War* (1962), p. 145-46.

41. Ismay, *Memoirs,* p. 227.

42. Churchill, *The Grand Alliance,* pp. 384-87, 393.

43. Dean Acheson, *Present at the Creation* (1969), p. 34.

44. Langer and Gleason, *The Undeclared War,* p. 338; *F. R., 1941,* vol. 1, pp. 757-61.

45. *F. R. , 1941,* vol. 1, pp. 766-67.

46. Charles E. Bohlen, *Witness to History, 1929-1969* (1973), p. 125.

47. G-2 rpt., Feb. 5, 1941, in *Pearl Harbor Hearings,* Pt. 21, Exhibit 182, p. 4718; WPD rpt., "Miscellaneous Notes on 'National Objectives' of the United States in War Against Axis Powers," 1940, MM, OPD Exec. 4, Item 5, Defense Policies Folder.

48. Watson, *Chief of Staff,* p. 390.

49. Wedemeyer, *Wedemeyer Reports!,* pp. 1-35, 443; interview with Wedemeyer, Jan. 5, 1970. Wedemeyer was Embick's son-in-law.

50. *F. R., 1941,* vol. 1, pp. 789-90; memo, Berle to Hopkins, July 30, 1941, Harry L. Hopkins Papers, Box 123, FDRL. See also memo from Propaganda and Press Sec. of Justice Dept. to State Dept., July 22, 1941, DS, 740.0011 EW 1939/12764.

51. Tel., Berle to all diplomatic officers, July 22, 1941, DS, 861.51/ 2869.

52. Langer and Gleason, *The Undeclared War,* p. 557.

53. *F. R., 1941,* vol. 1, p. 182; see also Lynn E. Davis, *The Cold War Begins* (1971), pp. 11-12.

54. Memo, Dunn to Hull, Aug. 2, 1941, DS, 740.0011 EW 1939/1584

55. Langer and Gleason, *The Undeclared War,* pp. 540-41.

56. *F. R., 1941,* vol. 1, p. 342; Sherwood, *Roosevelt and Hopkins,* p. 311; Eden, *The Reckoning,* pp. 315-16.

57. *F. R., 1941,* vol. 1, pp. 351-52.

58. Sherwood, *Roosevelt and Hopkins,* pp. 333-43; see also *F. R., 1941,* vol. 1, p. 183.

59. Tel., Biddle to Hull, Aug. 10, 1941, DS, 740.0011 EW 1939/1442

60. Elliot Roosevelt, ed., *FDR: His Personal Letters, 1928-1945,* vol. 2 (1950), pp. 1195-96; Stimson Diary, Aug. 1, 1941.

61. *F. R., 1941,* vol. 1, pp. 819-21.

62. Langer and Gleason, *The Undeclared War,* p. 668.

63. *F. R., 1941,* vol. 1, pp. 820-21.

64. Churchill. *The Grand Alliance,* pp. 455-57.

65. Ibid., p. 457; Eden, *The Reckoning,* pp. 317-18; Maisky, *Memoirs,* pp. 185-86, 190-92; J. R. M. Butler and J. M. A. Gwyer, *Grand Strategy,* vol. 3 (1964), pp. 197-99.

66. Churchill, *The Grand Alliance,* pp. 458-67.

67. Woodward, *British Foreign Policy,* p. 156.

68. Ibid., p. 156.

69. James Leasor, *War at the Top* (1959), p. 158.

70. Butler and Gwyer, *Grand Strategy,* vol. 3, pp. 208-11; see also *F. R., 1941,* vol. 1, pp. 656-57.

71. Tel., Johnson to Hull, Sept. 17, 1941, DS, 740.0011 EW 1939/15404.

72. Tel., Johnson to Hull, Oct.27, 1941, DS, 740.0011 EW 1939/16886; Hadley Cantril, ed., *Public Opinion, 1935-1946* (1951), p. 1108.

73. Sherwood, *Roosevelt and Hopkins,* pp. 393-94.

74. Churchill, *The Grand Alliance,* pp. 542-51.

75. Ibid., p. 546.

76. Churchill, *The Grand Alliance,* pp. 551-52.

77. *F. R., 1941,* vol. 1, pp. 654-55.

78. Churchill, *The Grand Alliance,* pp. 528-30.

79. Eden, *The Reckoning,* p. 326.

80. Ibid., pp. 326-27; tels., Thurston to Hull, Nov. 20 and 21, 1941, DS, 740.0011 EW 1939/16792 and 16793; Churchill, *The Grand Alliance,* pp. 531-33; Maisky, *Memoirs,* pp. 202-3.

81. *F. R., 1941,* vol. 1, pp. 192-94.

82. Ibid., p. 188.

83. Ibid., pp. 194-95; Cordell Hull, *The Memoirs of Cordell Hull,* vol. 2 (1948), pp. 1165-66; tel., Winant to Hull, Dec. 9, 1941, DS, 740.0011 EW 1939/17248.

84. Churchill, *The Grand Alliance,* pp. 623-24; Eden, *The Reckoning,* pp. 328-33.

85. *F. R., 1941,* vol. 1, pp. 204-5.

86. Eden, *The Reckoning,* pp. 334-38.

87. Ibid., pp. 338-52; see also *F. R., 1942,* vol. 3, pp. 495-503.

88. Churchill, *The Grand Alliance,* pp. 694-95.

89. Ibid., pp. 632-33.

90. Ibid., pp. 645-47.

91. As of Dec. 24, however, only 25 percent of the tonnage pledged had been shipped; see George C. Herring, *Aid to Russia* (1973), pp. 42-46.

92. Churchill, *The Grand Alliance, pp. 630-31.*

93. Arthur Bryant, *The Turn of the Tide* (1957), p. 225.

94. Churchill, *The Grand Alliance,* pp. 647-59. The COS prepared
a similar, though more defense-minded, memo; Butler and Gwyer, *Grand
Strategy,* vol. 3, pp. 340-48.

95. *F.R.: The Conferences at Washington, 1941-1942, and Casablanca,
1943* (1968), pp. 56-58; Henry H. Arnold, *Global Mission* (1949), p. 275.

96. Churchill, *The Grand Alliance,* pp. 664-65; emphasis in original.

97. See directly below; *F. R.: Washington and Casablanca,* p. 61.

98. Ibid., pp. 240, 258-64.

99. Sumner Welles, *Seven Decisions That Shaped History* (1950),
pp. 139-41.

100. Ibid. and Sumner Welles, *Where Are We Heading?* (1946), pp. 18-19.
The JCS replaced the Joint Board to mesh with the COS in forming the CCS.
Henceforth, Army-Navy comms. were known as "joint" comms.; "com-
bined" denoted U.S.-U.K. comms.

101. Churchill, *The Grand Alliance,* pp. 694-96.

102. *F. R.: Washington and Casablanca,* pp. 145, 210-17. Butler and Gwye
Grand Strategy, vol. 3, pp. 357-58, claim that the United States acquiesced b
cause of the shipping shortage and the subsequent impossibility of providing
an alternative strategy.

103. WPD rpt., "Notes on Agenda Proposed by British," Dec. 21, 1941,
MM, OPD Exec. 4, Folder 2; Arnold, *Global Mission,* pp. 303-04.

104. Memo, Embick to CofS, Jan. 1942, MM, WPD 4511-37.

105. Notes by Eisenhower, Jan. 2, 1942, OCMH, OPD Historical Unit File
Item 3; Alfred D. Chandler, Jr., ed., *The Papers of Dwight David Eisenhower,*
vol. 1 (1970), pp. 39, 46.

106. Joseph W. Stilwell Diary, Jan. 2, 3, 8, and 13, 1942, Stilwell Paper
Hoover Institute, Stanford, Calif., partially reprinted in Theodore White,
ed., *The Stilwell Papers* (1948), p. 25.

107. Stimson Diary, Jan. 3 and 4, 1942; *F. R.: Washington and Casablanca,* p. 239; memo, CofS to Pres., Jan. 9, 1942, MM, WPD 4511-43;
White, *The Stilwell Papers,* pp. 20-23.

108. *F.R.:Washington and Casablanca,* pp. 11, 47-50, 54-55, 64, 72, 153-5
244-45, 248-50, 255-56; ltr., Bullitt to Pres., Dec. 27, 1941, Roosevelt Paper
PSF, West Africa Folder; Steel, *The First Offensive,* pp. 46-53.

109. White, *The Stilwell Papers,* pp. 15-16; see also pp. 17-42 and
Stilwell Diary for Dec. and Jan.

110. Butler and Gwyer, *Grand Strategy,* vol. 3, p. 352.

CHAPTER 2: THE AMERICAN INITIATIVE

1. J.R.M. Butler and J.M.A. Gwyer, *Grand Strategy,* vol. 3 (1964), p. 56
Maurice Matloff and Edwin M. Snell, *Strategic Planning for Coalition Warf
1941-1942* (1953), p. 176.

2. Maurice Matloff, *Strategic Planning for Coalition Warfare, 1943-1944* (1959), p. 12; Forrest C. Pogue, *George C. Marshall,* vol. 2, *Ordeal and Hope* (1966), p. 314.

3. Richard W. Steele, *The First Offensive, 1942* (1973), pp. 76-80.

4. Hadley Cantril, ed., *Public Opinion, 1935-1946* (1951), p. 1176.

5. Matloff and Snell, *Strategic Planning, 1941-1942,* pp. 154-55.

6. Henry H. Arnold, *Global Mission* (1949), p. 306.

7. See, for example, paraphrase of tel., Faymonville to Marshall, Dec. 19, 1941, MM, RG 165, WDCSA, Secretariat, Confs. 1938-1942, Box 887; tel. 846, Chaney to Marshall, Mar. 21, 1942, MM, WDCSA, Russia (Super Secret); and memo, Lee to CofS, Jan. 1, 1942, MM, WPD 4457-40.

8. See above, pp. 18-19, tel., Thurston to Hull, Dec. 17, 1941, Roosevelt Papers, PSF Safe: ABCD Folder.

9. See Alfred D. Chandler, Jr., ed., *The Papers of Dwight David Eisenhower,* vol. 1 (1970), p. 118.

10. JPWC 7, "Demand for United Nations Offensive," with enclosure, Mar. 21, 1942, MM, RG 218, CCS 385 (3-21-42).

11. Memo, Lee, ACofS, G-2, to CofS, "Possibility of a Negotiated Russo-German Settlement," Feb. 12, 1942, Hopkins Papers, Box 105, Russia Folder.

12. Chandler, *The Eisenhower Papers,* vol. 1, pp. 149-55, emphasis in original; see also pp. 73, 75, 118-19, 122-23, 142, 145-48.

13. Stimson Diary, Feb. 24, 1942.

14. Memo, Arnold to CofS, "Employment of Army Air Forces," Mar. 3, 1942, Henry H. Arnold Papers, Box 39, SOF, 1941-1945, LOC.

15. Memo, King to Pres., "Areas of Responsibility," Mar. 5, 1942, NH, King Papers.

16. Stimson Diary, Mar. 5, 1942

17. Paraphrase of rpt. from Col. Fellers to War Dept., Mar. 4, 1942, Roosevelt Papers, PSF, Russia 1942-1943; min., JCS 4 mtg., Mar. 7, 1942, MM, CCS 381 (3-5-42) (2).

18. Stimson Diary, Mar. 6 and 7, 1942.

19. Winston S. Churchill, *The Second World War*, vol. 4, *The Hinge of Fate* (1950), pp. 194-199; Butler and Gwyer, *Grand Strategy*, vol. 3, p. 574.

20. Stimson Diary, Mar. 8, 1942.

21. Ltrs., Arnold to Chaney and Portal, Mar. 9, 1942, Arnold Papers, SOF, 1941-1945, Corres.–Commanders-in-the-Field Folder.

22. Robert Sherwood, *Roosevelt and Hopkins* (1950), pp. 518-19.

23. William D. Leahy, *I Was There* (1950), pp. 84-85.

24. Stimson Diary, Mar. 16, 1942.

25. Churchill, *The Hinge of Fate*, p. 201.

26. Stimson Diary, Mar. 20, 1942.

27. All JUSSC studies, Feb. 18-Mar. 14, 1942, in MM, CCS 381 (1-30-42) (1). See also Ray S. Cline, *Washington Command Post* (1951), p. 147.

28. Covering ltr. from JPS in JCS 23, and memo, Smith to Dykes, "Strategic Deployment of the Land, Sea and Air Forces of the U.S.," Mar. 14 and 16, 1942, MM, CCS 381 (1-30-42) (1).

29. Ibid., App. II to JPS 2/6 in JCS 23, Mar. 14, 1942.

30. Chandler, *The Eisenhower Papers*, vol. 1, pp. 205-8, emphasis in original; see also Cline, *Washington Command Post*, pp. 149-54. OPD replaced WPD by the Gen. Staff reorganization of Mar. 9, 1942.

31. Cline, *Washington Command Post*, pp. 143-54; Butler and Gwyer, *Grand Strategy*, vol. 3, pp. 566-71.

32. Min., JCS 7 mtg., Mar. 23, 1942, MM, CCS 381 (1-30-42) (1); the British plan is also in this file. See also Cline, *Washington Command Post*, p. 153.

33. Stimson Diary, Mar. 25, 1942; Henry L. Stimson and McGeorge Bundy, *On Active Service in Peace and War* (1947), pp. 416-18.

34. Reprinted in Butler and Gwyer, *Grand Strategy*, vol. 3, pp. 675-81; see also Matloff and Snell, *Strategic Planning, 1941-1942,* p. 383. Ironically, the code names came from the original British plan.

35. CPS 26/1, Apr. 3, 1942, MM, CCS 381 (3-23-42), Pt. 2; Richard M. Leighton and Robert W. Coakley, *Global Logistics and Strategy, 1940-1943* (1955), pp. 358-59.

36. Memo, King to Marshall, "Strategic Deployment in the Pacific Against Japan," Mar. 29, 1942, NH, King Papers.

37. Arnold, *Global Mission*, pp. 304-5; Ernest J. King and Walter M. Whitehill, *Fleet Admiral King* (1952), pp. 390-91.

38. See Stimson Diary, Feb. 14, 1942.

39. See Cantril, *Public Opinion*, pp. 1176, 1178; ltr., Barth to MacLeish, Office of Facts and Figures, Mar. 27, 1942, DS, 740.0011 EW 1939/20691; Steele, *The First Offensive*, pp. 81-93.

40. Anthony Eden, *The Memoirs of Anthony Eden, Earl of Avon: The Reckoning* (1965), pp. 370-71.

41. *F.R., 1942*, vol. 3 (1961), pp. 517-18.

42. Ibid., p. 101; *F.R., 1941*, vol. 1 (1958), pp. 337-39; disp., Biddle to Hull, Jan. 7 and 10, 1942, DS, 740.0011 EW 1939/18730 and 19031; unsigned memo, European Affairs Div. to Atherton, Jan. 24, 1942, DS, 740.0011 EW 1939/18780.

43. *F.R., 1942*, vol. 3, pp. 504-12; Cordell Hull, *The Memoirs of Cordell Hull*, vol. 2 (1948), pp. 1166-70.

44. *F.R., 1942*, vol. 3, p. 521. For a different interpretation, see Robert A. Divine, *Roosevelt and World War II* (1969), pp. 85-88.

45. *F. R., 1942,* vol. 3, pp. 432-33, 527-28; tel., Thurston to Hull, Feb. 24, 1942, DS, 861.415/68; tels., Thurston and Johnson to Hull, Feb. 28 and Mar. 7, 1942, DS, 740.0011 EW 1939/19847 and 20007.

46. *F.R., 1942,* vol. 3, pp. 536-38.

47. Nancy H. Hooker, ed., *The Moffat Papers* (1956), p. 380.

48. Churchill, *The Hinge of Fate,* p. 327.

49. Hopkins saw the peace threats as a bluff to get aid, and as early as Mar. 6 he felt that Britain was willing to sign a treaty because she could not open a second front; see Jan Ciechanowski, *Defeat in Victory* (1947), pp. 96, 100-1.

50. *F.R., 1942,* vol. 3, pp. 521-26, 532-33; Eden, *The Reckoning,* pp. 375-76.

51. Churchill, *The Hinge of Fate,* p. 201.

52. John M. Blum, *From the Morgenthau Diaries,* vol. 3 (1967), pp. 80-82. A week earlier, however, Stalin had complained that while Britain had fulfilled her commitments, the United States "had lamentably failed to do so." See *F.R., 1942,* vol. 3, pp. 437-38.

53. See above, p. 33, and Eden, *The Reckoning,* p. 376.

54. Memo by Welles of conversation with Polish foreign minister and ambassador, with ltr. and enclosures for Roosevelt, Feb. 19, 1942, DS, 740.0011 EW 1939/19850.

55. Stimson Diary, Mar. 27, 1942.

56. Disp., Biddle to Hull for Roosevelt, Hull and Welles, Mar. 16, 1942, DS, 740.0011 EW 1939/20790; see also disp., Biddle to Hull, Feb. 20, 1942, DS, 740.0011 EW 1939/20193.

57. Transcript of interview by Ray S. Cline with Wedemeyer, Oct. 17, 1945, OCMH, OPD Historical Unit File; min., OCMH seminar, Feb. 27, 1948, in Cline's original draft of *Washington Command Post,* National Archives and Records Center, Suitland, Md.; author's interview with Wedemeyer, Jan 5, 1970; Samuel E. Morison, *History of U.S. Naval Operations in World War II,* vol. 2, *The Invasion of France and Germany* (1957), p. 8.

CHAPTER 3: SECOND-FRONT DIPLOMACY

1. Winston S. Churchill, *The Second World War,* vol. 4, *The Hinge of Fate* (1950), pp. 313-14, emphasis in original.

2. Robert Sherwood, *Roosevelt and Hopkins* (1950), pp. 536-38.

3. Ibid., p. 526; Albert C. Wedemeyer, *Wedemeyer Reports!* (1958), pp. 112-13, claims he informed British planners at this time that a second front would also block postwar Soviet expansion.

4. Churchill, *The Hinge of Fate*, pp. 316-17.

5. Lord Moran, *Churchill: Taken from the Diaries of Lord Moran* (1966), p. 38.

6. Arthur Bryant, *The Turn of the Tide* (1957), pp. 274, 298.

7. Tel., Churchill to Roosevelt, Mar. 7, 1942, Roosevelt Papers, MRF, Box 2.

8. George H. Gallup, *The Gallup Poll*, vol. 1 (1972), p. 328; Dennis E. Harris, "The Diplomacy of the Second Front" (Ph.D. diss., 1969), pp. 117-19.

9. Memo for the record by Arnold, Apr. 1, 1942, Arnold Papers, Box 180, CF, White House Apr.-May 1942 Folder.

10. Churchill, *The Hinge of Fate*, pp. 316-24; Sir John Kennedy, *The Business of War* (1957), p. 224.

11. Bryant, *The Turn of the Tide*, pp. 285-90; James Leasor, *War at the Top* (1959), p. 184.

12. See min., 23 COS mtg., Apr. 9, 1942, and Apr. 14 Defense Cabinet mtg., COS 42 and 42 (0), MM, CCS 381 (3-23-42), Pt. 3; Sherwood, *Roosevelt and Hopkins*, p. 523; Churchill, *The Hinge of Fate*, pp. 317-18.

13. CM-IN 3457, Marshall to McNarney, Apr. 13, 1943, MM, OPD Exec. 1, Item 5c.

14. The 1943 statement was added in pen to the min. of the CCS 16 mtg., Apr. 21, 1942, MM, CCS 334 (3-10-42) (mtgs. 11-20).

15. Anthony Eden, *The Memoirs of Anthony Eden, Earl of Avon: The Reckoning* (1965), p. 377; Churchill, *The Hinge of Fate*, pp. 322-24.

16. Richard M. Leighton and Robert W. Coakley, *Global Logistics and Strategy, 1940-1943* (1955), p. 377; JPS 1, "Amphibious Training," Apr. 14, 1942, MM, CCS 381 (1-30-42) (1).

17. Memo for the record by Arnold, Apr. 1, 1942, Arnold Papers, Box 180, CF, White House Apr.-May, 1942 Folder.

18. *F.R., 1942*, vol. 3 (1961), pp. 542-43.

19. Ibid., pp. 535-36; J.R.M. Butler and J.M.A. Gwyer, *Grand Strategy*, vol. 3 (1964), p. 592.

20. Ivan M. Maisky, *Memoirs of a Soviet Ambassador* (1967), p. 261; *F.R., 1942*, vol. 3, pp. 543n.81, 556; Churchill, *The Hinge of Fate*, pp. 330-31; Eden, *The Reckoning*, p. 378; Ministry of Foreign Affairs of the USSR, *Russia: Correspondence Between the Chairman of the Council of Ministers of the U.S.S.R. and the Presidents of the U.S.A. and the Prime Ministers of Great Britain During the Great Patriotic War of 1941-1945* [hereafter cited as *Stalin's Correspondence*], vol. 2 (1957), pp. 23-24.

21. Maisky, *Memoirs*, p. 268.

22. Alexander Werth, *Russia at War, 1941-1945* (1964), p. 380.

23. David Dilks, ed., *The Diaries of Sir Alexander Cadogan, 1938-1945* (1972), p. 454.

24. Butler and Gwyer, *Grand Strategy*, vol. 3, p. 593; Eden, *The Reckoning*, p. 380.

25. Churchill, *The Hinge of Fate*, p. 332.

26. Ibid., pp. 332-35; tel., Churchill to Roosevelt, May 28, 1942, Roosevelt Papers, MRF, Box 2.

27. *F.R., 1942*, vol. 3, 140-45, 558-59, 561-65; tel., Biddle to Hull, Apr. 27, 1942, DS, 741.6111/9; memo, Welles to Roosevelt, Apr. 18, 1942, DS, 740.0011 EW 1939/21079 3/4; tel., Winant to Hull, Apr. 23, 1942, DS, 740.00119 EW 1939/964; Cordell Hull, *The Memoirs of Cordell Hull*, vol. 2 (1948), pp. 1172-73; Eden, *The Reckoning*, pp. 380-82.

28. *F.R., 1942*, vol. 3, p. 560.

29. Ibid., pp. 564-65.

30. Butler and Gwyer, *Grand Strategy*, vol. 3, p. 620. Brooke considered JUPITER a "nightmare" without any strategic prospects; see Bryant, *The Turn of the Tide*, p. 274.

31. Tel., Churchill to Roosevelt, May 28, 1942, Roosevelt Papers, MRF, Box 2, partially reprinted in Churchill, *The Hinge of Fate*, p. 340.

32. *F.R., 1942*, vol. 3, pp. 566-74, has abridged min. for May 29; this account uses unabridged min., Hopkins Papers, Box 126, Molotov Visit Folder, and Cordell Hull Papers, LOC, Box 50.

33. Ibid. The Soviets in early May had angrily rejected the SLEDGE-HAMMER concept; see *F.R., 1942*, vol. 3, p. 441.

34. Sherwood, *Roosevelt and Hopkins*, pp. 561-63.

35. Forrest C. Pogue, *George C. Marshall*, vol. 2, *Ordeal and Hope* (1966), p. 324.

36. Sherwood, *Roosevelt and Hopkins*, p. 568.

37. Churchill, *The Hinge of Fate*, pp. 259-61; Maurice Matloff and Edwin M. Snell, *Strategic Planning for Coalition Warfare, 1941-1942* (1953), pp. 229-32; Richard W. Steele, *The First Offensive, 1942* (1973), pp. 129-34; memo, King to JCS, "Russian Munition Protocol," May 1, 1942, NH, King Papers; memos, Marshall to Pres. and JCS to CCS, "Transport Airplanes for Russia," Apr. 27-28, 1942, MM, WDCSA Russia and JCS geographic series, CCS 400. 3295 USSR (2-27-42), Sec. 1, Pt. 1; min., CCS 16 mtg., Apr. 21, 1942, MM, CCS 334 (3-10-42) (mtgs. 11-20).

38. Sherwood, *Roosevelt and Hopkins*, pp. 568, 570.

39. Ibid., pp. 568-70; tel., Roosevelt to Churchill, May 31, 1942,

Roosevelt Papers, MRF, Box 2. He replaced "August" with "1942" but added that weather precluded delay until year's end.

40. Sherwood, *Roosevelt and Hopkins*, pp. 574-75.

41. Ibid., p. 577; *F.R., 1942*, vol. 3, p. 587.

42. Alfred D. Chandler, Jr., ed., *The Papers of Dwight David Eisenhower* (1970), vol. 1, pp. 278, 315, 328; Matloff and Snell, *Strategic Planning, 1941-1942*, pp. 210-19; Pogue, *Marshall*, vol. 2, p. 326; ltr., CofS to Portal, May 6, 1942, Arnold Papers, Box 113, OF 1938-1946, War Plans Folder; MM, OPD 381 Gen. (Sec. II), 62. Marshall responded to the report by setting up ETO in England under Eisenhower.

43. Sherwood, *Roosevelt and Hopkins*, p. 577.

44. Ibid., p. 577.

45. Charles E. Bohlen, *Witness to History 1929-1969* (1973), p. 128.

46. Sherwood, *Roosevelt and Hopkins*, pp. 580-81.

47. Ibid., pp. 582-83; min., CCS 24 mtg., June 10, 1942, MM, CCS 381 (3-23-42), Sec. I, Pt. 3.

48. Bryant, *The Turn of the Tide*, pp. 300-3, 315; Churchill, *The Hinge of Fate*, pp. 346-48; Butler and Gwyer, *Grand Strategy*, vol.3, p. 599.

49. Eden, *The Reckoning*, p. 383; Sir Llewellyn Woodward, *British Foreign Policy in the Second World War* (1962), p. 197.

50. Woodward, *British Foreign Policy*, p. 197.

51. Butler and Gwyer, *Grand Strategy*, vol. 3, p. 596.

52. Ibid., pp. 596-97, 682-83.

53. Ibid., pp. 597, 621-22; Sherwood, *Roosevelt and Hopkins*, pp. 582-83; *F.R.: The Conferences at Washington, 1941-1942, and Casablanca, 1943* (1968), pp. 419-20.

54. See *F.R., 1942*, vol. 3, pp. 445, 598-99, 608-9, 612-14; tel., Standley to Hull, July 17, 1942, DS, 740.0011 EW 1939/13212A.

CHAPTER 4: THE POLITICS OF TORCH

1. Stimson Diary, June 17, 1942; memo by Arnold of June 17 White House Conf., Arnold Papers, Box 180, CF, White House May 20-Aug. 7, 1942 Folder; *F.R.: The Conferences at Washington, 1941-1942, and Casablanca, 1943* (1968), pp. 457-60; memo, CofS to Pres., "GYMNAST Operation," June 16, 1942, MM, RG 407, OPD Registered Document 5, drafts in OPD Exec. 10, Item 53.

2. Winston S. Churchill, *The Second World War*, vol. 4, *The Hinge of Fate* (1950), pp. 381-82.

3. *F.R.: Washington and Casablanca*, pp. 473-75.

4. Arthur Bryant, *The Turn of the Tide* (1957), pp. 324-27.

5. *F.R.: Washington and Casablanca*, pp. 422-43, 465-67.

6. Bryant, *The Turn of the Tide,* p. 328; Stimson Diary, June 21, 1942.

7. *F.R.: Washington and Casablanca*, pp. 434-35, 468-69, 478-79.

8. J.R.M. Butler and J.M.A. Gwyer, *Grand Strategy*, vol. 3 (1964), p. 627.

9. Stimson Diary, June 22, 1942.

10. "Notes on War Council Meeting," June 29, 1942, MM, WDCSA, SW Confs., II. See also *F.R.: Washington and Casablanca*, pp. 436-38, 473-74, 476; Stimson Diary, June 22-25, 1942.

11. Lord Moran, *Churchill: Taken from the Diaries of Lord Moran* (1966), p. 48.

12. Butler and Gwyer, *Grand Strategy*, vol. 3, pp. 629-31.

13. Churchill, *The Hinge of Fate*, pp. 433-35.

14. Albert C. Wedemeyer, *Wedemeyer Reports!* (1958), p. 146.

15. Stimson Diary, June 21, 1942.

16. "Notes on War Council Meeting," June 22, 1942, MM, WDCSA, SW Confs., II.

17. Kent R. Greenfield, *American Strategy in World War II* (1963), p. 7.

18. Henry L. Stimson and McGeorge Bundy, *On Active Service in Peace and War* (1947), p. 424.

19. Min., JCS 24 mtg., July 10, 1942, MM, CCS 334 (6-23-42).

20. Ibid.

21. Wedemeyer, *Wedemeyer Reports!*, p. 158.

22. Memo, CofS and CNO to Pres., July 10, 1942, MM, OPD 381 Gen. (Sec. II), p. 73.

23. Stimson later stated it was a bluff (Stimson and Bundy, *On Active Service*, pp. 424-25) as did Forrest C. Pogue (*George C. Marshall*, vol. 2, *Ordeal and Hope* [1966], pp. 340-41), but American statements and actions cast doubt upon such claims and the British took the threat seriously. See above, p. 34; directly below; Stimson Diary, July 12-17, 1942; Churchill, *The Hinge of Fate*, pp. 439-40; David Dilks, ed., *The Diaries of Sir Alexander Cadogan, 1938-1945* (1972), p. 462.

24. Tel., Roosevelt to Marshall, July 14, 1942, MM, WDSCA, BOLERO, Super Secret; drafts in Roosevelt Papers, MRF, Churchill-FDR messages, Strays Box. See also papers with July 10 memo in MM, OPD 381 Gen. (Sec. II), 73; Maurice Matloff and Edwin M. Snell, *Strategic Planning for Coalition Warfare, 1941-1942* (1953), pp. 270-72.

25. Memo, Wedemeyer to Handy on "Resume of Action Taken by JCS," MM, OPD Exec. 5, Item 1, Tab 10.

26. Stimson Diary, July 15, 1942.

27. Memo, Marshall to King, July 15, 1942, MM, WDCSA 381 War Plans, Folder 1.

28. Ibid.

29. Robert Sherwood, *Roosevelt and Hopkins* (1950), pp. 603-5; Matloff and Snell, *Strategic Planning, 1941-1942*, pp. 384-85.

30. Sherwood, *Roosevelt and Hopkins*, pp. 602-3.

31. Tel., Marshall to Eisenhower, July 16, 1942, MM, OPD Exec. 5, Item 9.

32. Alfred D. Chandler, Jr., ed., *The Papers of Dwight David Eisenhower* (1970), vol. 1, pp. 388-92, emphasis in original. Eisenhower later admitted in *Crusade in Europe* (1948), pp. 68-71, that launching SLEDGEHAMMER would have been a mistake.

33. Min., July 20 and 22 mtgs. and July 28 summary of conf. by CofS and CNO to Pres., MM, CCS 381 (3-23-42), Pt. 3, Sec. 2.

34. Harry C. Butcher, *My Three Years with Eisenhower* (1946), p. 29.

35. Sherwood, *Roosevelt and Hopkins,* p. 610, full text in Roosevelt Papers, PSF, Box 125, Hopkins Folder.

36. CCS 94 is in Butler and Gwyer, *Grand Strategy*, vol. 3, pp. 684-85. Samuel E. Morison, *History of U.S. Naval Operations in World War II*, vol. 11, *The Invasion of France and Germany* (1957), p. 14, states it was King's idea, and that the CNO wrote this quote.

37. Min., CCS 32 mtg., July 24, 1942, MM, CCS 334 (5-26-42), Pt. 3, Sec. 2; Butler and Gwyer, *Grand Strategy*, vol. 3, pp. 636-38; Michael Howard, *Grand Strategy*, vol. 4 (1972), pp. xx-xxv; Bryant, *The Turn of the Tide*, pp. 341-42.

38. Butler and Gwyer, *Grand Strategy*, vol. 3, pp. 635-36.

39. See Sherwood, *Roosevelt and Hopkins*, pp. 602-3; CM-OUT 7303, McNarney to Marshall, July 25, 1942, OPD Exec. 5, Item 9.

40. Sherwood, *Roosevelt and Hopkins*, pp. 611-12; Stimson Diary, July 25, 1942.

41. Memo, Smith to JCS, "Notes on a Conference Held at the White House at 8:30 P.M., July 30, 1942," Aug. 1, 1942, MM, OPD Exec. 5, Item 1, Tab 14.

42. Samuel E. Morison, *Strategy and Compromise* (1958), p. 38. See also Roosevelt's memo on Stimson July 25 memo, July 29, 1942, Hopkins Papers, Box 115; Elliot Roosevelt, ed., *FDR: His Personal Letters, 1928-1945* (1950), vol. 2, pp. 1337-39; Hadley Cantril, ed., *Public Opinion, 1935-1946* (1951), pp 1062-64; Eisenhower, *Crusade in Europe*, p. 195; Pogue, *Marshall*, vol. 2, p. 402; and above, n. 1, 2, and 3.

43. Memo, Wedemeyer to CofS, undated, MM, RG 165, ABC 381 (9-25-41), Sec. VII, Paper 9.

44. Min., JCS 26 mtg., July 28, 1942, MM, CCS 334 (6-23-42).

45. Memo, Arnold to CofS, "Strategic Decisions," undated, Arnold Papers, Box 50, OF 1932-1946, Germany Folder.

46. Stimson Diary, Aug. 7, 1942; Stimson and Bundy, *On Active Service*, p. 426.

47. Memo for the record by Arnold, Aug. 11, 1942, Arnold Papers, Box 3, Misc. Corres., Aug.-Dec. 1942 Folder. See also JCS 32-35 mtgs., MM, CCS 334 (6-23-42) (mtgs. 21-40); CCS 381 (6-24-32), Secs. 1 and 2; Matloff and Snell, *Strategic Planning, 1941-1942;* pp. 281, 296, 321-22.

48. See above, n. 1, 2, 15, and 33.

49. Churchill, *The Hinge of Fate*, pp. 267-70.

50. Ivan M. Maisky, *Memoirs of a Soviet Ambassador* (1967), p. 283.

51. Churchill, *The Hinge of Fate*, pp. 270-71.

52. Ernest J. King and Walter M. Whitehill, *Fleet Admiral King* (1952), p. 406.

53. Maisky, *Memoirs*, pp. 292-95; *F.R., 1942*, vol. 3 (1961), pp. 451-52; William D. Leahy Diary, July 31, 1942, Leahy Papers, LOC; memo, Welles to Marshall, Aug. 3, 1942, MM, OPD 041 (State Dept.), Sec. I, Case 10; July and Aug. tels., DS, 740.00119 EW 1939; DS, 740.0011 EW 1939/23272, 23456, 23448 1/2, and 23620.

54. Churchill, *The Hinge of Fate*, p. 475.

55. *F.R., 1942*, vol. 3, p. 619.

56. Ibid. p. 619.

57. All quotes from official British min., Hopkins Papers, Box 126A, Churchill-Harriman-to-Moscow Folder, and Churchill, *The Hinge of Fate*, pp. 480-83.

58. Sir Arthur Tedder, *With Prejudice* (1966), p. 330.

59. Sir John Kennedy, *The Business of War* (1957), p. 275.

60. Churchill, *The Hinge of Fate*, pp. 486-91.

61. Bryant, *The Turn of the Tide*, pp. 373-74.

62. Moran, *Churchill*, p. 64.

63. Churchill, *The Hinge of Fate*, pp. 491-92.

64. Moran, *Churchill*, p. 66.

65. Ibid., pp. 68-70; Churchill, *The Hinge of Fate*, pp. 496-502.

66. See *F.R., 1942*, vol. 3, pp. 634-35; tel., Standley to Hull, Aug. 19, 1942, DS, 740.0011 EW 1939/23631.

67. See Chandler, *The Eisenhower Papers,* vol. 1, pp. 433-99: Howard, *Grand Strategy*, vol. 4, pp. 111-28; Matloff and Snell, *Strategic Planning, 1941-1942*, pp. 285-91; MM, OPD Exec. 5, Item 9 and Exec. 10, Item 53; MM, CCS 381 (7-24-42), Sec. 1 and 1a.

68. Moran, *Churchill*, pp. 78-79.

69. Chandler, *The Eisenhower Papers*, vol. 1, pp. 499-501.

70. Churchill, *The Hinge of Fate*, p. 651.

71. Supp. min., CCS 38 mtg., Aug. 28, 1942, MM, CCS 334 (5-26-42).

72. Ltr., Roosevelt to Marshall and King, Aug. 12, 1942, Roosevelt Papers, MRF, Box 15; see also above, n. 42.

73 Kennedy, *The Business of War*, pp. 261-63.

74. See Dennis Harris, "The Diplomacy of the Second Front" (Ph.D. diss., 1969), pp. 257-59; Cantril, *Public Opinion,* p. 1064.

75. Churchill, *The Hinge of Fate*, p. 530.

CHAPTER 5: THE CONSEQUENCES OF TORCH

1. Alfred D. Chandler, Jr., ed., *The Papers of Dwight David Eisenhower*, vol. 1 (1970), pp. 570-73.

2. Tel., Churchill to Roosevelt, Sept. 22, 1942, Roosevelt Papers, MRF, Box 2.

3. Stimson Diary, Sept. 23, 1942.

4. See proposed tel., Roosevelt to Churchill, prepared by Army planners between Oct. 2 and 6, 1942, Roosevelt Papers, MRF, Box 1.

5. See memo, Gen. St. Clair Streett, Theater Group Chief, OPD, to Arnold, "British and American Participation in the Caucasus," Nov. 30, 1942, MM, OPD Exec. 1, Item 11; WDCSA Russia (Super Secret) and OPD 381 Russia 6 and 7.

6. Winston S. Churchill, *The Second World War*, vol. 4, *The Hinge of Fate* (1950), pp. 564-66; tel., Churchill to Roosevelt, Sept. 14, 1942, Roosevelt Papers, MRF, Box 3.

7. Memo, Marshall to Pres., "Proposed Anglo-American Air Force for Operation in the Caucasian Area," Sept. 18, 1942, Hopkins Papers, Box 126, Aid to Russia Folder.

8. Richard M. Leighton and Robert W. Cloakley, *Global Logistics and Strategy, 1940-1943* (1955), p. 586.

9. Memo by King on conf. with Pres., Aug. 21, 1942, NH, King Papers

10. Tel., Roosevelt to Churchill, Oct. 5, 1942, Roosevelt Papers, MRF, Messages: FDR-Churchill "Strays" Box.

11. Churchill, *The Hinge of Fate*, pp. 578-80.

12. Ibid., p. 581; *F.R., 1942,* vol. 3 (1961), pp. 459-76, 637-48; Joseph Stalin, *The Great Patriotic War of the Soviet Union* (1945), pp. 56-70; rpts. from London and New York OSS offices, Sept. 21 and Dec. 7,

1942, MM, RG 226, OSS 21377 S, and 24927 R; *Stalin's Correspondence,*
vol. 2, pp. 37-38. For VELVET, see Richard C. Lukas, "The VELVET
Project," *Military Affairs* 28 (Winter 1964): 145-62, and Richard C. Lukas,
Eagles East (1970), pp. 139-64.

13. Cards to Roosevelt demanding a second front fell from 25,000 in Oct.
to 6,000 in Nov.; in Britain, Churchill's popularity reached new heights.
See Roosevelt Papers, OF 4675-6, Box 51, Second Front; tel., Winant to
Hull, Nov. 29, 1942, DS, 841.00/1612.

14. Harley Notter, *Postwar Foreign Policy Preparation, 1939-1945*
(1950), p. 162.

15. Ltr., Roosevelt to Daniels, Nov. 10, 1942, Roosevelt Papers, PPF,
Josephus Daniels.

16. *Stalin's Correspondence,* vol. 2, p. 39; *F.R., 1942,* vol. 3, pp. 478-81.

17. Michael Howard, *Grand Strategy,* vol. 4 (1972), pp. 205-6, 225-28.

18. Churchill, *The Hinge of Fate,* pp. 649-50.

19. Ibid., pp. 649-50.

20. CM-IN 3805, Smith to AGWAR for Marshall, Nov. 11, 1942, MM,
OPD Exec. 5, Item 5, Tab 11/11, paraphrased in Robert Sherwood,
Roosevelt and Hopkins (1950), pp. 656-57.

21. Tel., Churchill to Roosevelt, Nov. 13, 1942, Roosevelt Papers,
MRF, Box 3; see also Churchill, *The Hinge of Fate,* pp. 630-31.

22. Howard, *Grand Strategy,* vol. 4, pp. 61, 229, 617-20; CCS 124
Brief, MM, CCS 381 (11-16-42).

23. Churchill, *The Hinge of Fate,* p. 562.

24. Ibid., p. 562.

25. Ibid., p. 651.

26. Ibid., pp. 650-53.

27. *Stalin's Correspondence,* vol. 1, pp. 78-82.

28. Tels., Churchill to Roosevelt, Dec. 2, 7, 10, and 12, 1942, Roosevelt Papers, MRF, Box 3.

29. Churchill, *The Hinge of Fate,* pp. 655-58.

30. Sir John Kennedy, *The Business of War* (1957), p. 277.

31. Arthur Bryant, *The Turn of the Tide* (1957), pp. 427-37.

32. Ibid., pp. 435-37; Howard, *Grand Strategy,* vol. 4, pp. 208-16.

33. *Stalin's Correspondence,* vol. 1, pp. 75-82, vol. 2, pp. 39-44; *F.R.:
The Conferences at Washington, 1941-1942, and Casablanca, 1943*
(1968), pp. 491-500.

34. *F.R., 1942,* vol. 3, pp. 655-58; *Stalin's Correspondence,* vol. 2,
p. 43.

35. *Stalin's Correspondence,* vol. 2, p. 44.

36. Memo, Handy to CofS, "American-British Strategy," Nov. 8,

1942, MM, OPD, Exec. 1, Item 10a, Tab 13; 1 memo, Wedemeyer to ACofS OPD, "Considerations of Offensive Operations in the Mediterranean Subsequent to the Special Operation," Nov. 16, 1942, MM, ABC 381 (7-25-41), Sec. 4B, 80; unsigned OPD paper, "Strategic Lines of Action in European Theater," Nov. 25, 1942, MM, OPD Exec. 10, Item 63a; Stimson Diary, Dec. 12 and 14, 1942.

37. Policy Comm. rpt., "The Military and Psychological Effect on Russia of the TORCH Operation and the Drive of General Montgomery's Eighth Army," Dec. 19, 1942, MM ABC 334.3 Policy Comm. (1 Aug. 42), Sec. 3. See also ibid., "Weekly Strategic Resume," Nov. 28, Dec. 5 and 26, 1942; memo, Cols. Roberts and Blizzard to Wedemeyer, undated, "Outline of Strategy," and unsigned, untitled, undated paper in MM, OPD Exec. 1, Item 10a, Tab 15; memo, Col. Baumer to Blizzard, "Comparison of Bases for Initiation of Major Offensive Against Axis," Nov. 27, 1942, OCMH, OPD Historical Unit File, Item 20.

38. Leahy Diary, Sept. 20, Oct. 2, 1942; George H. Gallup, *The Gallup Poll*, vol. 1 (1972), p. 270.

39. JCS 152, memo, Arnold to JCS, "Strategic Policy for 1943," Nov. 16, 1942, MM, CCS 381 (11-16-42). See also in Arnold Papers ltr., Arnold to Spaatz, Sept. 2, 1942, Box 38, SOF 1941-1945, Corres.—Commanders-in-the-Field Folder; memos, Arnold to Hopkins, Sept. 3, Oct. 7, 1942, Box 42, OF 1932-1946, Folder 74, Papers 6 and 8; memo, Cols. C. P. Cabell and J. E. Smart to Arnold, Nov. 17, 1942, Journals, Nov. 1942 Folder.

40. Forrest C. Pogue, *George C. Marshall*, vol. 3, *Organizer of Victory* (1973), pp. 12-15. See also Maurice Matloff, "The 90-Division Gamble," in Kent R. Greenfield, ed., *Command Decisions* (1960), pp. 366-68; min., JPS 42 mtg., Oct. 21, 1942, MM, CCS 334 Jt. Staff Planners (10-14-42).

41. "Notes Taken at Meeting in Executive Office of the President," Nov. 25, 1942, MM, CCS 334 (11-10-42); min. of White House mtg., Dec. 10, 1942, MM, OPD Exec. 5, Item 2, Tab 42.

42. JCS 167, "Basic Strategic Concept for 1943," Dec. 11, 1942; min., JCS 46 mtg., Dec. 12, 1942, MM, CCS 381 (8-27-42), Sec. 1.

43. *F.R.: Washington and Casablanca*, pp. 735-38.

44. Ibid., pp. 738-52; see also CPS 49/1 and 49/2, "Planning for Operations Subsequent to TORCH," with attached CPS min., Nov. 17-Dec. 3, 1942, MM, CCS 381 (11-16-42).

45. Sherwood, *Roosevelt and Hopkins*, p. 656.

46. Stimson Diary, Nov. 23, 1942.

47. Memo, Gens. S. D. Embick and Muir S. Fairchild, "Comments on CCS 135/1 and 135/2," Jan. 4, 1943, MM, ABC 381 (9-25-41), Sec. VII,

emphasis in original. See also memo by Stimson of conf. with Hull and
Knox, Dec. 29, 1942, MM, OPD Exec. 5, Item 2, Tab 53; memo, Lt. Col.
D. P. Armstrong, SS, OPD, to Chief, S&P, OPD, "Report of Visit to Middle East," Jan. 12, 1943, MM, ABC 381 Middle East (3-10-42), Sec. 1-A.

48. JCS 167 series, including JSSC papers, min., JCS 49 mtg., and JPS
rpt., Jan 5 to 10, 1943, MM, CCS 381 (8-27-42), Sec. 1; JSSC 4/1, "Operations Subsequent to TORCH," Dec. 31, 1942, MM, CCS 381 (11-16-42).
See also MM, CCS 381 (8-27-42), Secs. 1 and 2; Kent R. Greenfield, *American Strategy in World War II* (1963), p. 31.

49. Min., JCS 49 mtg., Jan. 5, 1943, MM, CCS 381 (8-27-42), Sec. 1.

50. Sherwood, *Roosevelt and Hopkins*, pp. 641-43.

51. *F.R.: Washington and Casablanca,* pp. 505-6.

52. Ibid., pp. 509-11.

53. Ibid., pp. 510-13.

54. Ibid., pp. 536-94; Churchill, *The Hinge of Fate*, pp. 676-77;
Bryant, *The Turn of the Tide*, p. 541; Sir Hastings Ismay, *The Memoirs of General Lord Ismay* (1960), p. 286.

55. Min., JCS 52 mtg., Jan. 16, 1943, MM, CCS 334 (1-14-43).

56. Ibid.; *F. R.: Washington and Casablanca,* pp. 583-84, 594-98, 631.

57. Min., JCS 52 mtg., Jan. 16, 1943, MM, CCS 334 (1-14-43).

58. *F.R.: Washington and Casablanca*, pp. 601-4, 614-22. Over 50 per
cent of U.S. combat troops were in the Pacific at this time; see Leighton
and Coakley, *Global Logistics, 1940-1943*, p. 662.

59. Bryant, *The Turn of the Tide*, p. 449.

60. Pogue, *Marshall*, vol. 3, pp. 26-30.

61. *F.R.: Washington and Casablanca*, pp. 627-37, 760-61.

62. Ibid., pp. 629-30, 634.

63. *Stalin's Correspondence,* vol. 2, p. 50.

64. Bryant, *The Turn of the Tide*, p. 445.

65. *F.R.: Washington and Casablanca*, p. 629.

66. Ibid., p. 629; Elliot Roosevelt, *As He Saw It* (1946), p. 100.

67. Memo, Roosevelt to JCS with notation by Pres. that it was delivered orally, Jan. 20, 1943, Roosevelt Papers, MRF, Box 19.

68. *F.R.: Washington and Casablanca*, pp. 791-98; see also pp. 649-52,
659-60, 677-79, 688-89, 764-73, 785-91.

69. Ibid., p. 631; see also pp. 716-18, 785-89.

70. Ibid., pp. 632-33, 708-11; Ernest J. King and Walter M. Whitehill,
Fleet Admiral King (1952), p. 421.

71. *F.R.: Washington and Casablanca*, pp. 782-85, 803-7.

72. Roosevelt, *As He Saw It*, p. 117.

73. *F. R.: Washington and Casablanca,* p. 708.

74. Ltr., Wedemeyer to Handy, Jan. 22, 1943, MM, OPD Exec. 3, Item 1a, paper 5; see also Albert C. Wedemeyer, *Wedemeyer Reports!* (1958), pp 169-70, 189-92.

75. Bryant, *The Turn of the Tide,* pp. 458-59.

76. Sherwood, *Roosevelt and Hopkins*, p. 675, and notes dictated by Hopkins, Jan. 23, 1943, Hopkins Papers, Sherwood collection, Box 137, Casablanca Folder.

77. Leahy Diary, Feb. 2, 1943.

78. Kennedy, *The Business of War*, pp. 282, 285.

79. Chandler, *The Eisenhower Papers*, vol. 2, pp. 927-29.

80. *F.R.: Washington and Casablanca*, pp. 632-33, 708-11.

CHAPTER 6: THE MERGING OF OLD AND NEW ISSUES

1. Ltr., Wedemeyer to Handy, Jan. 22, 1943, MM, OPD Exec. 3, Item 1a, Paper 5; memo, Wedemeyer to Deputy CofS, "Report of Mission Headed by General Devers," Apr. 28, 1943, MM, OPD 381 Security (Sec. III), 118.

2. Maurice Matloff, *Strategic Planning for Coalition Warfare, 1943-1944* (1959), pp. 106-11; see also Ray S. Cline, *Washington Command Post* (1951), pp. 235-42.

3. Gordon A. Harrison, *Cross-Channel Attack* (1951), pp. 46-47; Richard M. Leighton and Robert W. Coakley, *Global Logistics and Strategy, 1943-1945* (1968), pp. 48-49; unsigned OPD rpt., Feb. 23, 1943, MM, OPD Exec. 1, Item 16; min., JCS 69 and 71 mtgs., Mar. 23 and 30, 1943, MM, CCS 334 (1-14-43) and (3-29-43); JCS 243 series, MM, CCS 381 (8-27-42), Sec. 2.

4. *F.R.: The Conferences at Washington and Quebec, 1943* (1970), pp. 12-14.

5. Leighton and Coakley, *Global Logistics, 1943-1945*, p. 29; Sir Frederick Morgan, *Overture to Overlord* (1950), p. 71; CCS 199/1, "Survey of Present Strategic Situation," Apr. 23, 1943, and CCS 169 series, CCS 381 (8-27-42), Sec. 2; min., CCS 81-82 mtgs., Apr. 23 and 30, 1943, MM, CCS 334 (2-25-43) (mtgs. 70-88).

6. *F.R., 1943*, vol. 2 (1964), p. 326.

7. Min., White House mtg., Apr. 6, 1943, and supp. min., JCS 75 mtg., Apr. 20, 1943, MM, CCS 334 (3-29-43); CCS 169 series, MM, CCS 381 (8-27-42); Leighton and Coakley, *Global Logistics, 1943-1945*, p. 29.

8. Stimson Diary, Apr. 28 and May 3, 1943.

9. Arnold, "Observation Memorandum as of May 1, 1943," Arnold Papers, Box 3, Misc. Corres., 1943; ltr., Maj. Gen. H. D. Ingles, Deputy

Theater Commander, ETO, to Marshall, May 6, 1943, MM, OPD Exec. 3, Item 1c, Paper 4.

10. Memo, Theodore Achilles, European Affairs Div. to Hull, Welles, and Atherton, Apr. 3, 1943, DS, 740.0011 EW 1939/29067.

11. Leahy Diary, Feb. 10, 1943.

12. Ltr., Stimson and Hull to Pres., Apr. 13, 1943, MM, OPD Exec. 3, Item 1a, Paper 86.

13. JWPC3 and JPS memo, "Agenda for Next United Nations Conference," Apr. 24 and 26, 1943, MM, CCS 381 (4-24-43), Sec. 1, Pt. 1; supp. min., JCS 76 mtg., Apr. 27, 1943, MM, CCS 334 (3-29-43).

14. SS 74, "Probable British Proposals for Further Operations in 1943 and 1944 in the European-African Areas," Apr. 14, 1943, MM, ABC 381 SS (7 Jan. 43) (Nos. 2-95), Tab 74; see also unsigned, undated OPD rpt. with app., "Strategic Considerations," MM, ABC 381 (9-25-42), Sec. VII, Papers 16 and 17.

15. JCS 283-283/1, "Current British Policy and Strategy in Relationship to That of the United States," May 3, 1943, MM, CCS 381 (4-24-43), Sec. 3.

16. Ibid.; JSSC memo, "Probable Russian Reaction to Anglo-American Operations in the Aegean," May 5, 1943, MM, CCS 381 (9-5-43).

17. George H. Gallup, *The Gallup Poll*, vol. 1 (1972), p. 370.

18. Matloff, *Strategic Planning, 1943-1944*, pp. 117-19.

19. JWPC 14, " Conduct of the War 1943-1944," an amplification of JCS 290, May 7, 1943, MM, CCS 381 (4-24-43), Sec. 1, Pt. 1.

20. Ibid.; see also unsigned, undated OPD paper, "U.S.-British Strategy," MM, OPD Exec. 10, Item 69.

21. See Apr. SS rpts., MM, ABC 381 SS (7 Jan. 43) (Nos. 2-95), Tabs 54/1-3, 57, 75, 79; memo, Hull to Marshall, May 3, 1943, MM, OPD Exec. 10, Item 57; Matloff, *Strategic Planning, 1943-1944*, pp. 120-24; Leighton and Coakley, *Global Logistics, 1943-1945*, pp. 59-61; Ch. 22 of Cline's original unpub. work "Washington Command Post."

22. JCS 286, 288, and 293 series, MM, CCS 381 (3-23-42) and (4-24-43).

23. Min., JCS 78 mtg., May 8, 1943, MM, CCS 334 (3-29-43).

24. Memo, Leahy for JCS to Pres., "Recommended Line of Action at Coming Conference," May 8, 1943, Roosevelt Papers, MRF, Naval Aide's File, Gen. Corres.

25. See below, pp. 101, 109-111.

26. William D. Leahy, *I Was There* (1950), pp. 157-58.

27. Stimson Diary, May 10 and 12, 1943; for differing interpretations of this mtg., see Matloff, *Strategic Planning, 1943-1944,* pp. 124-25, and Leighton and Coakley, *Global Logistics, 1943-1945*, p. 62.

28. Michael Howard, *Grand Strategy*, vol. 4 (1972), p. 327.

29. Memo, Strong, G-2, to CofS, "Russian Reaction to Operations, June, 1943," Jan. 28, 1943, MM, WDCSA, Russia.

30. *Stalin's Correspondence*, vol. 1, p. 89; see also William H. Standley and Arthur A. Ageton, *Admiral Ambassador to Russia* (1955), pp. 453-54.

31. Tel., Churchill to Roosevelt, Feb. 3, 1943, Roosevelt Papers, MRF, Box 3.

32. Howard, *Grand Strategy*, vol. 4, p. 328.

33. Memo, CofS to Pres., "Message to Mr. Stalin," and tel., Roosevelt to Churchill, Feb. 5, 1943, MM, OPD Exec. 10, Item 63a.

34. *Stalin's Correspondence,* vol. 1, pp. 93-94.

35. Ibid., vol. 1, pp. 94-106, vol. 2, pp. 55-59.

36. *F.R., 1942*, vol. 3 (1961), pp. 197-212, 290-91; *F.R., 1943*, vol. 2, pp. 969-70, 974-75, 978-1003; *F.R., 1943*, vol. 3 (1963), pp. 314-29, 332-80, 506-9. See also Roosevelt Papers, Mar. tels. from Earle, MRF, Box 15a, and Jan.-Mar. Papers, PSF, Box 17, Poland Folder; disp., Biddle to Hull, Jan. 20, 1943, DS, 840.50/1256; DS, 740.0011 EW 1939/24630, 27293, 27518, 28101, 18720, 18607.

37. Stimson Diary, Dec. 18, 1942.

38. Two unsigned memos from American Republics Div. to Chapin, Dec. 20, 1942, DS, 711.61/871 1/2.

39. OSS Interoffice Memo, Mar. 2, 1943, OSS 29551 R; see also Leahy Diary, Mar. 31, 1943.

40. Memo, Berle to Lehman, Mar. 24, 1943, Hull Papers, Box 90, SF, Folder 403.

41. "The Weekly Strategic Resume," Jan. 23, 1943, MM, ABC 334.3 Policy Comm. (1 Aug. 42), 3.

42. Memo, Arnold to CofS, "Heavy Bombers for Russia," Feb. 23, 1943, MM, OPD 452.1 Russia (Sec. 1), Case 24.

43. Ibid., memo, Handy to CofS, "Heavy Bombers for Russia," Mar. 8, 1943. See also rpt. by Lt. Col. Park, Jan. 23, 1943, and memo, Col. Bratton, Chief, Intelligence Group, to ACofS, OPD (attn: Gen. Wedemeyer), "United States-U.S.S.R. Policy," Mar. 5, 1943, MM, ABC 334.3 Policy Comm. (1 Aug. 42), 1 and 4, Tab 20; memo, Wedemeyer to Handy, Dec. 19, 1942, MM, OPD 381 Russia; Albert C. Wedemeyer, *Wedemeyer Reports!* (1958), pp. 185-86; Jan Ciechanowski, *Defeat in Victory* (1947), p. 130.

44. See above, pp. 39, 183 n. 3.

45. Ltr., Biddle to Welles, June 18, 1942, DS, 740.0011 EW 1939/ 23023.

46. Memo, Sikorski to Marshall, Dec. 22, 1942, MM, OPD 381 Gen.

114; same memo to Welles, DS, 740.0011 EW 1939/26678 1/2.

47. Unsigned Dept. memo to Atherton attached to ibid.

48. Min., JCS 52 mtg., Jan. 16, 1943, MM, CCS 334 (1-14-43).

49. OSS rpt., Dec. 24, 1942, OSS 25921.

50. Howard, *Grand Strategy*, vol. 4, p. 329.

51. Memo, Bullitt to Roosevelt, Jan. 27, 1943, Roosevelt Papers, PSF, Box 1, Bullitt Folder, reprinted in part in Orville H. Bullitt, ed., *For the President* (1972), pp. 573-80. Kennan served under Bullitt in Moscow during the 1930s.

52. Ibid. Bullitt also sent this memo to Hull and discussed it with Leahy.

53. Wedemeyer, *Wedemeyer Reports!*, pp. 228-30.

54. William C. Bullitt, "How We Won the War and Lost the Peace," *Life*, 25 (Aug. 30, 1948): 91-94.

55. *F.R., 1943*, vol. 3, pp. 17, 22, 36, 39.

56. Ibid, p. 26.

57. See Cordell Hull, *The Memoirs of Cordell Hull*, vol. 2 (1948), pp. 1284-85; memo, King to Knox, "Postwar Security Force," Apr. 13, 1943, NH, King Papers.

58. Memo, Arnold to Hopkins, "BOLERO Operations," Apr. 9, 1943, Arnold Papers, Box 43, OF 1932-1946, Folder 90.

59. Memo, Marshall to Handy, Mar. 30, 1943, MM, WDCSA (Super Secret), I, and OPD Exec. 10, Item 57.

60. See below, pp. 94, 105, 117-123; Morgan, *Overture to Overlord*, p. 54. COSSAC prepared three RANKIN plans for differing degrees of German deterioration; Case C was for total collapse.

61. Winston S. Churchill, *The Second World War*, vol. 4, *The Hinge of Fate* (1950), pp. 754-55.

62. *F.R., 1943*, vol. 3, pp. 358-60, 372-74, 400-2, 404-5; *Stalin's Correspondence*, vol. 1, pp. 120-30; Hull, *Memoirs*, vol. 2, pp. 1268-69; unsigned memo, "Notes on Relations with the Soviet Union," Apr. 26, 1943, Hull Papers, Box 51, Folder 155; OSS rpt., Mar. 30, 1943, OSS 25743 S; tels., Earle to Roosevelt, Apr. 1943, Roosevelt Papers, MRF, Box 15a; memo, Berle to European Affairs Div., Mar. 26, 1943, DS, 740.0011 EW 1939/29001.

63. CCS Russian Combat Estimate, Apr. 1, 1943, MM, JCS Geographic Series, CCS 350.05 USSR (4-1-42).

64. *Stalin's Correspondence*, vol. 2, pp. 63-64.

65. See Leahy, *I Was There*, pp. 157-58.

66. Min., JCS 79 mtg., May 10, 1943, MM, CCS 334 (3-29-43).

67. Ibid., supp. min.

68. *F.R.: Washington and Quebec*, pp. 25-27.

69. Ibid., pp. 29-30.

70. See JCS 286, 288 and 293 series, MM, CCS 381 (3-23-42) and (4-24-43); min., JCS 84-85 mtgs., May 18-19, 1943, MM, CCS 334 (3-29-43).

71. Lord Moran, *Churchill: Taken from the Diaries of Lord Moran* (1966), p. 102; for a contrary viewpoint, see Leighton and Coakley, *Global Logistics, 1943-1945,* pp. 62-63.

72. Memo, Bullitt to Pres., May 12, 1943, Roosevelt Papers, PSF, Box 1, Diplomatic Corres., Bullitt Folder, reprinted in Bullitt, *For the Persident*, pp. 591-94.

73. Henry L. Stimson and McGeorge Bundy, *On Active Service in Peace and War* (1947), p. 527; Stimson Diary, May 17 and 19, 1943, Stimson comments on Bullitt memo, May 14, 1943, Stimson Papers.

74. See Matloff, *Strategic Planning, 1943-1944*, pp. 130-31; min., JCS 81-85 mtgs., May 14-19, 1943, MM, CCS 334 (3-29-43); MM, CCS 381 (4-24-43), Secs. 1-5.

75. *F.R.: Washington and Quebec*, p. 45.

76. Arthur Bryant, *The Turn of the Tide* (1957), p. 508.

77. *F.R.: Washington and Quebec*, pp. 43-44, 53-54, 81-84, 93, 101-2, 112-16, 222-29, 238-39, 273-81.

78. Bryant, *The Turn of the Tide,* pp. 504-509.

79. See JCS 286, 288 and 293 series, MM, CCS 381 (3-23-42) and (4-24-43); min., JCS 83-85 mtgs., May 17-19, 1943, MM, CCS 334 (3-29-43).

80. *F.R.: Washington and Quebec*, pp. 36-48, 52-56, 77-84, 93-96, 101-2, 112-16, 232, 257-72; Bryant, *The Turn of the Tide*, pp. 504-8.

81. Forrest C. Pogue, *George C. Marshall*, vol. 3, *Organizer of Victory* (1973), p. 208.

82. Sir Hastings Ismay, *The Memoirs of General Lord Ismay* (1960), p. 296; Mark Clark, *Calculated Risk* (1950), p. 66.

83. Bryant, *The Turn of the Tide*, pp. 508-10.

84. *F.R.: Washington and Quebec*, pp. 121-22, 281-82, 346-73.

85. Ibid., pp. 193-95; Churchill, *The Hinge of Fate* (1950), p. 810; Moran, *Churchill*, p. 104.

86. Bryant, *The Turn of the Tide*, p. 513.

87. Leahy Diary, May 24, 1943.

88. Stimson Diary, May 17, 25, and 27, 1943; see also Bryant, *The Turn of the Tide*, p. 514.

89. Bryant, *The Turn of the Tide*, pp. 509, 515.

90. Ernest J. King and Walter M. Whitehill, *Fleet Admiral King* (1952), p. 443.

91. Stimson Diary, May 27, 1943.

92. *F. R.: Washington and Quebec,* pp. 49-50.

93. Stimson Diary, May 11, 1943.

94. *F. R.: Washington and Quebec,* pp. 167-68.

95. Memo by Gen. Hull, "Analysis of TRIDENT and Anfa Conferences," May 25, 1943, MM, OPD Exec. 5, Item 10, Tabs 8-9.

96. See *Stalin's Correspondence,* vol. 1, pp. 93-106.

97. Churchill, *The Hinge of Fate,* pp. 810-13; *F.R.: Washington and Quebec,* pp. 379-87; *Stalin's Correspondence,* vol. 2, pp. 67-69.

CHAPTER 7: THE SUMMER CRISES

1. Ray S. Cline, *Washington Command Post* (1951), pp. 317-18.

2. Min. of mtgs. at Eisenhower's Villa, May 29 and 31, 1943, and App. A to May 31 mtg., MM, CCS 381 (4-23-43), Sec. 1.

3. Ibid. In *Crusade in Europe* (1948), p. 167, Eisenhower claimed Brooke had privately said he would "be glad to reconsider the cross-Channel project, even to the extent of eliminating" it "from accepted allied strategy." In Arthur Bryant's *The Turn of the Tide* (1957), p. 521, Brooke flatly denied the charge.

4. Min., May 29, 31, and June 3, 1943 mtgs., MM, CCS 381 (4-23-43), Sec. 1.

5. Ibid.; Winston S. Churchill, *The Second World War,* vol. 4, *The Hinge of Fate* (1950), p. 817; Lord Moran, *Churchill: Taken from the Diaries of Lord Moran* (1966), pp. 109-12.

6. Stimson Diary, June 8, 1943; min., JCS 91 mtg., June 8, 1943, MM, CCS 334 (5-21-43).

7. Stimson Diary, June 1, 1943; see also June 4-28, 1943, and Leahy Diary, June 11 and 17, 1943.

8. Henry L. Stimson and McGeorge Bundy, *On Active Service In Peace and War* (1947), pp. 429-31; Stimson Diary, Aug. 4, 1943 rpt.

9. Gordon A. Harrison, *Cross-Channel Attack* (1951), p. 87; Alfred D. Chandler, Jr., ed., *The Papers of Dwight David Eisenhower,* vol. 2 (1970), pp. 1261-62; memo, Strong, G-2, to CofS, " 'HUSKY' Exploitation," July 15, 1943, MM, ABC 381 SS (7 Jan. 43) (Nos. 2-95), Tab 57/1; min., CCS 102 mtg., July 16, 1943, MM, CCS 334 (5-19-43).

10. Winston S. Churchill, *The Second World War,* vol. 5, *Closing the Ring* (1951), pp. 35-36.

11. Stimson and Bundy, *On Active Service,* pp. 432-33; Stimson Diary, Aug. 4, 1943 rpt.

12. Michael Howard, *Grand Strategy*, vol. 4 (1972), pp. 564-65.

13. Sir John Kennedy, *The Business of War* (1957), pp. 294-95.

14. Memo, Somervell to CofS, "Planning," July 20, 1943, MM, ABC 381 (9-25-41), Sec. VII; see also Maurice Matloff, *Strategic Planning for Coalition Warfare, 1943-1944* (1959), pp. 179-84.

15. CCS 268/6-9, "Post-HUSKY Operations, North African Theater," July 21-26, 1943, MM, CCS 381 (4-23-43), Sec. 2; min., CCS 103 mtg. and sp. mtg., July 23 and 26, 1943, MM, CCS 334 (5-19-43); Bryant, *The Turn of the Tide*, pp. 550-51.

16. Churchill, *Closing the Ring*, pp. 55-59.

17. Rpt. by sp. subcomm., Cols. W. W. Bessell and R. C. Lindsay, "Conduct of the War," July 25, 1943, MM, OPD 381 Security Sec. VIIB, 218; see also unsigned OPD papers, "Notes re Strategic Policy—U.S. vs. U.K.," undated, and "Agreements with British with Respect to Future Operations," Aug. 8, 1943, MM, ABC 381 (9-25-42), Sec. VII.

18. Memo, OPD to Marshall, "Notes for Use in Conference with President," July 22, 1943, MM, OPD Exec. 5, Item 11, Paper 1.

19. Memo, Col. W. E. Todd, Deputy Chief, S&P, to ACofS, OPD, "Special JCS Meeting of July 26, 1943," MM, OPD Exec. 5, Item 11, Paper 2.

20. Churchill, *Closing the Ring*, pp. 55-59.

21. Min., JCS sp. mtg., July 26, 1943, MM, CCS 334 (5-21-43).

22. Memo, Hull to Handy, July 17, 1943, MM, ABC 381 SS (7 Jan. 43) (Nos. 96-126/3), Tab 111; sp. subcomm. rpt. cited in n. 17; JPS 231, "Operations in the European-Mediterranean Area, 1943-1944—Adequacy of TRIDENT Strategy," July 26, 1943, MM, CCS 381 (6-7-43), Sec. 1.

23. *F.R.: The Conferences at Washington and Quebec, 1943* (1970), pp. 486-96.

24. Min., JPS 89 mtg., Aug. 4, 1943, MM, CCS 334 Jt. Staff Planners (3-24-43). For differing interpretations of this split and the final JCS decision, see Harrison, *Cross-Channel Attack*, pp. 92-94; Matloff, *Strategic Planning, 1943-1944*, pp. 165-79; Richard M. Leighton and Robert W. Coakley, *Global Logistics and Strategy, 1943-1945* (1968), pp. 178-85.

25. Min., JCS 100 mtg., Aug. 6, 1943, MM, CCS 334 (5-21-43).

26. *F.R., 1943*, vol. 3 (1963), pp. 519-20, 536-37; *F.R.: The Conferences at Cairo and Tehran, 1943* (1961), pp. 5-7.

27. *F.R., 1943*, vol. 3, p. 658.

28. *Stalin's Correspondence*, vol. 2, pp. 70-71.

29. David Dilks, ed., *The Diaries of Sir Alexander Cadogan, 1938-1945* (1972), pp. 534-35.

30. *Stalin's Correspondence*, vol. 1, pp. 133-35, vol. 2, p. 72.

31. Sir Llewellyn Woodward, *British Foreign Policy in the Second World War*, vol. 2 (1971), p. 556.

32. *Stalin's Correspondence*, vol. 1, pp. 136-38, vol. 2, pp. 73-76.

33. Ibid, vol. 1, pp. 140-41.

34. *F.R.: Cairo and Tehran*, pp. 10-12.

35. Woodward, *British Foreign Policy* (1962), p. 561.

36. Ibid., pp. 562-63; *F.R., 1943*, vol. 2, pp. 121, 143, 1011, vol. 3, pp. 420-57, 548-54, 560-63; Herbert Feis, *Churchill, Roosevelt and Stalin* (1967), pp. 136, 142-43; Julius W. Pratt, *Cordell Hull* (1964), pp. 613-14; tels., Biddle, McClintlock, and Winant to Hull, June 26, 30 and July 27, 1943, DS, 740.00119 EW 1939/1530, 1515, 1091; tels., Messersmith and Standley to Hull, July 10 and 29, 1943, DS, 740.0011 EW 1939/ 30122 and 30455; OSS rpt. from Foreign Nationalities Branch, "Development of Polish-Russian Antagonism in the United States," June 24, 1943, OSS 37797 S.

37. Tel., Churchill to Roosevelt, June 28, 1943, Roosevelt Papers, MRF, Box 3; Woodward, *British Foreign Policy*, p. 243.

38. *F. R., 1943,* vol. 3, pp. 553-59, 682-97; tels., Standley and Johnson to Hull, Aug. 12 and 16, 1943, DS, 740.0011 EW 1939/30675 and 30701; tels., Standley to Hull, July 22 and Aug. 3, 1943, and circular, Berle to Diplomatic Missions in Other American Republics, Aug. 19, 1943, DS, 862.01/299, 326 and 359A.

39. SS rpt., "Course of Action for the United States in the Event Russia and Germany Effect a Compromise Peace in July and August, 1943," undated, MM, ABC 381 SS (7 Jan. 43) (Nos. 131-159), Tab 131; memo, Wedemeyer to Marshall, Aug. 5, 1943, MM, ABC 384 Europe Sec. 1A, 5 Aug. 43.

40. See above, pp. 87-91.

41. Memo, Brig.-Gen. E. P. Sorenson, ACofS, Air, Intelligence Div., to Arnold, "Reconsideration of Invasion Timing," Aug. 4, 1943, Arnold Papers, Journals, Aug. 1-15, 1943 Folder.

42. See sp. subcomm. rpt. cited in n. 17.

43. JWPC 62, "United Nations Course of Action on Termination of the War with the European Axis," July 20, 1943, MM, CCS 387 EUROPE (7-20-43), Box 578, geographic series; memo, Col. R. T. Maddocks, GSC, to Col. Roberts, July 23, 1943, MM, ABC 381 SS (7 Jan. 43) (Nos. 2-95), Tab 90; memo, Somervell to CofS, "Planning," July 20, 1943, MM, ABC 381 (9-25-41), Sec. VII.

44. London OSS Correspondent rpt., June 16, 1943, OSS 37453 S.

45. See below, pp. 116-123.

46. Min., JCS 100 mtg., Aug. 6, 1943, MM, CCS 334 (5-21-43).

47. Ibid.

48. Min., JPS 91 mtg., Aug. 7, 1943, MM, CCS 334 Jt. Staff Planners (3-24-43).

49. JCS 443 Rev., "QUADRANT and European Strategy," Aug. 6, 1943, MM, CCS 381 (5-23-43), Sec. 1; min., JCS 101 mtg., Aug. 7, 1943, MM, CCS 334 (8-7-43).

50. Min., JCS 101 mtg., Aug. 7, 1943, MM, CCS 334 (8-7-43).

51. *F.R.: Washington and Quebec*, pp. 467-72, with handwritten comments on copy in MM, OPD 381 Security Case 217, Sec. VIIA, Pt. 2; Matloff, *Strategic Planning, 1943-1944*, pp. 176-79.

52. Min., JCS 101-103 mtgs., Aug. 7-10, 1943, MM, CCS 334 (8-7-43).

53. *F.R.: Washington and Quebec*, pp. 472-82, emphasis in original.

54. Ibid.

55. JPS 189, "Preparations for the Next U.S.-British Staff Conference," May 25, 1943, MM, CCS 381 (5-25-43), Sec. 1.

56. Memo, Wedemeyer to Marshall, June 8, 1943, MM, OPD Exec. 8, Book 10, Paper 68.

57. JWPC 30/11, "Thoughts for QUADRANT," Aug. 4, 1943, MM, CCS 381 (5-25-43), Sec. 1.

58. Memo, JSSC to JCS, "Procedure for Chiefs of Staff at Conference," Aug. 9, 1943, MM, CCS 381 (10-17-43), Sec. 1B; min., JPS 93 mtg., Aug. 11, 1943, MM, CCS 334 Jt. Staff Planners (3-24-43).

59. JCS 443 Rev., "QUADRANT and European Strategy," Aug. 6, 1943, MM, CCS 381 (5-24-43), Sec. 1.

60. Churchill, *Closing the Ring*, pp. 99-100.

61. Stimson and Bundy, *On Active Service*, pp. 429-34, full memo in Stimson Diary; ltr., Stimson to Pres., Aug. 4, 1943, Roosevelt Papers, PSF, Stimson Folder.

62. Ltr., Roosevelt to Stimson, Aug. 8, 1943, Roosevelt Papers, PSF, Stimson Folder.

63. *F.R.: Washington and Quebec*, pp. 482-83; min., JCS 103 mtg., Aug. 10, 1943, MM, CCS 334 (8-7-43).

64. Stimson Diary, Aug. 10, 1943; Stimson and Bundy, *On Active Service*, pp. 435-39.

65. Ibid.

66. Ibid.; *F.R.: Washington and Quebec*, pp. 498-503.

67. *F. R.: Washington and Quebec*, pp. 499-501. See also min., JCS 103 mtg., Aug. 10, 1943, MM, CCS 334 (8-7-43); ltr., Arnold to Kuter, Aug. 11, 1943, Arnold Papers, Journals, Aug. 1-15 Folder.

68. Stimson and Bundy, *On Active Service*, pp. 438-39.

CHAPTER 8: SHOWDOWN AT QUEBEC

1. *F.R.: The Conferences at Washington and Quebec, 1943* (1970), p. 864; John Ehrman, *Grand Strategy*, vol. 5 (1956), pp. 80-81, 88-92; Richard M. Leighton and Robert W. Coakley, *Global Logistics and Strategy, 1943-1945* (1968), pp. 200-1; Winston S. Churchill, *The Second World War*, vol. 5, *Closing the Ring* (1951), pp. 82-83, 203-4.

2. *F.R.: Washington and Quebec*, pp. 472-77, 483-84, 863-68.

3. Ibid., pp. 866-68, 1023-24.

4. Ibid., pp. 867-68.

5. Arthur Bryant, *The Turn of the Tide* (1957), p. 578.

6. Ibid., p. 579.

7. Min., JCS 104 mtg., Aug. 15, 1943, MM, CCS 334 (8-7-43).

8. Bryant, *The Turn of the Tide*, p. 576.

9. *F.R.: Washington and Quebec*, pp. 588-601, 1055-61; Alfred D. Chandler, Jr., ed., *The Papers of Dwight David Eisenhower*, vol. 2 (1970), pp. 1335-36.

10. *F.R.: Washington and Quebec*, p. 891 n. 8.

11. Ibid., pp. 1024-26, 1037-39.

12. Bryant, *The Turn of the Tide*, p. 581; Leighton and Coakley, *Global Logistics, 1943-1945*, pp. 203-4; Michael Howard, *Grand Strategy*, vol. 4 (1972), pp. 569-70.

13. Howard, *Grand Strategy,* vol. 4, pp. 508, 569-70.

14. Bryant, *The Turn of the Tide*, pp. 574-75, 578-79; Churchill, *Closing the Ring*, pp. 82-83, 203-4.

15. *F.R.: Washington and Quebec*, pp. 896-97, 942-43.

16. Final CCS rpt. in ibid., pp. 1121-32.

17. Harley Notter, *Postwar Foreign Policy Preparation, 1939-1945* (1950), p. 188.

18. *Stalin's Correspondence*, vol. 1, pp. 142 and 387n. 35.

19. Churchill, *Closing the Ring*, p. 81.

20. Naval Intelligence disp., Aug. 19, 1943, Roosevelt Papers, MRF, MR 300, Sec. 1; tels., Winant, Scotten, and Standley to Hull, Aug. 23-24, 1943, DS, 740.0011 EW 1939/30821, 30831-34, 30842; tel., Harrison to Hull, Aug. 24, 1943, DS, 740.0019 EW 1939/1607.

21. William H. Standley and Arthur A. Ageton, *Admiral Ambassador to Russia* (1955), p. 467, emphasis in original.

22. Min., JCS 104 mtg., Aug. 15, 1943, MM, CCS 334 (8-7-43).

23. Anthony Eden, *The Memoirs of Anthony Eden, Earl of Avon: The Reckoning* (1965), p. 466.

24. Memo, OSS Planning Group to JCS, "Manifesto to German People by Moscow National Committee of Free Germany," Aug. 6, 1943, MM, ABC 381 (9-25-41), Sec. VII, PG 40/1.

25. Ibid., app.

26. Ibid.

27. Ibid., memo, Wedemeyer to CofS, Aug. 10, 1943.

28. Memo, Dunn to Strong, Aug. 11, 1943, MM, OPD Exec. 9, Item 11, Papers 75 and 103.

29. Ibid., memos, Hull to Handy, Aug. 14, 1943, Handy to CofS.

30. JIC rpt., "Estimate of the Enemy Situation 1943-44, European-Mediterranean Area," July 19, 1943, MM, CCS 381 (6-7-43), Sec. 1.

31. *F.R.: Washington and Quebec*, pp. 910-11.

32. Ibid, p. 911.

33. Sir John Kennedy, *The Business of War* (1957), pp. 304-5.

34. Tel., Harriman to Roosevelt, July 5, 1943, Roosevelt Papers, PSF, Britain, 1943.

35. See Churchill, *Closing the Ring*, pp. 99-100.

36. Churchill, *Closing the Ring*, pp. 535-36; *F.R.: Washington and Quebec*, pp. 915, 932-34, 1044-46; *F.R., 1943*, vol. 4 (1964), pp. 141-48.

37. Churchill, *Closing the Ring*, pp. 536-37.

38. Cordell Hull, *The Memoirs of Cordell Hull*, vol. 2 (1947), p. 1231.

39. Interview with Henderson, Oct., 1969; ltr., Henderson to author, Aug. 1, 1970.

40. Draft of memo, Bullitt to Hull, Aug. 6, 1943, Hull Papers, Box 51, Corres., Folder 157; memo, Bullitt to Roosevelt, Aug. 10, 1943, Roosevelt Papers, PSF, Box 1, Diplomatic Corres., Bullitt Folder, reprinted in Orville H. Bullitt, ed., *For the President* (1972), pp. 595-99.

41. See above, p. 89; Lynn E. Davis, *The Cold War Begins* (1974), pp. 79-80.

42. *F. R.: Washington and Quebec,* pp. 624-27, emphasis in original. This memo apparently became the basis for later JCS judgments on the USSR; see JCS 506 series, "Instructions Concerning Duty as Military Observer at American-British-Soviet Conference," Sept.-Oct. 1943, MM, CCS 337 (9-12-43), Sec. 1; *F. R., 1944*, vol. 1 (1966), pp. 700-3; *F. R.: The Conferences at Malta and Yalta, 1945* (1955), pp. 107-8.

43. JCS memo for Information 121, "Strategy and Policy: Can America and Russia Cooperate?," Aug. 22, 1943, MM, CCS 092 USSR (8-22-43), emphasis in original.

44. For further information on this memo, see covering memo, Donovan to Deane, ibid.; memo, Col. Ordway to Col. Roberts, Aug. 27, 1943, MM, OPD Exec. 9, Item 11, Paper 107; ltr., Special Asst. to Director, Research

and Analysis, OSS, to Col. R. J. Laux, CAD, Jan. 20, 1944, MM, RG 165, CAD 388 (9-17-43) (1).

45. Min., JCS 111 mtg., Aug. 23, 1943, MM, CCS 334 (8-7-43); *F.R.: Washington and Quebec*, pp. 940, 1010-18; Gabriel Kolko, *The Politics of War* (1968), pp. 29-30, argues that RANKIN was a purely political plan to block Russian expansion into Europe. The analysis in this work shows such a motive to be one of many. John L. Gaddis, *The United States and the Origins of the Cold War, 1941-1947* (1972), p. 76, n. 23, disputes Kolko's claim. He argues that Kolko offers "no firm evidence" and that COSSAC's summary of RANKIN "noted specifically that the plan was to be carried out *in cooperation with* the Russians" (emphasis in original). COSSAC's actual statement was that "close attention should be devoted *to the question* of collaboration with the U.S.S.R." (*F.R.: Washington and Quebec,* pp. 1018, my emphasis). Such attention was not given, and RANKIN was never mentioned to the Soviets.

46. *F.R.: Washington and Quebec*, p. 942.

47. Ibid., pp. 1086-87.

48. Herbert Feis, *Churchill, Roosevelt and Stalin* (1967), p. 172.

49. *F.R.: Washington and Quebec*, pp. 966-67.

50. Churchill, *Closing the Ring*, pp. 93-94.

CHAPTER 9: OVERLORD IN TROUBLE

1. Lord Moran, *Churchill: Taken from the Diaries of Lord Moran* (1966), p. 117.

2. *F.R.: The Conferences at Washington and Quebec, 1943* (1970), pp. 1212-15, 1287-90; see also Winston S. Churchill, *The Second World War,* vol. 5, *Closing the Ring* (1951), p. 131.

3. Memo, Hull to CofS, Sept. 9, 1943, MM, OPD Exec. 10, Item 63b; min., sp. JCS mtg., Sept. 9, 1943, MM, CCS 334 (8-7-43).

4. *F.R.: Washington and Quebec*, pp. 1222-24, 1290-92.

5. Churchill, *Closing the Ring*, p. 205.

6. Ibid., pp. 205-9; Alfred D. Chandler, Jr., ed., *The Papers of Dwight David Eisenhower*, vol. 3 (1970), pp. 1460-63, 1484-87.

7. Chandler, *The Eisenhower Papers*, vol. 3, pp. 1487-89.

8. Unsigned OPD memo to CofS, " Future Operations in the Eastern Mediterranean," Oct. 5, 1943, MM, ABC 381 SS (7 Jan. 43) (Nos. 131-159), Tab 154; see also Tab 157.

9. JSSC enclosure to min., JCS 117 mtg., Oct. 5, 1943, MM, CCS 334 (9-19-43).

10. Ibid., min., JCS 117 mtg.; Marshall's handwritten comments on Eisenhower's Oct. 5 tel., Roosevelt Papers, MRF, Box 15.

11. Churchill, *Closing the Ring*, pp. 210-11; Chandler, *The Eisenhower Papers*, vol. 3, p. 1492.

12. Churchill, *Closing the Ring*, pp. 536-38; see also pp. 126-30.

13. Ibid., p. 538; John Ehrman, *Grand Strategy*, vol. 5 (1956), pp. 86-87.

14. Ehrman, *Grand Strategy*, vol. 5, p. 88.

15. Arthur Bryant, *Triumph in the West* (1959), pp. 31-32.

16. Leahy Diary, Oct. 7, 1943.

17. Ibid.; Churchill, *Closing the Ring*, pp. 211-12.

18. Churchill, *Closing the Ring*, pp. 212-13.

19. Ibid., pp. 214-15; memo, Marshall to Leahy, Oct. 8, 1943, Arnold Papers, Box 3, Misc. Corres. 1943 Folder.

20. Churchill, *Closing the Ring*, pp. 215-16.

21. Ibid., pp. 216-18; Chandler, *The Eisenhower Papers*, vol. 3, pp. 1494-98.

22. Chandler, *The Eisenhower Papers*, vol. 3, pp. 1504-05; JCS 531 and 531/1, Oct. 13, 1943, MM, CCS 370 (9-13-43).

23. Ehrman, *Grand Strategy*, vol. 5, p. 100; *F. R.: The Conferences at Cairo and Tehran, 1943* (1961), p. 34.

24. Bryant, *Triumph in the West*, pp. 34-35.

25. *F.R.: Washington and Quebec*, pp. 1159-60; *Stalin's Correspondence*, vol. 1, pp. 150-51, vol. 2, pp. 86-93.

26. *F.R., 1943*, vol. 3 (1963), pp. 696-97.

27. See ibid., pp. 567-68; Churchill, *Closing the Ring*, pp. 261-62; Cordell Hull, *The Memoirs of Cordell Hull*, vol. 2 (1948), pp. 1271-72.

28. *F. R., 1943,* vol. 1 (1963), pp. 534-36.

29. Hull, *Memoirs*, vol. 2, p. 1264.

30. OSS rpt., "Anglo-Soviet Relations," Aug. 28, 1943, OSS 49603 R.

31. For Deane's instructions, see above, Ch. 8, n. 42.

32. *F.R., 1943*, vol. 1, pp, 577-78, 771-81; tel., Hull to Roosevelt, Oct. 22, 1943, Roosevelt Papers, MRF, Box 9.

33. *F.R., 1943*, vol. 1, pp. 602-3.

34. Ibid., pp. 628-29, 635, 638-39, 686; Hull, *Memoirs,* vol. 2, pp. 1285-87, 1294-99, 1308-09.

35. Hull, *Memoirs*, vol. 2, pp. 1313-15.

36. CM-IN 18659, Deane to JCS, Oct. 30, 1943, Roosevelt Papers, MRF, Box 9.

37. Memo, JWPC to JIC, Oct. 9, 1943, MM, CCS 381 (10-4-43) JIC 142M.

38. See James M. Burns, *Roosevelt* (1970), p. 350.
39. Anthony Eden, *The Memoirs of Anthony Eden, Earl of Avon: The Reckoning* (1965), p. 483.
40. Churchill, *Closing the Ring*, pp. 285-87.
41. Ibid., p. 288.
42. Moran, *Churchill*, pp. 130-31.
43. Churchill, *Closing the Ring*, p. 247; *F.R.: Cairo and Tehran*, pp. 34, 37-39, 110-12.
44. Churchill, *Closing the Ring*, pp. 143-47, 288-90.
45. Maurice Matloff, *Strategic Planning for Coalition Warfare, 1943-1944* (1959), p. 263; David Dilks, ed., *The Diaries of Sir Alexander Cadogan, 1938-1945* (1972), pp. 570-71.
46. Ehrman, *Grand Strategy*, vol. 5, p. 100; *F.R., 1943,* vol. 1, p. 689.
47. *F.R., 1943*, vol. 1, p. 657.
48. Churchill, *Closing the Ring*, pp. 291-93.
49. *F. R., 1943,* vol. 1, pp. 644, 655-62; Hull, *Memoirs*, vol. 2, p. 1301.
50. Sir Llewellyn Woodward, *British Foreign Policy in the Second World War* (1962), p. 326n.1.
51. Hull, *Memoirs*, vol. 2, p. 1312; Eden, *The Reckoning*, p. 483; *F.R., 1943*, vol. 1, p. 689.
52. *F.R., 1943*, vol. 1, pp. 693-94, 697-98; Eden, *The Reckoning*, pp. 483-84.
53. *F.R.: Cairo and Tehran*, pp. 190-92.
54. Eden, *The Reckoning*, p. 486; Woodward, *British Foreign Policy*, pp. 338-39.
55. *F.R.: Cairo and Tehran*, pp. 150-51.
56. Richard M. Leighton and Robert W. Coakley, *Global Logistics and Strategy, 1943-1945* (1968), pp. 232-35; Ehrman, *Grand Strategy*, vol. 5, p. 74.
57. Matloff, *Strategic Planning, 1943-1944,* p. 263.
58. *F.R.: Cairo and Tehran*, pp. 411-13; Samuel E. Morison, *History of U.S. Naval Operations in World War II*, vol. 11, *The Invasion of France and Germany* (1957), p. 23.
59. Supp. min., CCS 126 mtg., Nov. 5, 1943, MM, CCS 334 (8-17-43).
60. Chandler, *The Eisenhower Papers*, vol. 3, pp. 1529-30.
61. CM-OUT, JCS to Deane, with attached memo, Marshall to Leahy, Oct. 28, 1943, MM, CCS 381 (3-23-42), Pt. 5.
62. Stimson Diary, Oct. 28, 29, 31, 1943.
63. *F.R., 1943*, vol. 3, pp. 589-90; see also tels., Harriman to Pres. and Hull, Nov. 7 and 9, 1943, Roosevelt Papers, MRF, Boxes 6 and 21.
64. CM-IN 18276, 5951, 7461, Deane to JCS, Oct. 29, Nov. 9 and 11,

1943, Roosevelt Papers, MRF, Box 9, and MM, CCS 381 (3-23-42), Pt. 6; John R. Deane, *The Strange Alliance* (1947), p. 35.

65. Stimson Diary, Nov. 11, 1943.

66. For other possible rationales, see John A. Bailey, "Lion, Eagle and Crescent" (Ph.D. diss., 1969), pp. 218-22.

CHAPTER 10: FINAL ARGUMENTS AND DECISION

1. Draft OPD memo, Marshall to Roosevelt, "Conduct of the European War," Nov. 8, 1943, MM, ABC 381 SS (7 Jan. 43) (Nos. 2-95), Tab 90. See also SS rpt., "Operations in the Balkans," Nov. 2, 1943, ibid., Tab 172; memo, Lincoln to ACofS, OPD, "Turkish Participation in the War," Nov. 18, 1943, MM, OPD Exec. 17, Item 22; JCS 533 series, "Recommend Line of Action at Next U.S.-British Staff Conference," Nov., 1943, MM CCS 381 (10-17-43), Secs. 1 and 2; *F.R.: The Conferences at Cairo and Tehran, 1943* (1961), pp. 210-13.

2. Memo, Col. E. H. Maguire, Chief, Theater Group, to ACofS, G-2, "Russian Reaction to a Postponement or Failure to Mount a Cross-Channel Operation," Nov. 18, 1943, MM, OPD Exec. 9, Item 13, Paper 112.

3. Draft OPD memo cited in n. 1, emphasis in original; see also undated OPD rpt., "United Nations Courses of Action in Case SEXTANT Decisions Do Not Guarantee OVERLORD," MM, OPD Exec. 17, Item 22.

4. *F.R.: Cairo and Tehran*, pp. 203-9; Robert Sherwood, *Roosevelt and Hopkins* (1950), p. 766.

5. JCS 533/3, memo from King, "Preparations for the Next United States-British Staff Conference," Oct. 24-25, 1943, MM, CCS 381 (10-17-43), Sec. 1; see also unsigned OPD memo to CofS, "Message from General Deane with Reference to Possible Russian Desire for Increased Activity in the Mediterranean," Nov. 10, 1943, MM, ABC 381 SS (7 Jan. 43) (Nos. 160-195), Tab 181/1.

6. *F.R.: Cairo and Tehran*, pp. 39-47, 49-50.

7. Ibid., pp. 41, 47-48.

8. Ibid., pp. 54-55, 60-61, 64; see also Robert Beitzell, *The Uneasy Alliance* (1972), pp. 249-61.

9. *F.R.: Cairo and Tehran*, pp. 55-69, 71-72, 77-79.

10. Ibid., pp. 72n. 3, 79, 82-83, 87; *Stalin's Correspondence*, vol. 1, pp. 175-76.

11. *F.R.: Cairo and Tehran*, pp. 195, 248-53.

12. Ibid., pp. 259-60.

13. Memo. SS to Acting Chief, SS, "Notes on RANKIN," Oct. 26, 1943, MM ABC 381 SS (7 Jan. 43) (Nos. 131-159), Tab 159; memo, Handy to CofS, "Brief of Proposed Revision of Outline Plan for RAN-KIN-Case 'C'," Oct. 13, 1943, MM, OPD Exec. 9, Item 13, Paper 82; memo, Handy to CofS, Nov. 2, 1943, MM, OPD 381 Security (Sec. VIIB), 226; JCS 577 series, Nov. 4-18, 1943, MM, CCS 381 (8-20-43); min., JCS 124-125 mtgs., Nov. 17 and 18, 1943, MM, CCS 334 (11-15-43); min., JPS 114 mtg., Nov. 22, 1943, MM, CCS 334 Jt. Staff Planners (9-20-43).

14. *F.R.: Cairo and Tehran*, pp. 195, 253-56.

15. Ibid., pp. 254-55, 261. Marshall reported, however, that Roosevelt wanted an Allied occupation of Berlin, and his pencil line went through the city; see Maurice Matloff, *Strategic Planning for Coalition Warfare, 1943-1944* (1959), pp. 341-42.

16. *F.R.: Cairo and Tehran*, pp. 253-55.

17. Ibid., p. 330.

18. Ibid., pp. 330-33.

19. Ibid., pp. 336-37, 407-11.

20. Theodore H. White, ed., *The Stilwell Papers* (1948), p. 245.

21. Forrest C. Pogue, *George C. Marshall*, vol. 3, *Organizer of Victory* (1973), pp. 306-7.

22. CM-OUT 8182, Gen. Hull to Handy, Nov. 20, 1943, MM, OPD Exec. 5, Item 14; *F.R.: Cairo and Tehran*, pp. 265-66.

23. War Dept. message to AMSME, Nov. 23, 1943, MM, OPD Exec. 5, Item 15, Folder 2.

24. Min., JCS 127 and 129 mtgs., Nov. 22 and 24, 1943, MM, CCS 334 (11-15-43), partially reprinted in *F.R.: Cairo and Tehran*, pp. 301-3, 327-29.

25. Min., JCS 130 mtg., Nov. 25, 1943, MM, CCS 334 (11-15-43).

26. JCS 611 and 611/1, " 'OVERLORD' and the Mediterranean," Nov. 26, 1943, MM, CCS 381 (3-23-42), Pt. 6.

27. *F.R.: Cairo and Tehran*, pp. 349-50, 380, 395-97; see also Richard M. Leighton, "OVERLORD versus the Mediterranean at the Cairo-Tehran Conferences," in Kent R. Greenfield, ed., *Command Decisions* (1960), pp. 269-70.

28. Min., JCS 131 mtg., Nov. 26, 1943, MM, CCS 334 (11-15-43).

29. Ibid.; *F.R.: Cairo and Tehran,* pp. 363-64.

30. *F.R.: Cairo and Tehran*, pp. 364-65.

31. Ibid., p. 365; Arthur Bryant, *Triumph in the West* (1959), pp. 57-58; Henry H. Arnold, *Global Mission* (1949), p. 464.

32. *F.R.: Cairo and Tehran*, p. 365.

33. Elliot Roosevelt, *As He Saw It* (1946), pp. 151, 156.

34. Lord Moran, *Churchill: Taken from the Diaries of Lord Moran* (1966), pp. 140-42.

35. Matloff, *Strategic Planning, 1943-1944*, pp. 365-67n.44.

36. Bryant, *Triumph in the West*, p. 60.

37. Min., JCS 132 mtg., Nov. 28, 1943, MM, CCS 334 (11-15-43); *F.R.: Cairo and Tehran*, pp. 477-82.

38. *F.R.: Cairo and Tehran*, p. 481.

39. All references to this mtg. in ibid., pp. 487-508. Included in this volume are the Bohlen and CCS min. of each plenary mtg.; the two sets are complementary and are used here in conjunction.

40. Sherwood, *Roosevelt and Hopkins*, p. 780.

41. See *F.R.: Cairo and Tehran*, pp. 259-60, 477-82; min., JCS 131 and 132 mtgs., Nov. 26 and 28, 1943, MM, CCS 334 (11-15-43).

42. Roosevelt, *As He Saw It*, p. 203.

43. See Leighton, "Overlord vs. the Mediterranean," p. 272.

44. *F.R.: Cairo and Tehran*, pp. 515-28.

45. All references to this mtg. in ibid., pp. 533-52.

46. Charles E. Bohlen, *Witness to History, 1929-1969* (1973), pp. 151-5

47. David Dilks, ed., *The Diaries of Sir Alexander Cadogan, 1938-1945* (1972), p. 582; see also *F.R.: Cairo and Tehran*, pp. 553-55, 836.

48. *F.R.: Cairo and Tehran*, pp. 553-54; Winston S. Churchill, *The Second World War*, vol. 5, *Closing the Ring* (1951), pp. 373-74.

49. *F.R.: Cairo and Tehran*, pp. 554-55.

50. Bryant, *Triumph in the West*, p. 64.

51. Moran, *Churchill*, p. 149.

52. Dilks, *The Cadogan Diaries*, p. 582.

53. Bohlen, *Witness to History*, pp. 152-53.

54. *F.R.: Cairo and Tehran*, pp. 555-63.

55. Ibid., 563-64.

56. Churchill, *Closing the Ring*, pp. 377-80. Churchill had used this argument during the earlier plenary mtg.; see *F.R.: Cairo and Tehran*, pp. 536, 543.

57. *F.R.: Cairo and Tehran*, pp. 565, 576-79, 587, 652.

58. Ibid., p. 582.

59. Dilks, *The Cadogan Diaries*, p. 581.

60. Ibid., p. 581; *F.R.: Cairo and Tehran*, pp. 582-85, 837; Sir John Kennedy, *The Business of War* (1957), p. 314.

61. Message, Marshall to Stimson, Dec. 2, 1943, MM, OPD Exec. 10, Item 63a (Pt. 2).

62. Ltr., McCloy to Stimson, Dec. 2, 1943, Stimson Papers; Stimson Diary, Dec. 5, 1943.

63. Memo, Bohlen to Dunn, attached to memo by Prof. S. H. Cross, Sept. 7, 1943, Hull Papers, Box 52, Corres., Folder 159.

64. Ltr., Roosevelt to Harriman, Dec. 1, 1943, Hopkins Papers, Sherwood Collection, Box 115, Book 3, Footnotes.

65. Bohlen, *Witness to History*, p. 158.

CHAPTER 11: AFTERMATH, SUMMARY AND CONCLUSIONS

1. Forrest C. Pogue, *George C. Marshall*, vol. 3, *Organizer of Victory* (1973), pp. 263-68, 318-21.

2. Lord Moran, *Churchill: Taken from the Diaries of Lord Moran* (1966), p. 155; Henry H. Arnold, *Global Mission* (1949), p. 474.

3. William D. Leahy, *I Was There* (1950), pp. 213-14.

4. Winston S. Churchill, *The Second World War*, vol. 5, *Closing the Ring* (1951), pp. 429-41; Trumbull Higgins, *Soft Underbelly* (1968), pp. 137-53.

5. Arthur Bryant, *Triumph in the West* (1959), pp. 125-34, 157-68.

6. Maurice Matloff, *Strategic Planning for Coalition Warfare, 1943-1944* (1959), pp. 414-26, 467-74, and "The ANVIL Decision," in Kent R. Greenfield, ed., *Command Decisions* (1960), pp. 383-400; Winston S. Churchill, *The Second World War*, vol. 6, *Triumph and Tragedy*, pp. 57-71, 716-23.

7. Churchill, *Triumph and Tragedy*, pp. 72-81, 206-43, 283-325.

8. John R. Deane, *The Strange Alliance* (1947), p. 153.

9. Churchill, *Triumph and Tragedy*, p. 9.

10. Milovan Djilas, *Conversations with Stalin* (1962), pp. 73, 81.

11. David Dilks, ed., *The Diaries of Sir Alexander Cadogan, 1938-1945* (1972), p. 597.

12. *F.R., 1944*, vol. 4 (1966), pp. 813-54, 862-63, 951, 1035-37.

13. Deane, *The Strange Alliance*, p. 98.

14. Sir Llewellyn Woodward, *British Foreign Policy During the Second World War* (1962), p. 291.

15. Memo, Stettinius to Hull, Oct. 26, 1943, Hull Papers, Box 52, Corres., Folder 161.

16. *F.R., 1944*, vol. 4, pp. 902-14.

17. Memo, Stimson to Marshall, "Our Military Reserves," May 10, 1944, MM OPD Exec. 10, Item 57, Paper 42.

18. Matloff, *Strategic Planning, 1943-1944*, p. 497.

19. Informal OPD Notes on Rumanian Armistice Terms Proposed by USSR, Apr. 10, 1944, MM, ABC 381 SS (7 Jan. 43) (Nos. 227-241/7), Tab 231.

20. Sir Llewellyn Woodward, *British Foreign Policy During the Second World War*, vol. 3 (1971), pp. 110-11.

21. Anne Armstrong, *Unconditional Surrender* (1961), pp. 86-93; Matloff, *Strategic Planning, 1943-1944*, pp. 430-31.

22. Armstrong, *Unconditional Surrender*, pp. 86-93; William M. Frankl "Zonal Boundaries and Access to Berlin," *World Politics* 16 (Oct. 1963): 1-24.

23. Ray S. Cline, *Washington Command Post* (1951), p. 331. See also Matloff, *Strategic Planning, 1943-1944*, pp. 503, 523-24; min., JCS 126 mtg., Nov. 19, 1943, MM, CCS 334 (11-15-43); memo by Handy, July 28 1944, MM, OPD Exec. 2, Item 11; Arnold Papers, Box 45, OF, Folder 147 "Postwar Planning."

24. James M. Burns, *Roosevelt* (1970), p. 428.

25. Sir John Kennedy, *The Business of War* (1957), pp. 305-14.

26. James Nelson, ed., *General Eisenhower on the Military Churchill* (1970), p. 42.

27. Winston S. Churchill, *The Second World War*, vol. 3, *The Grand Alliance* (1950), p. 28.

28. Pogue, *Marshall*, vol. 3, p. 315.

29. Dean Acheson, *Sketches from Life of Men I Have Known* (1959), pp. 163-64, and *Present at the Creation* (1969), pp. 141-42.

30. See Samuel P. Huntington, *The Soldier and the State* (1957), pp. 326-33, for an interesting reversal of this argument.

___BIBLIOGRAPHICAL NOTES___

Any historian dealing with World War II faces numerous problems in regard to the size and availability of unpublished research materials. U. S. Army records alone weigh 17,120 tons and fill 188 miles of filing cases. The history based on these records is scheduled to include eighty volumes. Of necessity one must be highly selective in the use of documents and rely heavily on official histories. Records used in this study were chosen on the basis of information supplied by these histories and the National Archives, and they include most of the important documents presently available.

Until recently, access to those documents was severely limited. Original research for this work required a personal security check, limitation on the number of notes allowed, and a review of those notes as well as the final manuscript. The ensuing frustrations were only compounded by the insistence of the agencies involved that this process did not equal censorship, but "freedom of information" for which one should be grateful. Fortunately, recent declassification decisions have been putting an end to this system. Since declassification is still in process, however, much research becomes dated even before it is finished because of the gradual opening of previously closed records and publication of additional document collections. Extra trips and manuscript revisions are the inevitable results. Furthermore, many documents simply remain closed to unofficial researchers.

The most valuable material for this study is in Record Groups 59, 165, and 218 of the National Archives. Group 59 contains State Department records and is a necessary supplement to the *Foreign Relations* series. High-level strategic planning papers of the Army are in 165, while 218 contains the papers and minutes of the joint and combined committees. Some of these are reprinted in *Foreign Relations,* and that series should be consulted before exploring these Record Groups. Other archival material of the armed forces is of secondary importance for this study. OSS records are helpful, but the unofficial researcher is limited to the files of the Research and Analysis Branch and cannot cite authors or trace papers through committees. Nevertheless, the information available is valuable.

While memoirs and biographies abound, they cannot replace the complete unpublished papers for key individuals. Most important are the Roosevelt papers, especially the President's Secretary's File, which includes his correspondence with important individuals, and the Map Room File, which contains the complete Churchill-Roosevelt correspondence and key military documents. While most of these papers are open, some remain under security regulations.

Also important are the papers of Arnold, Hopkins, Hull, Leahy, Stilwell, and Stimson. The Arnold papers contain much useful and previously unnoticed material on the Army's concern with political issues and Roosevelt's conferences with his military advisers; and the Leahy, Stilwell, and Stimson diaries provide fascinating and informative day-to-day, inside accounts of many of the issues discussed in this study. One should consult the memoirs of these men and Sherwood's biography of Hopkins before looking at these collections, however, since they reprint many of the important documents. Arnold's papers are controlled by the Air Force, Leahy's by his family, and Hull's by the State Department; the others are controlled by the libraries housing them. Most of the documents in these collections are open.

While memoirs are an extremely valuable source for this era, one must remember that they are often written to justify the writer's position and thus cannot be accepted at face value. With the above caveat, Churchill's six-volume work is essential, as are the memoirs of Arnold, Bohlen, Eden King, Leahy, Moran, Stimson, and Wedemeyer. Bryant's two volumes based on Brooke's diary are very useful, but Kennedy's memoirs should be read concurrently as an important corrective to some of Bryant's claim Chandler's compilation of the Eisenhower papers is much more informative than the general's memoirs. Unfortunately, neither Roosevelt, Marsh nor Hopkins wrote memoirs, but Burns, Pogue, and Sherwood have provided excellent biographies.

The complete Big Three wartime correspondence is now open and available in published form. During the 1950s, the Soviet government reprinted Stalin's correspondence with the two Western leaders, while portions of the Churchill-Roosevelt collection were reprinted in the prime minister's memoirs. Contrary to popular belief, Churchill's work omitted

into that complete correspondence for this work was done at the Roosevelt
Library in Hyde Park before the recent publication of an edited collection,
Lowenheim et. al., *Roosevelt and Churchill: Their Secret Wartime Correspondence* (New York: E. P. Dutton and Co., Inc., 1975), and two microfilm
collections (Roosevelt Library).

The official Army histories by Cline, Matloff and Snell, and Leighton
and Coakley are invaluable, as are the official British volumes on grand strategy.
Higgins' essay traces the historical debate over Anglo-American strategy
in these works and the unofficial histories. In the diplomatic sphere, a new
and complete history is badly needed. Feis and McNeill are both dated,
Langer and Gleason stop in 1941, and Woodward's unabridged work is only
partially finished. Important new insights can be found in the volumes
by Kolko, Gaddis, and Beitzell.

Interviews, correspondence, and articles provided useful but largely
supplementary information. Dissertations were quite important, and the
unpublished manuscripts by Kittredge and Cline invaluable.

__SELECTED BIBLIOGRAPHY__

MANUSCRIPT COLLECTIONS

Henry H. Arnold Papers, Division of Manuscripts, Library of Congress, Washington, D. C.
Harry L. Hopkins Papers, Franklin D. Roosevelt Library, Hyde Park, N. Y.
Cordell Hull Papers, Division of Manuscripts, Library of Congress, Washington, D. C.
William D. Leahy Papers, Division of Manuscripts, Library of Congress, Washington, D. C.
Franklin D. Roosevelt Papers, Franklin D. Roosevelt Library, Hyde Park, N. Y.
Joseph W. Stilwell Papers, Hoover Institute, Stanford, Calif.
Henry L. Stimson Papers, Division of Manuscripts, Sterling Memorial Library, Yale University, New Haven, Conn.

UNITED STATES GOVERNMENT ARCHIVES

Archives of the Department of the Army, Modern Military Branch, Military Archives Division, National Archives and Records Service, Washington, D. C.
  Record Group 107. Records of the Office of the Secretary of War.
  Record Group 165. Records of the War Department General and Special Staffs: American-British Conversations File, Civil Affairs Division File, Operations Division Decimal and Executive Files, War Department Chief of Staff Army File, and War Plans Division Decimal File.

Record Group 218. Records of the Joint and combined Chiefs of Staff

Record Group 226. Records of the Office of Strategic Services.

Record Group 331. Records of Allied Operational and Occupationa Headquarters, World War II: Supreme Headquarters, Allied Expeditionary Forces, G-3 and Secretary General Staff Files.

Record Group 332. Records of United States Theaters of War, Worl War II: European Theater of Operations File.

Record Group 334. Records of Interservice Agencies: United States Military Mission to Moscow File.

Archives of the Department of the Army, Office of the Chief of Military History, General Reference Branch, Historical Services Division, Washington, D.C.: Operations Division Diary and Historical Unit File.

Archives of the Department of the Army, Office of the Chief of Military History, National Records Center, Suitland, Md.: Bulky files for *Unite States Army in World War II,* Cline and Matloff volumes.

Archives of the Department of State, National Archives and Records Service, Washington, D. C., Record Group 59.

Operational Archives of the Naval History Division of the Department of the Navy, Washington, D. C.: Operational Division Plans, COMINCH; Ernest J. King Personal Papers; Samuel Morison Collection; War Plans Division Strategic Plans.

PERSONAL INTERVIEWS AND CORRESPONDENCE

Hon. Loy W. Henderson, Department of State (ret.); Major General Frank N. Roberts, U. S. Army (ret.); General Albert C. Wedemeyer, U. S. Arm (ret.).

PUBLISHED GOVERNMENT RECORDS AND OFFICIAL HISTORIES

Blumenson, Martin. *Salerno to Cassino.* In Office of the Chief of Military History, Department of the Army, *U. S. Army in World War II: The Mediterranean Theater of Operations.* Washington, D. C.: U. S. Govern ment Printing Office, 1969.

Butler, J. R. M. *Grand Strategy.* Vol. 2, *September, 1939-June, 1941.* United Kingdom Military Series. J. R. M. Butler, gen. ed., *History of the Second World War.* London: Her Majesty's Stationery Office, 195 _____. and J. M. A. Gwyer. *Grand Strategy.* Vol. 3, *June, 1941-August, 1942.* United Kingdom Military Series. J. R. M. Butler, gen. ed., *History of the Second World War.* London: Her Majesty's Stationery Office, 1964.

Cline, Ray S. *Washington Command Post: The Operations Division.* In
  office of the Chief of Military History, Department of the Army,
  U. S. Army in World War II: The War Department. Washington, D.C.:
  U. S. Government Printing Office, 1951.
Conn, Stetson and Byron Fairchild. *The Framework of Hemispheric
  Defense.* In Office of the Chief of Military History, Department of
  the Army, *U. S. Army in World War II: The Western Hemisphere*
  Washington, D. C.: U. S. Government Printing Office, 1960.
Craven, Wesley F. and James L. Cate, eds. *The Army Air Forces in World War
  II.* 7 vols. Chicago: University of Chicago Press, 1948-1949.
Department of State. *Foreign Relations of the United States: Diplomatic
  Papers.* Washington, D. C.: U. S. Government Printing Office.
        1941, 7 vols., 1956-1963.
        1942, 6 vols., 1960-1963.
        1943, 6 vols., 1963-1965.
        1944, 7 vols., 1965-1967.
        The Conferences at Washington, 1941-1942, and Casablanca, 1943.
            1968.
        The Conferences at Cairo and Tehran, 1943. 1961.
        The Conferences at Washington and Quebec, 1943. 1970.
        The Conferences at Malta and Yalta, 1945. 1955.
Ehrman, John. *Grand Strategy.* Vol. 5, *August, 1943-September, 1944.*
  United Kingdom Military Series. J. R. M. Butler, gen. ed., *History of
  the Second World War.* London: Her Majesty's Stationery Office, 1956.
Garland, Lieutenant-Colonel Albert N. and Howard M. Smyth. *Sicily and
  the Surrender of Italy.* In Office of the Chief of Military History, Department
  of the Army, *U. S. Army in World War II: The Mediterranean Theater of
  Operations.* Washington, D. C.: U. S. Government Printing Office, 1965.
Greenfield, Kent R. *American Strategy in World War II: A Reconsideration.*
  Baltimore, Md.: The Johns Hopkins University Press, 1963.
_____, ed. *Command Decisions.* Washington, D. C.: U. S. Government Printing
  Office, 1960.
_____. *The Historian and the Army.* New Brunswick, N.J.: Rutgers
  University Press, 1954.
Harrison, Gordon A. *Cross-Channel Attack.* In Office of the Chief of
  Military History, Department of the Army, *U. S. Army in World War II:
  The European Theater of Operations.* Washington, D. C.: U. S. Government
  Printing Office, 1951.
Howard, Michael. *Grand Strategy.* Vol. 4, *August, 1942-September, 1943.*
  United Kingdom Military Series. J. R. M. Butler, gen. ed., *History of the
  Second World War.* London: Her Majesty's Stationery Office, 1972.

_____. *The Mediterranean Strategy in the Second World War.* London: Weidenfeld Nicolson, 1968.

Howe, George F. *Northwest Africa: Seizing the Initiative in the West.* In Office of the Chief of Military History, Department of the Army, *U. S. Army in World War II: The Mediterranean Theater of Operations.* Washington, D. C.: U. S. Government Printing Office, 1957.

Issrealjan, Victor. *The Anti-Hitler Coalition: Diplomatic Co-Operation Between the U. S. S. R., U. S. A. and Britain During the Second World War, 1941-1945.* Moscow: Progress Publishers, 1971.

Langer, William L. and S. Everett Gleason. *The Undeclared War, 1940-194* New York: Harper and Brothers, 1953.

Leighton, Richard M. and Robert W. Coakley. *Global Logistics and Strateg 1940-1943.* In Office of the Chief of Military History, Department of th Army, *U. S. Army in World War II: The War Department.* Washington, D. C.: U. S. Government Printing Office, 1955.

_____. *Global Logistics and Strategy, 1943-1945.* In Office of the Chief of Military History, Department of the Army, *U. S. Army in World War II: Th War Department.* Washington, D. C.: U. S. Government Printing Office, 1968.

Matloff, Maurice. *Strategic Planning for Coalition Warfare, 1943-1944.* In Office of the Chief of Military History, Department of the Army, *U. S. Army in World War II: The War Department.* Washington, D. C.: U. S. Government Printing Office, 1959.

_____ and Edwin M. Snell. *Strategic Planning for Coalition Warfare, 194 1942.* In Office of the Chief of Military History, Department of the Army, *U. S. Army in World War II: The War Department.* Washington, D. C.: U. S. Government Printing Office, 1953.

Ministry of Foreign Affairs of the USSR. *Russia: Correspondence Betweer the Chairman of the Council of Ministers of the U. S. S. R. and the Presidents of the U. S. A. and the Prime Ministers of Great Britain During the Great Patriotic War of 1941-1945.* 2 vols. Moscow: Foreign Languages Publishing House, 1957.

Morison, Samuel E. *History of U. S. Naval Operations in World War II.* 15 vols. Boston: Little, Brown and Co., 1947-1962.

_____. *Strategy and Compromise.* Boston: Little, Brown and Co., 1958.

Notter, Harley. *Postwar Foreign Policy Preparation, 1939-1945.* Department of State Publication 3580, General Foreign Policy Series 1 Washington, D. C.: U. S. Government Printing Office, 1950.

Pogue, Forrest C. *The Supreme Command.* In Office of the Chief of Milita History, Department of the Army, *U. S. Army in World War II: The European Theater of Operations.* Washington, D. C.: U. S. Governmen Printing Office, 1954.

Rothstein, Andrew, trans. *Soviet Foreign Policy During the Great Patriotic War: Documents and Materials.* 2 vols. London: Hutchinson and Co., 1944-1945.

79th Cong., 1st sess. *Hearings Before the Joint Committee on the Investigation of the Pearl Harbor Attack,* pursuant to Senate Cong. Res. 27, 39 parts. Washington, D. C.: U. S. Government Printing Office, 1946.

Stalin, Joseph. *The Great Patriotic War of the Soviet Union.* New York, 1945; reprint ed., Greenwood Press, 1969.

The War Reports of General of the Army George C. Marshall, Chief of Staff, General of the Army H. H. Arnold, Commanding General, Army Air Forces, and Fleet Admiral Ernest J. King, Commander-in-Chief of the United States Fleet and Chief of Naval Operations. Philadelphia and New York: J. P. Lippincott Co., 1947.

Watson, Mark S. *Chief of Staff: Prewar Plans and Preparations.* In Office of the Chief of Military History, Department of the Army, *U. S. Army in World War II: The War Department.* Washington, D. C.: U. S. Government Printing Office, 1950.

Williams, Mary H. *Chronology, 1941-1945.* In Office of the Chief of Military History, Department of the Army, *U. S. Army in World War II: Special Studies.* Washington, D. C.: U. S. Government Printing Office, 1960.

Woodward, Sir Llewellyn. *British Foreign Policy in the Second World War.* London: Her Majesty's Stationery Office, 1962.

_____. *British Foreign Policy in the Second World War,* 3 vols. London: Her Majesty's Stationery Office, 1971.

MEMOIRS, SPEECHES, PAPERS, AND BIOGRAPHIES

Acheson, Dean. *Present At the Creation: My Years in the State Department.* New York: W. W. Norton and Co., Inc., 1969.

_____. *Sketches from Life of Men I Have Known.* New York: Harper and Brothers, 1959.

Alexander, Field-Marshal Sir Harold, Earl of Tunis. *The Alexander Memoirs, 1940-1945.* Ed. by John North. London: Cassell, 1962.

Ambrose, Stephen. *The Supreme Commander: The War Years of General Dwight D. Eisenhower.* New York: Doubleday and Co., 1969.

Arnold, Henry H. *Gobal Mission.* New York: Harper and Brothers, 1949.

Bellush. Bernard. *He Walked Alone: A Biography of John G. Winant.* The Hague: Mouton, 1968.

Birkenhead, Earl of. *Halifax: The Life of Lord Halifax.* London: Hamish Hamilton, 1965.

Birse, A. H. *Memoirs of an Interpreter.* New York: Coward-McCann, Inc., 1967.

Blum, John M. *From the Morgenthau Diaries: Years of War, 1941-1945*. Boston: Houghton Mifflin Co., 1967.

Bohlen, Charles E. *Witness to History, 1929-1969*. New York: W. W. Norton and Co., Inc., 1973.

Bryant, Arthur. *Triumph in the West: A History of the War Years Based on the Diaries of Field-Marshal Lord Alanbrooke, Chief of the Imperial General Staff*. Garden City, N. Y.: Doubleday and Co., Inc., 1959.

_____.*The Turn of the Tide: A History of the War Years Based on the Diaries of Field Marshal Lord Alanbrooke, Chief of the Imperial General Staff*. Garden City, N. Y.: Doubleday and Co., Inc., 1957.

Bullitt, Orville H., ed. *For the President: Personal and Secret; Correspondence Between Franklin D. Roosevelt and William C. Bullitt*. Boston: Houghton Mifflin Co., 1972.

Burns, James M. *Roosevelt: The Soldier of Freedom, 1940-1945*. New York: Harcourt, Brace, Jovanovich, Inc., 1970.

Butcher, Harry C. *My Three Years with Eisenhower*. New York: Simon and Schuster, 1946.

Chandler, Alfred D., Jr., ed. *The Papers of Dwight David Eisenhower. The War Years, 1941-1945*. 5 vols. Baltimore, Md.: The Johns Hopkins University Press, 1970.

Churchill, Winston S. *The Second World War*. 6 vols. Boston: Houghton Mifflin Co., 1948-1953.

Ciechanowski, Jan. *Defeat in Victory*. Garden City, N. Y.: Doubleday and Co., Inc., 1947.

Clark, Mark. *Calculated Risk*. New York: Harper and Brothers, 1950.

Cunningham, Sir Andrew B. *A Sailor's Odyssey*. London: Hutchinson and Co., Ltd., 1951.

Current, Richard N. *Secretary Stimson: A Study in Statecraft*. New Brunswick, N.J.: Rutgers University Press, 1954.

Davies, Joseph E._Mission to Moscow_. New York: Simon and Schuster, 194

Deane, John R. *The Strange Alliance: The Story of Our Efforts at Wartime Cooperation with Russia*. New York: The Viking Press, 1947.

Dilks, David, ed. *The Diaries of Sir Alexander Cadogan, 1938-1945*. New York: G. P. Putnam's Sons, 1972.

Djilas, Milovan. *Conversations with Stalin*. Trans. by Michael B. Petrovich. New York: Harcourt, Brace and World, Inc., 1962.

Eden, Anthony. *The Memoirs of Anthony Eden, Earl of Avon: The Reckoning*. Boston: Houghton Mifflin Co., 1965.

Eisenhower, Dwight D. *Crusade in Europe*. New York: Doubleday and Co., 1948.

Farnsworth, Beatrice. *William C. Bullitt and the Soviet Union*. Bloomington: Indiana University Press, 1967.

Harriman, W. Averell. *American and Russia in a Changing World: A Half Century of Personal Observation.* Garden City, N. Y.: Doubleday and Co., Inc., 1971.

Hassett, William D. *Off the Record with F. D. R.* New Brunswick, N. J.: Rutgers University Press, 1958.

Hooker, Nancy H., ed. *The Moffat Papers: Selections from the Diplomatic Journals of Jay Pierrepont Moffat, 1919-1943.* Cambridge, Mass.: Harvard University Press, 1956.

Hull, Cordell. *The Memoirs of Cordell Hull.* 2 vols. New York: The Macmillan Co., 1948.

Ickes, Harold. *The Secret Diary of Harold Ickes.* 3 vols. New York: Simon and Schuster, 1954.

Ismay, Sir Hastings. *The Memoirs of General Lord Ismay.* New York: The Viking Press, 1960.

Israel, Fred, ed. *The War Diary of Breckinridge Long: Selections from the War Years, 1939-1944.* Lincoln: University of Nebraska Press, 1966.

Kennan, George F. *Memoirs, 1925-1950.* Boston: Little, Brown and Co., 1967.

Kennedy, Sir John. *The Business of War.* London: Hutchinson and Co., 1957.

King, Ernest J. and Walter M. Whitehill. *Fleet Admiral King: A Naval Record.* New York: W. W. Norton and Co., Inc., 1952.

Leahy, William D. *I Was There: The Personal Story of the Chief of Staff to Presidents Roosevelt and Truman Based on his Notes and Diaries Made at the Time.* New York: Whittlesey House, 1950.

Leasor, James. *War at the Top: Based on the Experiences of General Sir Leslie Hollis.* London: Michael Joseph, 1959.

Macmillan, Harold. *The Blast of War, 1939-1945.* New York: Harper and Row, 1967.

Maisky, Ivan M. *Memoirs of a Soviet Ambassador: The War, 1939-1943.* New York: Charles Scribner's Sons, 1967.

Moran, Lord (Charles Wilson). *Churchill: Taken from the Diaries of Lord Moran; The Struggle for Survival, 1940-1965.* Boston: Houghton Mifflin Co., 1966.

Morgan, Sir Frederick. *Overture to Overlord.* Garden City, N. Y.: Doubleday and Co., Inc., 1950.

Morison, Elting E. *Turmoil and Tradition: A Study of the Life and Times of Henry L. Stimson.* Boston: Houghton Mifflin Co,, 1960.

Nelson, James, ed. *General Eisenhower on the Military Churchill: A Conversation with Alistair Cooke.* New York: W. W. Norton and Co., 1970.

Pawle, Gerald. *The War and Colonel Warden: Based on the Recollections of Commander C. R. Thompson, Personal Assistant to the Prime Minister, 1940-1945.* New York: Alfred A. Knopf, 1963.

Pogue, Forrest C. *George C. Marshall.* 3 vols. New York: The Viking Press, 1963-1973.

Pope, Arthur U. *Maxim Litvinoff.* New York: L. B. Fisher, 1943.

Pratt, Julius W. *Cordell Hull.* Vol. 13 in Samuel F. Bemis and Robert H. Ferrell, eds., *The American Secretaries of State and Their Diplomacy.* New York: Cooper Square Publishers, 1964.

Roosevelt, Elliot. *As He Saw It.* New York: Duell, Sloan and Pearce, 1946.

_____, ed. *F. D. R.: His Personal Letters, 1928-1945.* 2 vols. New York: Duell, Sloan and Pearce, 1950.

Sherwood, Robert. *Roosevelt and Hopkins: An Intimate History.* Rev. ed. New York: Grossett and Dunlap, 1950.

Slessor, Sir John. *The Central Blue: Recollections and Reflections.* London: Cassell and Co., Ltd., 1956.

Standley, William H. and Arthur A. Ageton. *Admiral Ambassador to Russia.* Chicago: Henry Regnery Co., 1955.

Stimson, Henry L. and McGeorge Bundy. *On Active Service in Peace and War.* New York: Harper and Brothers, 1947.

Tedder, Sir Arthur. *With Prejudice: The War Memoirs of Marshal of the Royal Air Force Lord Tedder.* Boston: Little, Brown and Co., 1966.

Wedemeyer, Albert C. *Wedemeyer Reports!* New York: Henry Holt and Co., 1958.

Welles, Sumner. *Seven Decisions That Shaped History.* New York: Harper and Brothers, 1950.

_____. *The Time for Decision.* Cleveland: The World Publishing Co., 1944.

_____. *Where Are We Heading?* New York: Harper and Brothers, 1946.

Wheeler-Bennett, Sir John, ed. *Action This Day: Working with Churchill.* New York: St. Martin's Press, 1969.

White, Theodore, ed. *The Stilwell Papers.* New York: William Sloan Associates, Inc., 1948.

Winant, John G. *Letter from Grosvenor Square.* Boston: Houghton Mifflin Co., 1947.

GENERAL AND SPECIALIZED STUDIES

Armstrong, Anne. *Unconditional Surrender: The Impact of the Casablanca Policy upon World War II.* New Brunswick, N. J.: Rutgers University Press, 1961.

Baldwin, Hanson W. *Great Mistakes of the War.* New York: Harper and Brothers, 1949.

Beitzell, Robert. *The Uneasy Alliance: America, Britain, and Russia, 1941-1943.* New York: Alfred A. Knopf, 1972.

Cantril, Hadley, ed. *Public Opinion, 1935-1946,* Princeton, N. J.: Princeton
   University Press, 1951.
Coles, Harry L., ed. *Total War and Cold War: Problems in Civilian Control
   of the Military.* Columbus: Ohio State University Press, 1962.
Collier, Basil. *The Lion and the Eagle: British and Anglo-American
   Strategy, 1900-1950.* New York: G. P. Putnam's Sons, 1972.
Davis, Lynn E. *The Cold War Begins: Soviet-American Conflict over
   Eastern Europe.* Princeton, N.J.: Princeton University Press, 1974.
Divine, Robert A. *Roosevelt and World War II.* Baltimore, Md.:
   The Johns Hopkins University Press, 1969.
Feis, Herbert. *Churchill, Roosevelt and Stalin: The War They Waged and
   the Peace They Sought.* 2nd ed. Princeton, N. J.: Princeton University
   Press. 1967.
Fischer, Louis. *The Road to Yalta: Soviet Foreign Relations, 1941-1945.*
   New York: Harper and Row, 1972.
Fuller, J. F. C. *The Second World War 1939-1945.* New York: Duell,
   Sloan and Pearce, 1949.
Funk, Arthur L. *The Politics of TORCH: The Allied Landings and the
   Algiers Putsch, 1942.* Lawrence: The University Press of Kansas,
   1974.
Gaddis, John L. *The United States and the Origins of the Cold War, 1941-
   1947.* New York: Columbia University Press, 1972.
Gallup, George H. *The Gallup Poll: Public Opinion, 1935-1971.*
   3 vols. New York: Random House, 1972.
Gardner, Lloyd C. *Architects of Illusion: Men and Ideas in American
   Foreign Policy, 1941-1949.* Chicago: Quadrangle, 1970.
_____. *Economic Aspects of New Deal Diplomacy.* Boston:Beacon
   Press, 1964.
Herring, George C. *Aid to Russia, 1941-1946: Strategy, Diplomacy
   and the Origins of the Cold War.* New York: Columbia University
   Press, 1973
Higgins, Trumbull. *Soft Underbelly: The Anglo-American Controversy
   over the Italian Campaign, 1939-1945.* New York: The Macmillan
   Co., 1968.
_____. *Winston Churchill and the Second Front, 1940-1943.* New York:
   Oxford University Press, 1957..
Howard, Michael, ed. *Studies in War and Peace.* New York: The Viking
   Press, 1972.
_____, ed. *The Theory and Practice of War: Essays Presented to Captain
   B. H. Liddell Hart on His Seventieth Birthday.* New York: Frederick A.
   Praeger, 1965.

Huntington, Samuel P. *The Soldier and the State: The Theory and Politics of Civil-Military Relationships.* New York: Vintage, 1957.

Jones, Robert H. *The Roads to Russia: United States Lend-Lease to the Soviet Union.* Norman: University of Oklahoma Press, 1969.

Kolko, Gabriel. *The Politics of War: The World and United States Foreign Policy, 1943-1945.* New York: Random House, 1968.

Kuklick, Bruce. *American Policy and the Division of Germany: The Clash with Russia Over Reparations.* Ithaca, N.Y.: Cornell University Press, 1972.

Liddell Hart, B. H. *History of the Second World War.* New York: G.P. Putnam's Sons, 1970.

Lukas, Richard C. *Eagles East: The Army Air Forces and the Soviet Union, 1941-1945.* Tallahassee: Florida State University Press, 1970.

May, Ernest, ed. *The Ultimate Decision: The President as Commander in Chief.* New York: George Braziller, 1960.

McNeil, William H. *America, Britain and Russia: Their Cooperation and Conflict, 1941-1946.* Survey of International Affairs, 1939-1946. London: Oxford University Press, 1953.

Mosely, Philip E. *The Kremlin and World Politics: Studies in Soviet Policy and Action.* New York: Random House, 1960.

Neumann, William L. *After Victory: Roosevelt, Stalin and the Making of Peace.* New York: Harper and Row, 1967.

O'Connor, Raymond G. *Diplomacy for Victory: FDR and Unconditional Surrender.* New York: W. W. Norton and Co., Inc., 1971.

Roberts, Walter R. *Tito, Mihailovic and the Allies, 1941-1945.* New Brunswick, N. J.: Rutgers University Press, 1973.

Robertson, Terrence. *Dieppe: The Shame and the Glory.* London: Hutchinson and Co., 1963.

Rozek, Edward J. *Allied Wartime Diplomacy: A Pattern in Poland.* New York: John Wiley and Sons, Inc., 1958.

Smith Gaddis. *American Diplomacy During the Second World War, 1941-1945.* New York: John Wiley and Sons, Inc., 1966.

Smith, R. Harris. *OSS: The Secret History of America's First Central Intelligence Agency.* Berkeley: University of California Press, 1972.

Snell, John L. *Illusion and Necessity: The Diplomacy of Global War, 1939-1945.* Boston: Houghton Mifflin Co., 1963.

———. *Wartime Origins of the East-West Dilemma Over Germany.* New Orleans: The Phauser Press, 1959.

Steele, Richard W. *The First Offensive, 1942: Roosevelt, Marshall and the Making of American Strategy.* Bloomington: Indiana University Press, 1973.

Stein, Harold, ed. *American Civil-Military Decisions: A Book of Case Studies.*
  Birmingham: University of Alabama Press, 1963.
Taylor, A. J. P., et al. *Churchill Revised: A Critical Assessment.* New York:
  The Dial Press, Inc., 1969.
Ulam, Adam B. *Expansion and Coexistence: The History of Soviet Foreign Policy,
  1917-1967.* New York: Praeger, 1968.
Werth, Alexander. *Russia at War, 1941-1945.* New York: E. P. Dutton
  and Co., Inc., 1964.
Wheeler-Bennett, Sir John and Anthony Nicholls. *The Semblance of
  Peace: The Political Settlement After the Second World War.* New
  York: St. Martin's Press, 1972.
Williams, William A. *American-Russian Relations, 1781-1947.* New
  York: Rhinehart and Co., 1952.
———. *The Tragedy of American Diplomacy.* 2d rev. ed. New York:
  Delta, 1972.
Wilmot, Chester. *The Struggle for Europe.* New York: Harper and
  Row, 1952.
Wilson, Theodore A. *The First Summit: Roosevelt and Churchill at
  Placentia Bay, 1941.* Boston: Houghton Mifflin Co., 1969.

ARTICLES

Bullitt, William C. "How We Won the War and Lost the Peace."
  Life 25 (August 30, 1948): 82-97.
Chase, John L. "Unconditional Surrender Reconsidered."
  Political Science Quarterly 70 (June 1955): 258-79.
Conn, Stetson. "Changing Concepts of National Defense in the United
  States, 1937-1947." *Military Affairs* 28 (Spring 1964): 1-7
Fischer, George. "Genesis of U. S.-Soviet Relations in World War II.
  Review of Politics 12 (1950): 368-78.
Franklin, William M. "Zonal Boundaries and Access to Berlin." *World
  Politics* 16 (October 1963): 1-35.
Greene, Fred. "The Military View of American National Policy, 1904-
  1940." *American Historical Review* 66 (January 1961): 354-77.
Herring, George C., Jr. "Lend-Lease to Russia and the Origins of the
  Cold War, 1944-1946." *Journal of American History* 56 (June 1969):
  93-114.
Higgins, Trumbull. "The Anglo-American Historians' War in the
  Mediterranean, 1942-1945." *Military Affairs* 34 (October 1970):
  84-88.

Kuklick, Bruce. "The Genesis of the European Advisory Commission."
  Journal of Contemporary History 4 (October 1969): 189-201.
Leighton, Richard M. "OVERLORD Revisited: An Interpretation of
  American Strategy in the European War, 1942-1944."
  American Historical Review 68 (July 1963): 919-37.
Lukas, Richard C. "The VELVET Project: Hope and Frustration."
  Military Affairs 28 (Winter 1964): 145-62.
Matloff, Maurice. "The Soviet Union and the War in the West." *U. S.
  Naval Institute Proceedings* 82 (March 1956): 261-71.
May, Ernest R. "Political-Military Consultation in the United States."
  Political Science Quarterly 70 (June 1955): 161-80.
_____. "The United States, the Soviet Union and the Far Eastern War,
  1941-1945." *Pacific Historical Review* 24 (May 1955): 153-74.
Morton, Louis. "Soviet Intervention in the War with Japan." *Foreign
  Affairs* 40 (July 1961): 653-62.
Patterson, Thomas G. "The Abortive Loan to Russia and the Origins of
  the Cold War, 1943-1946." *Journal of American History* 14
  (June 1969): 70-92.
Pundeff, Marin. "Allied Strategy and the Balkans." *World Affairs
  Quarterly* 29 (1958): 25-52.
Ullman, Richard. "The Davies Mission and United States-Soviet Relations,
  1937-1941." *World Politics* 9 (January 1957): 220-39.
Warner, Geoffrey. "From Tehran to Yalta: Reflections on FDR's Foreign
  Policy." *International Affairs* 43 (July 1967): 530-36.

UNPUBLISHED STUDIES

Bailey, John A., Jr. "Lion, Eagle and Crescent: The Western Allies and
  Turkey in 1943; A Study of British and American Diplomacy in a
  Critical Year of War." Ph.D Dissertation, Georgetown University, 1969
Cline, Ray S. "Washington Command Post: The Operations Division."
  Original typed manuscript, Federal Records Center, Suitland, Md.
Dwan, John E. "Franklin D. Roosevelt and the Revolution in the
  Strategy of National Security: Foreign Policy and Military Planning
  Before Pearl Harbor." Ph.D. Dissertation, Yale University, 1954.
Eubanks, Richard.K. "The Diplomacy of Postponement: The United
  States and Russia's Western Frontier Claims During World War
  II." Ph.D. Dissertation, University of Texas, 1971.
Geberding, William P. "Franklin D. Roosevelt's Conception of the
  Soviet Union in World Politics." Ph.D. Dissertation, University
  of Chicago, 1959.

Hammersmith, Jack L. "American Diplomacy and the Polish Question, 1943-1945." Ph.D. Dissertation, University of Virginia, 1970.

Harris, Dennis E. "The Diplomacy of the Second Front: America, Britain, Russia and the Normandy Invasion." Ph.D. Dissertation, University of California-Santa Barbara, 1969.

Hawkes, James R. "Stalin's Diplomatic Offensive: The Politics of the Second Front, 1941-1945." Ph.D. Dissertation, University of Illinois, 1966.

Julian, Thomas A. "Operation Frantic and the Search for American-Soviet Military Collaboration, 1941-1944." Ph.D. Dissertation, Syracuse University, 1968.

Kittredge, Tracy. "U. S.-British Naval Cooperation, 1940-1945." Unfinished manuscript, Naval History Division of the Department of the Navy.

Levering, Ralph. "Prelude to Cold War: American Attitudes Toward Russia During World War II." Ph.D. Dissertation, Princeton University, 1971.

McIlvenna, Don E. "Prelude to D-Day: American Strategy and the Second Front Issue." Ph.D. Dissertation, Stanford University, 1966.

Morris, Max K. "Political-Military Coordination in the United States Armed Forces." Ph.D. Dissertation, Fletcher School of Law and Diplomacy, 1968.

Wyckoff, Theodore. "The Office of the Secretary of War Under Henry L. Stimson, 1940-1945." Unpublished manuscript, Office of the Chief of Military History, Department of the Army, Washington, D. C., 1960.

INDEX

72-73, 75-76; and Mediterranean, 65, 80-81, 102, 111; and 1942 second front, 29-35, 41, 48-49; at QUADRANT Conference, 113-15, 120-21; Soviet Union and, 69, 89, 120-21, 128-30, 137, 161. *See also* Japan; Pacific-first strategy
Pearl Harbor, 21-22, 25-26, 29
Peripheral strategy. *See* British strategy; Mediterranean
Persia. *See* Iran
Philippines, 7, 27
Pisa-Ancona-Rimini line, 143. *See also* Italy, invasion of
Planning Group, OSS. *See* Office of Strategic Services
Poland, 158; boundaries of, 43-44, 153; government of, 15, 39, 44, 65, 86, 91
Policy Committee, OPD. *See* Operations Division, U.S. Army General Staff
Po line. *See* Italy, invasion of
Portal, General Sir Charles, 75, 142
Portugal, 8, 12-13, 26
Public Opinion, 12, 121; in Britain, 19, 37, 41, 51-54, 97; and cross-Channel vs. Mediterranean debate, 82-84, 93-94, 99, 101, 107, 135; and 1942 second front plan, 28-31, 35-36, 40, 53, 161; and North Africa, 6, 58, 63, 67, 191 n.13; and Pacific, 25-26, 28-29, 36, 40-41, 70, 93-94, 101
QUADRANT Conference: and Anglo-American strategy, 112-16, 164; dispute over accords of, 133, 135-36; and Soviet Union, 116-23, 128-29, 132, 204 n.42
Quebec Conference. *See* QUADRANT Conference

RANKIN, 90-91, 101, 106, 138, 164, 197 n.60; CCS directive for, 94, 96; at *Iowa* discussions, 137-39; at QUADRANT Conference, 117-23, 205 n.45; at Tehran Conference, 143, 151
Research and Analysis, OSS. *See* Office of Strategic Services
Rhodes. *See* ACCOLADE; Aegean
Rome. *See* Italy, invasion of
Rommel, General Erwin, 5, 20, 27-28, 52-53, 71; British plans for, 18, 20-21, 23, 57, 62, 64-66
Roosevelt, Elliot, 76-77, 142
Roosevelt, Franklin D., xii, 9-10, 71, 107, 130, 163-68; at ARCADIA Conference, 23-26; and Bullitt, 88-89, 93, 120, 130; and Cairo-Tehran Conferences, 136-56; at Casablanca Conference, 75-78; and Churchill, 17, 32-33, 38-41, 46-48, 51, 54, 63, 65-69, 101, 103, 109, 127, 131, 136-37; and Far East, 101, 141-42, 155-56; and *Iowa* discussions, 137-39, 209 n.15; and Joint Chiefs of Staff, 55-59, 73-74, 84-85, 91, 110-11, 137-39; and Mediterranean, 5-10, 67, 101, 109-11, 125, 127, 132-33; and 1942 second front, 29, 32-43, 45-49, 51-52, 161-62, 166; and North Africa, 6-9, 12, 23, 25-27, 29, 49-60, 63, 67, 166; and public opinion, 6, 12, 28, 36-37, 51, 63, 67, 84, 161; and QUADRANT Conference, 114-15, 119, 123; and Soviet Union, 17-18, 21, 24, 36-38, 42-49, 51, 66, 89-91, 110, 161-62; and Stalin, 17, 38, 42, 47, 67, 69, 73-74, 76, 85,

About the Author
Mark A. Stoler is an associate professor of history at the University of
Vermont in Burlington and specializes in American diplomatic and
military history. He is presently preparing materials on the military view
of American national policy during World War II and George Aiken's
work on the Senate Foreign Relations Committee.